Created in God's Image

Created in God's Image

An Introduction to Feminist Theological Anthropology

Michelle A. Gonzalez

ORBIS BOOKS

Maryknoll, New York 10545

Founded in 1970, Orbis Books endeavors to publish works that enlighten the mind, nourish the spirit, and challenge the conscience. The publishing arm of the Maryknoll Fathers and Brothers, Orbis seeks to explore the global dimensions of the Christian faith and mission, to invite dialogue with diverse cultures and religious traditions, and to serve the cause of reconciliation and peace. The books published reflect the views of their authors and do not represent the official position of the Maryknoll Society. To learn more about Maryknoll and Orbis Books, please visit our website at www.maryknoll.org.

Manufactured in the United States of America.
Manuscript editing and typesetting by Joan Weber Laflamme.

Library of Congress Cataloging-in-Publication Data

Gonzalez, Michelle A.
    Created in God's image : an introduction to feminist theological anthropology / Michelle A. Gonzalez.
        p. cm.
    Includes bibliographical references and index.
    ISBN-13: 978–1–57075–697–9
    1. Feminist theology. 2. Theological anthropology. I. Title.
    BT83.55.G66 2007
    233.082—dc22

                                                    2006032997

For Byron and Byron Manuel

Contents

Introduction

No other text has affected women in the Western world as much as that found in the opening chapters of Genesis.

For two millennia now the Judeo-Christian tradition has placed man a little lower than the angels and woman a little higher than the demons.

Genesis opens with two creation stories, accounts that have captured theological and popular imagination for centuries. Whether the writings of the earliest Christian thinkers, contemporary debates on intelligent design versus evolution, or a Simpsons cartoon's humorous reinterpretation of Adam and Eve, perhaps no other section of the Hebrew scriptures and Christian Bible has provoked as much creativity and debate as the first three chapters of Genesis. My study focuses on interpretations of the first of these creation stories, creation in seven days, and the pivotal line in the story found in verse 27:

> So God created humankind in his image,
> in the image of God he created them;
> male and female he created them.

This statement has been a central point of contention and a foundation for Christian understandings of men and women for centuries. The notion that humanity is created in the image of God, distinguishing us from the rest of creation, and the exact meaning of that image continue to mystify and to challenge the religious imagination of Christians. While it can be argued that the second, often popularized creation story of Adam, Eve, and the Fall has influenced Christian understandings of the human in a more profound manner, it is the egalitarian image of humanity offered in Genesis 1 that is our focus. Because Genesis 1 offers such an egalitarian vision of the sexes, the manner in which this understanding of men and women has been rejected, misrepresented, and revived throughout Christianity is vital for uncovering the construction of male and female identity within Christian history. The second creation story is not entirely ignored, but it instead will be examined in relationship to the first.

A key point of controversy for Christian thinkers is the relationship between men and women and whether Genesis 1:27 undermines a hierarchical categorization of the sexes. As this book demonstrates, contrary to the spirit of the passage, male Christian authors have argued for centuries that creation in the image of God as male and female does not necessarily lead to an egalitarian relationship between men and women. Women are seen as possessing the image deficiently, for example, or only in relationship with men. Interpretations such as these have falsely denied the full image of God in women, equated her with bodiliness, and elevated man as the ultimate representation of rationality and spirituality, the expression of the image in its fullness. A central emphasis of this study is the manner in which interpretations of Genesis 1:27 have shaped Christian understandings of the relationship between men and women.

The focus of this study, therefore, is not a biblical passage but the interpretation of a biblical passage. This is a very important distinction from the onset. I am not a biblical scholar, nor do I claim an expertise in the Hebrew scriptures, although biblical scholars inform my work, especially in the following chapter. Instead, I examine how historical and contemporary interpretations of creation in the image of God shape Christian understandings of men and women. This has implications not

only for those who claim Christianity as a religion, but also for
cultures in which Christianity is the majority religion and has
a profound influence on shaping the dominant cultural ethos.
This is a book about theological anthropology, the area in
Christian theology that examines the nature of the human, our
relationship with one another, and our relationship with our
Creator. My focus on gender can be situated within contemporary feminist theology, an explosive academic, pastoral, and
grassroots movement that emerged on the theological landscape in the second half of the twentieth century. While feminist theology is a fairly recent arrival to the Christian theological scene, the question of gender has been a central concern for
theology and philosophy since the inception of these disciplines.

This Introduction sets the stage for future chapters, examining the questions, dialogue partners, sources, and methodology that inform this study. I begin by introducing the discipline
of systematic theology, my area of expertise, and the place of
theological anthropology within that discipline. I then turn to
the importance of gender within theological anthropology. This
section clarifies some of the terms and categories employed
throughout this study. The third section introduces feminist
theology, emphasizing the global nature of this theological
movement. I conclude by offering an outline of the remainder
of the text.

Theological Anthropology
within Systematic Theology

The classic definition of theology comes from Saint Anselm,
who defined it as "faith seeking understanding." Literally
translated, the word *theology* breaks down to *theos* (God) and
logos (word); theology is therefore discourse about God (God-
talk). Theology, however, cannot simply be defined as discourse
about God, for the human capacity to know the divine is limited by our very humanity. Instead, theology refers to discourse

surrounding human experience of the divine. Theology is a human attempt to describe divine being, an exploration of the human experience of revelation. We can only speak of our response to God's initiative in human life. In order to tap into that human experience of the divine, theology draws from philosophy, literature, the arts, liturgy, and church teachings, to name a few. In fact, the sources of theology are only limited by the sources of human expression. In more recent decades the praxeological dimension of the theological task has come forth, as reflected in Peruvian theologian Gustavo Gutiérrez's definition of theology as "critical reflection on Christian praxis in light of the Word."[1] Since humanity's experience of the divine saturates every aspect of human expression, even the most mundane, everyday act can become a resource for theology.

There are several different types of theology: biblical, systematic, historical, pastoral, and philosophical. The sources, themes, and questions of a particular theologian are limited by his or her focus. This book falls into the area of systematic theology. Systematic theology is critical reflection on communal Christian responses to God's revelation. Systematic theologians attempt to articulate in a cohesive manner the faith expressions of Christian communities, both historical and contemporary. While drawing from history, however, systematic theology is a fairly recent player on the theological field (some would argue as late as the twentieth century). As noted by Francis Schüssler Fiorenza, *systematic theology* is at times an ambiguous term, for sometimes the term *theology* points to all areas of theological studies and other times it is used to designate systematic theology exclusively. *Theology* is also sometimes placed in contrast to *religious studies* (the former referring to a confessional approach), and other times the terms are used interchangeably. Recognizing the diversity within systematic theology, however, Fiorenza finds the constants of scripture, tradition, experience, and method to unite theological writings.[2] Most systematic theologians attempt to address the contemporary situation, building on the history of Christian theology. Several theologians who are categorized in this discipline neither named their method as systematic nor saw their work as systematic theologies. The *system* in systematic does not imply a closed framework that imprisons God's revelation into human categories. Instead, *system* refers to coherence, the method (approach) of a particular theologian (or theological school), and the shared loci that often categorize this discipline.

European and European American male voices have historically dominated the area of systematic theology, often working very closely with the discipline of philosophy. While offering a vital contribution to the field, they are but one perspective within global theological writings. In addition, an attempt to elaborate an abstract universal theology characterized many of the writings of early systematic theologians. Recent contributions by third-world, US minority, and feminist theologies, as well as the growing dialogue between theologians and postmodern, poststructuralist, and postcolonial philosophies have emphasized the contextuality of all theological elaborations. Every systematic theology is a contextual theology, even if it does not claim or recognize its own sociocultural, political, and historical limitations. This does not promote relativism. However, in today's academic landscape the ability for any voice to speak in a detached, ahistorical, and universal manner has been severely (and thankfully) challenged. While the relationship between systematics and philosophy is in no way over, systematic theologians are no longer "monogamous." Instead, their eyes have wandered to other disciplines, such as sociology, critical theory, literary theory, cultural anthropology, the arts, and political science. This interdisciplinary approach can only aid theologians in their quest to understand and articulate humanity's experience and expression of God's presence in their lives.

A diversity of theological approaches has characterized Christian theology since its inception. These approaches, with their sources and norms, are characterized in modern theology as theological method. The theological method of a particular theologian or theological school is distinctly shaped by the culture, geography, and sociopolitical context from which a theology emerges. Whether this contextuality is acknowledged or not, it is a characteristic of all theologies. Feminist theologian Anne E. Carr observes:

> As the broad set of Christian traditions developed and the work of theological reflection became more refined, it was always marked by its historical and geographical setting and by the social location and experience of the theologians involved, just as it was marked by the cultural, ecclesial, and personal experience of its intended readers. Changes in theological method often occurred in relation to transformations in the wider culture, in philosophical thinking, and in other fields of human thought.[3]

The extent to which a theology should adapt to its cultural context or how much it should remain loyal to the Christian tradition, however, remains today a topic open to much debate.

What is not open for debate are the sources for theology, which are generally accepted to be scripture, tradition, reason, and experience. "For the most part, previous theologians assumed these elements in their work, appealing to the central authority of the Bible as it was interpreted in their times, to the authority of earlier theologians or philosophers, to church councils or the pope, to rational argumentation, or to common experience, both cultural and personal."[4] Depending on a particular theologian's intellectual slant or denominational affiliation, these four will have varying degrees of importance in his or her corpus. Theologians who attempt to expand the sources of systematic theology often return to these four as a normative framework for their writings.[5]

One area where one sees an inconsistent level of commitment within systematic theology is in its relationship with the church. Some theologians remain closely tied to church teachings, and their corpus is very much shaped by the issues of their institutional affiliation. For others, the institutional church is of little concern. Serene Jones defines Christian theology as the "long line of theologians who have shared in the critical task of helping the church reflect on its present-day witness and practice to see if it continues to be faithful to the revelation of God manifest in Scripture, tradition, and the ongoing life of the Christian community."[6] Jones's definition situates her work in the context of the church while not becoming an uncritical servant of the church. This is the position of many contemporary systematic theologians, especially those feminist theologians that are explored in this book.

Systematic theology is characterized by several classic loci or themes that are shared areas of emphasis for theologians. They include Christology (the identity and meaning of Jesus Christ), methodology (discussed above), concept of God, Pneumatology (the Holy Spirit), ecclesiology (the church), Mariology (Mary), soteriology (salvation), and eschatology (last things). This book is located in one such locus, theological anthropology. Within systematic theology the study of what it means to be human, created in the image and likeness of God, falls under the heading of theological anthropology. This has implications for both our relationship with our Creator and our relationship with one another. Theological anthropology speaks to humanity's relationship with the divine and the interrelationship of the human community. Since the writings of the earliest Christians, theologians have attempted to understand and explain what it means to be a creature of God. For every generation of Christians the significance of our humanity is constantly being reinterpreted based on our sociocultural, historical, and political context. There is no one unified anthropology, but rather various anthropologies that are shaped by the diverse communities that struggle to interpret God's revelation.

As defined by Kristen E. Kvam, the term *theological anthropology* emerges from "the Greek work *anthrōpos*, which signifies 'human.' . . . The adjective *theological* underscores that this study differs from the study of humanity in anthropology

as a social-scientific discipline. . . . The term *theological* stresses
that this field of study explores religious considerations of what
it means to be God's human creatures."[7] Kvam observes that
for centuries anthropology did not stand alone as a theological focus but was often nestled into writings on Christology or
the doctrine of creation. Kvam also notes that historically anthropology was labeled the doctrine of man, though there is
now a move to more gender-inclusive language. Kvam warns,
however, that this move to inclusivity can often eclipse the function of gender in theological anthropologies. Men are often
held as paradigmatic for human experience and women's experiences are ignored. In a sense then, given the privileging of
men's experience, the doctrine of man can be seen at times as
a more appropriate name for this field of study.

Classic theological anthropologies have often emphasized
our spiritual relationship with the divine and downplayed its
implications for our concrete existence. Otherwise put, "The
main focus of theological anthropology has tended to be the
supernatural orientation of humankind as beings created (in
the words of Gen 1:27) 'in the image of God' *(imago Dei)*. As
a result of this focus, the other, more material side of existence
has been overshadowed, even obscured."[8] This passage
emerges from a recent collaborative rewriting of systematic
theology that emphasizes the constructive nature of the theological task. As the authors of the chapter on the human being indicate, there are three issues that challenge contemporary theological anthropologies: freedom and responsibility
(in light of relativist approaches to ethics and an awareness of
the contextual nature of our understandings of sin and evil),
identity and alterity (in reference to difference at the level of
the individual and community), and time and memory (in
light of contemporary emphases on expediency).[9] This book
is sympathetic to these concerns. Theological anthropology
must remain firmly grounded in the contemporary situation
and not fall into abstract speculation that ignores the very
materiality of human life.

A pressing concern for theological anthropology is the relationship between humanity as described in the opening chapters of Genesis (falling from God's original creation, and consequently becoming deficient) and the new creation that Christians claim is found in Christ. The classic formulation of this new creation is found in Paul's letter to the Galatians when he writes, "There is no longer Jew or Greek, there is no longer slave or free, there is no longer male and female; for all of you are one in Christ Jesus" (Gal 3:28). How one constructs the relationship between the old and the new remains a central question for theological anthropology, one that has plagued Christians since New Testament times.

> If the emphasis is placed on the contrast between the new humanity in Christ and the old, it becomes easy to wonder whether the differences of (for example) gender and race that are overcome in Christ are part of God's good creation or signs of some defect in the created order. On the other hand, if the abiding significance of these differences is affirmed, then it might seem to follow that social practices designed to reinforce them should be preserved.[10]

At the root of this question is the meaning of our historical particularity in light of salvation history. Another concern that emerges from this discussion is the role of sin and evil within theological anthropology. These are classic topics that are discussed under this heading. In this text my treatment of sin is limited to its relationship to the story of the Fall. However, sin or original sin is not the focus of this study.[11] Instead, my discussion of sin emphasizes how gender has shaped out notions of sinfulness in reference to the Genesis accounts.

Gender and Theological Anthropology

One dimension of our historical particularity that has been the subject of debate within Christian theology since its inception has been the question of gender. In other words, what does it mean to be created male and female and how should the relationship between the two sexes be defined by Christian theology? Far from being a recent concern raised by contemporary theologians, this is a fundamental question in the history of theology and philosophy. Refuting the claim that philosophers have only begun to look at the concepts of female and male in the last two centuries, Prudence Allen writes, "Careful research reveals, however, that nearly every single philosopher over the first two thousand years of western philosophy thought about the identity of woman in relation to man. This astonishing discovery means that the concept of woman has been a fundamental area of philosophical research since the sixth century B.C."[12] What *is* a fairly recent arrival is the feminist hermeneutic that has informed approaches to gender and sexual identity in the last fifty years.

Liberation theologies exploded onto the theological arena in the 1960s. These theologies emphasize a preferential option for the marginalized, a rewriting of Christian history, and theology from the underside. They propose alternative Christian visions grounded in both traditionally marginalized sources and rereadings of voices "canonized" within the theological tradition. The invisibility of women within religious history and institutions fueled the outrage and fervor behind feminist theology. "Women are not only the 'silent majority' but we are also the 'silenced majority' in the Roman Catholic Church," Elisabeth Schüssler Fiorenza stresses. "This deliberate or unconscious silencing of women in the Church engenders our ecclesial and theological invisibility."[13] The 1968 publication of Mary Daly's *Church and the Second Sex* marks the birth of this movement in the United States.[14] Many consider Schüssler Fiorenza, along with Daly and Rosemary Radford Ruether, the foremothers of feminist theology. In their work one finds a hesitancy to give Christian tradition, scripture, and theology any sort of normative status due to their androcentric foundation. Therefore, women's experiences and struggles for liberation often become the central commitment and norm in their work. Fundamental to these theologians' work is recovering women's intellectual histories and the implications of this task. Through privileging gender as a primary analytic category, feminist theologians seek to highlight the ideologies operating in historical and current understandings of Christian tradition.

Though many list white European American women as the foremothers of feminist theology, feminist theology today is a global movement. While their voices are often marginalized or ignored, feminist theologians are writing and struggling within the Third World and among US minorities. Their theological writings offer an alternative vision, one that is shaped by the complexity of oppression (for example, racism, ethnic prejudice, and/or classism) that characterizes their contemporary reality. This text is intentionally global in its sources, attempting to give a full picture of feminist theology throughout the world. A vital dimension of the work of feminist theologians is the self-critical nature of their endeavors. This was always not the case. However, with growing voices among US minority and third-world women, the multilayered intricacy of oppression is now a central concern for feminists.

Feminist theologians all argue that the Christian tradition has produced some very damaging and oppressive understandings of women. Women traditionally have been seen as inferior to men, linked with corporality, and second-rate compared to the more spiritual and rational male, leading to their subordination under male authority. Feminist theologians argue that the theological anthropology operating within the greater part of the Christian tradition, one that Christians today have inherited, is patriarchal in nature, based on an androcentric world view that fuels sexist attitudes toward women. One might ask at this juncture, then, why feminist theologians do not merely abandon Christianity as a lost cause. Some feminist theologians, though a small minority, have in fact done that.[15] However, the majority of feminist theologians argue that this sexist anthropology is the result of a misinterpretation of the Christian tradition and very much in contrast to what Jesus Christ intended for humanity. My text falls within this line of thought, embracing a critical approach to the Christian tradition that seeks to uncover the manner in which sexism has functioned within theological anthropology in order to reveal an egalitarian vision of male and female that stands firmly within Christian teachings.

As the book title and the opening section of this Introduction indicate, the *imago Dei* is the central theme around which I center my study of theological anthropology in historical and contemporary Christianity. Genesis 1:27 is central not only for Christian understandings of the human but also for feminist claims for an egalitarian anthropology. Based on Christianity's reduction of women to corporality and the flesh, the body will also be a key player throughout this text. Because of her association with bodiliness, woman is often interpreted within the Christian tradition as reflecting the image of God in a flawed or lesser manner. The body is also often interpreted as that which impedes us from true union with God or from reaching our full potentiality as faithful Christians. Therefore, I repeatedly turn to the theme of the body and embodiment throughout the text.

A quick clarification of terms is appropriate at this juncture. When I speak of *biological sex* I am referring to the biological, embodied distinction between men and women. The word *gender* refers to the social construction of masculine and feminine identity or the socially acquired roles of men and women. Often these two have become confused within the Christian tradition, when biology is interpreted as destiny and is used to justify socially constructed gender roles (that is, women are "naturally" more nurturing). *Patriarchy,* which literally means "rule of the father," refers to the social, economic, and political relations that validate male sovereignty within households. This model is transferred to society at large, and also includes children and slaves. *Sexism* refers to the hierarchical gender stereotyping of men over women. *Androcentrism,* from the Greek term meaning "male-centeredness," is the world view in which males are normative and women are subordinate.

Overview of This Study

This book has an agenda. I am very blunt in this claim, though simultaneously acknowledging that all books have an agenda, whether the author explicitly reveals it or not. The aims of this book are multilayered. On one level, my intention is to introduce the area of theological anthropology within the corpus of Christian theology. Adding to that is the emphasis on gender in historical and contemporary understandings of the human, with special emphasis on the *imago Dei.* A third level of this study is its historical character, tracing the history of the interpretation of a central Christian notion, the *imago Dei,* and its implications for Christian understandings of humanity. Because my hermeneutic is situated within the corpus of global feminist theologies, this study also offers an introduction to the major questions and themes surrounding theological anthropology within contemporary feminist theology. These four layers inform and also structure this study.

Chapter 1 focuses on early Christian understandings of the *imago Dei.* We begin on ground zero of the *imago Dei,* the creation story found in chapter 1 of the book of Genesis. While attention will be given to the second creation story, Genesis 1 is the focus. My *exegesis,* or interpretation, of this text emphasizes feminist biblical scholarship, looking at varying manners in which contemporary scholars approach and understand this central passage. My analysis also explores the implications of this text for Christian scriptures, most notably Pauline theology. The last scriptural section briefly examines the role of the Bible within Christian theology and the manner in which it functions as a source and norm for historical and contemporary reflection. The last section of this chapter explores the philosophical foundations that inform early Christian reflections on the *imago Dei*, most notably the philosophies of Plato and Aristotle. Though not Christian sources, these philosophers lay the foundation for early Christian and medieval theological elaborations on this theme.

The lengthy historical survey of Christian theological writings on the *imago Dei* found in Chapter 2 is pivotal for this study. Here we cover a lot of ground, exploring how the centrality of the *imago Dei* became cemented within Christian tradition. My treatment is in no way exhaustive but instead centers on the major figures and ideas that shaped Christian tradition. Beginning with the church fathers, one finds even in early Christianity a variety of approaches and understandings of the divine image. This section concludes with Augustine, arguably one of the most, if not the most influential Christian theologian, especially on issues of gender and the body. The second section centers on medieval theologians, with the lengthiest treatment on Thomas Aquinas, whose theological anthropology remains the foundation of contemporary Vatican understandings of male and female even today. Of central importance for the church fathers and medieval theologians is the role of the body and its relationship to the *imago Dei*. Section three explores the European Protestant Reformations through the theology of Martin Luther. The chapter concludes with a transition into the modern era, looking at the influential philosophies of René Descartes and Immanuel Kant. After playing a central role in Christian understandings of the human, for several centuries the *imago Dei* "disappeared" as a principal focus within theology, only to be revived by European theologians in the twentieth century.

My overview of twentieth-century notions of the divine image centers on the work of four essential theologians within Christian theology: Karl Rahner, Karl Barth, Paul Tillich, and Hans Urs von Balthasar. My decision to focus on thinkers rather than broader ideas in Chapter 3 is informed in part by the shift in theological method within modern theology. Rather than creating a typology of numerous thinkers and offering a cursory glance at this or that comment on the *imago Dei*, I have chosen to offer more in-depth analyses of these four anthropologies and their implications for the contemporary reader. It would be difficult, if pressed, to find a student or teacher of Christian theology who did not place these four as central figures, and in many ways contemporary theology continues to respond to the visions of the human proposed by them. These four also recast the very role of anthropology within Christian theology, offering varying ways to understanding the starting point and nature of the theological task.

Chapter 4 offers an introduction to feminist theology, emphasizing the role of gender within this theology and the problematization of the concept of woman and man. Prior to the work of feminist theologians, notions of male and female had remained relatively stable concepts within Christian theology. With the contributions of feminists of color around the globe and the introduction of critical theory within theology, the manner and even the possibility of speaking of men and women as essentialized collectives become contested. After introducing the methodology and sources of feminist theology, this chapter turns to debates on the question of gender identity and the role of sexism in light of the broader concerns of feminist theologians. The central point of contention is women's experience and whether or not it can remain a viable category and starting point for contemporary feminist theologies.

Feminist theological anthropologies are the central focus of Chapter 5. Here I explore the various approaches feminist theologians embrace regarding understandings of the human. The *imago Dei* plays a central role. Donna Teevan argues that the *imago Dei* is the linchpin for the egalitarian claims of feminist theologians: "Attention to women's experience in Catholic feminist theology tends to be rooted in a conviction that women are made in God's image and called to participation in the project of building up the reign of God. Thus, the well-being of women—understood not in isolation but in relation to

God, other human beings, and the earth—serves as a goal and criterion of adequacy for feminist theology."[16] While speaking primarily of Catholic theologians, Teevan's claims can be applied to all feminist theologies. The creation of male and female in the image of God becomes a foundation for many of the broader claims within feminist theology. This chapter emphasizes feminist theologians' rejection of anthropologies based on gender complementarity and their constructive proposals of egalitarian, relational, and communal understandings of humanity.

Chapter 6 centers on my constructive proposal for a Christian theological anthropology informed by the hermeneutic of feminist theologies. The chapter draws from and critiques the multitude of sources explored throughout the text, offering a vision of the human that is grounded in yet critical of the Christian tradition. The centerpiece of this chapter is a trinitarian anthropology that understands the *imago Dei* as relational and dynamic. Far from proposing a blanket rejection of past interpretations, this vision is informed by historical sources, many of which are often too quickly discarded for their patriarchal undertones. As Robin May Schott points out regarding feminist work in philosophy, "If feminists do not analyze the way sexism has functioned in philosophical theories, then feminist theory risks becoming a utopian alternative that leaves untouched existing forms of thought."[17] The same could be said of theology. One must take a simultaneously critical and constructive stance.

This study concludes with suggestions for further research in this area. My hope is that this book will serve not only as an introductory text but also as a starting point for dialogue. With the rise of a Vatican-sanctioned "new feminism" within Catholic circles and the supposed failure of liberationist discourses such as feminist theology being touted in the halls of the academy, debates surrounding gender and biological sex within Christianity will continue to plague theology as long as the discipline exists. This has been the case since the first Christian theological writings, in fact within those that predate them, and the nature of men and women will continue to remain a central question and debate topic for theologians. This text can be seen as one voice in this ongoing and critical discussion.

Created in God's Image

certian texts privileged ← *scripture* ↓ *interpretations imposed on scripture* → *philosophical ideas that fueled* ↓ *Plato* ✗ *aristotle*

Chapter 1

Foundations:
Scripture and Philosophy

This chapter begins in the beginning, as the opening words to the book of Genesis proclaim. Any study of a central theme or idea in Christian theology inevitably commences with the Bible, for scripture is a foundational starting point for so many Christian ideas. However, some of those ideas are not necessarily found in the text itself but are interpretations imposed on a given passage in scripture. Also, certain texts are often privileged at the expense of others in order to impose a particular ideology or world view. After examining the creation stories in Genesis, I consider the philosophical ideas that fueled many central Christian interpretations of these texts through the philosophy of Plato and Aristotle. It may seem odd to pair the Bible with these non-Christian sources, but as this book demonstrates, they share an equal weight in the manner in which they inform Christian visions of the human.

Our journey opens with the book of Genesis and the creation accounts found in chapters 1 and 2—3. As Phyllis Trible has so thoughtfully written: "The Bible is a pilgrim wandering through history to merge past and present. Composed of diverse traditions that span centuries, it embraces claims and counterclaims in witness to the complexities and ambiguities of existence."[1] The method of this text embraces that spirit of

1

pilgrimage as we travel through the various interpretations of Genesis and the manner in which they have shaped Christian understandings of men and women. This chapter begins with an analysis of the Genesis 1 creation story. This is the most detailed section of the chapter, given our emphasis on the *imago Dei*. This is followed by two shorter scripture sections focusing on the Genesis 2—3 creation story and New Testament implications for the Genesis 1 account. My approach to scripture is informed by Sandra M. Schneiders's dialogical theory of interpretation in which the interaction between the text and the reader creates meaning. The text, thus, does not have one right meaning; it is instead "a linguistic structure that is susceptible of a number of valid readings by different readers or the same reader at different times." Meaning is not found in the text but "in the interaction between text and reader."[2] The author, therefore, does not control the meaning of a given text. After examining scripture in that spirit, the second half of this chapter studies Plato and Aristotle with a treatment of the function of gender in each of their philosophies.

Genesis

Before entering into a study of Genesis, it is important to highlight that, like several of the books in the Hebrew scriptures, Genesis is not one book but several books that have been edited together into one. This explains the existence of the two creation stories with their differing accounts and theological perspectives. The book of Genesis, most scholars concede, is the result of four sources written during four different historical eras. This is known as the four-source theory, which emerged from the belief that numerous sources lay behind Genesis and consequently the Pentateuch. The four documents are J (Yahwist, tenth century BCE), E (Elohist, eighth century BCE), D (Deutero-canonic, seventh century BCE), and P (Priestly, sixth century BCE). The first creation story, Genesis 1:1–2:4a, is Priestly (P), while Genesis 2:4b-3:25 is Yahwistic (J). Thus, while found in the first chapter of Genesis, creation in seven days is a much later source.

Ancient theory held that Moses wrote the Pentateuch; that claim was later modified to state that he only wrote parts of it. During the eighteenth and nineteenth centuries scholars began to explore whether or not he wrote *any* part of the Hebrew scriptures. Through careful study (known as source criticism), inconsistencies emerged that challenged the theory of single authorship. They include duplication of phrases (why would Moses say it twice?), contradictions, different names for the deity, different theological perspectives, different styles and vocabularies, and broken narratives. It is from this research that the four-source theory, or documentary hypothesis, emerged. The Yawhist (J) is the oldest source. Its language is simple and direct and includes the earliest invocation of the name Yahweh. The J author is also heavy on anthropomorphisms, describing God in human terms or with human attributes. The Elohist (E) source includes lots of human emotion. God is often revealed in dreams, and the author frequently speaks of the fear of God. The Deutero-canonic (D) source is the core source of the book of Deuteronomy and primarily consists of Moses' speeches. A school compiled the Priestly (P) source. It has a very orderly and stately rhythm and emphasizes worship, ritual, and sacrifice. By 400 BCE all four sources were put together, with the P source serving as the framework.

Structurally Genesis can be divided into two parts. The first part, chapters 1—11, is often described as mythic history. This section contains stories situated in primeval time. The original purpose of these stories was religious instruction not scientific guidelines; they were meant to teach moral lessons. They teach us about God's care for us and our resistance of God. In chapters 12—50 one finds the stories of the mothers and fathers (matriarchs and patriarchs) of Israel. The Hebrew scriptures tell the particular story of a particular people, namely, the Jewish community. While the focus of this book is Christian interpretations of these texts, one must always be aware that there exists a body of Jewish literature that offers its own set of interpretations of Genesis 1—3 based on the beliefs of Judaism. Jewish intellectual Philo (20–50 BCE), for example, interprets Genesis 1 as the creation of spiritual beings and the second creation account as the creation of corporeal beings. Interpretations of Genesis 1:1—2:4a and 2:4b—3:24 and their relationship have varied throughout history and continue to be a source of contention even today. Traditional Christian readings have emphasized a hierarchical depiction of the creation accounts, highlighting the second at the expense of the first. This interpretation most often depicts woman's subordination as part of the order of creation. While more egalitarian readings have flared up throughout Christian history, these are few and far between and are most often silenced by the dominant voices.

Genesis 1:1—2:4a

The Priestly creation story found in Genesis 1 was written in the sixth century BCE during the Jewish exile in Babylon. The trauma of the exile led Jews to write a creation narrative that emphasized God's power over chaos. This is clearly seen in the opening lines of the story, where God takes the dark formless void that is the earth and heavens and creates, in a very ordered fashion, the universe as we know it today. God speaks, and creation begins. The Priestly story of creation in seven days is influenced by the Babylonian poem the *Enuma elish*. Both stories emphasize chaos over order, the creation of dry land, and people. There are differences, however. In the *Enuma elish* the material for creation emerges when Marduk kills the goddess Tiamat. The world is created from the corpse of this goddess. The human is created from the blood of evil gods, and humans are to be servants of the gods. No such goddess is killed to form the matter of creation in Genesis 1; instead, humans are formed when God speaks them into existence.

In this section the focus of my analysis is on the sixth day of creation, when humanity comes into existence. In Genesis 1:26 God proclaims, "Let us make humankind in our image, according to our likeness; and let them have dominion over the fish of the sea, and over the birds of the air, and over the cattle, and over all the wild animals of the earth, and over every creeping thing that creeps upon the earth." Two words are important to examine in this verse: "us" and "image." Scripture scholars have offered three explanations for the "us" in Genesis 1:26: the first is named plural of majesty—the word *Elohim* (a name for God) in Hebrew is in the plural but with a singular verb to show the vastness of God's power; a second explanation is that the "us" reveals the remnants of polytheism; a third option is that the "us" is merely a rhetorical device. The word "image" and the meaning of that term will become a central point of debate for Christian theologians. Interestingly, while the idea that the word "image" in this passage refers to a soul will become a prominent Christian interpretation, this sounds ludicrous to Judaism, since the Hebrews did not even have a word for soul. The idea that we are made up of a body and soul is a Greek idea, one that heavily emphasized Christian interpretations of Genesis. Another manner in which image may be interpreted is tied to the notion of humans as representatives of God on earth. Like the ancient practice of sending a statue of a king in order to represent that king in absentia, so humans represent God in the earthly realm, which is why we are given dominion.[3]

Genesis 1:27 proclaims, "So God created humankind in his image, in the image of God he created them; male and female he created them." The Hebrew for *humankind* is *'adam*. The plural verb implies a collective, and *'adam* can be understood as a gender-inclusive word. While the phrase "image and likeness" distinguishes humanity from the rest of creation, what this metaphor actually means is open for speculation. Hebrew scripture scholar Claus Westermann argues that there are various possible interpretations:

To be made in God's image has meant: 1. Having certain spiritual qualities or capacities (soul, intellect, will). 2. Having a certain external (corporeal) form (i.e. upright carriage). 3. Having both the spiritual and corporeal features characteristic of humankind. 4. Being God's counterpart on earth; able to enter into partnership with God. 5. Being God's representative on earth (based on royal theology; humankind as God's viceroy/administrator.[4]

The creation of humans was an independent narrative that became incorporated into the creation of the world. In other words the creation of humanity was later added at the end of the larger creation account. In his interpretation Westermann holds that this passage, when referring to the image, is speaking of God's action, not the nature of humanity. "Gen 1:26f is not making a general and universally valid statement about the nature of humankind. . . . What the Old Testament says about the creation of humanity in the image of god has meaning only in its context, namely that of the process of the creation of human beings."[5] In spite of Westermann's claims, Christian theologians have used this passage as the starting point for understanding human nature, perhaps misinterpreting its intended message.

Within the work of feminist biblical scholars there are various interpretations of the Genesis passage. The starting point of our close read of Genesis 1 begins with the ground-breaking work of Phyllis Trible. Humans, Trible begins, are made in God's image without reference to nature (in the creation account, for example, fish are brought from water, animals from earth). Only humans are designated by their sexuality (male and female), a reference that belongs with the *imago Dei*, not their procreative abilities (which are shared with animals). Only humans receive dominion over the earth and are addressed directly. In her close read of Genesis 1:27 Trible notes that the verse only has seven words and actually reads (if one translates it more literally from the original Hebrew), "And-created God humankind in-his-image; / in-the-image-of-God created-he him; / male and-female created-he them." "Male and female" corresponds to "the image of God." The passage is poetic, where metaphor functions in order to reveal something about a lesser-known object (tenor) through a better-known element (vehicle). In Genesis 1:27 the vehicle "male and female" has a semantic correspondence with the tenor "image of God." In other words, the lesser element of the metaphor, "image of God," is in part illuminated by the better-known element, humanity. For Trible, the switch from singular to plural pronouns in the passage reveals that humanity *(hā-ʾādām)* consists of two creatures, male and female. "From the beginning humankind exists as two creatures, not as one creature with double sex."[6] Humankind exists in a unity that is at the same time sexually differentiated. Trible characterizes this as "distinction within harmony." Also, humanity as male and female reveals an egalitarian (not hierarchical) relationship between the sexes.

Another important point that arises from this verse is its ambiguity regarding the interpretation of male and female roles. Essentialist masculine and feminine attributes are not ascribed to male and female. The metaphor image of God both reveals and conceals something about the nature of God and the nature of humanity. There is a similarity and difference between created and Creator:

> But sexual differentiation of humankind is not thereby a description of God. Indeed, the metaphorical language of Genesis 1:27 preserves with exceeding care the otherness of God. If it depicts male and female in freedom and uniqueness, how much more does it uphold the transcendence of the deity. God is neither male nor female, nor a combination of the two. And yet, detecting divine transcendence in human reality requires human clues. Unique among them, according to our poem, is sexuality. God creates, in the image of God, male and female. To describe male and female, then, is to perceive the image of God; to

perceive the image of God is to glimpse the transcendence of God.[7]

In other words, the distinction of humanity as male and female does not imply any sort of sexuality within God. The metaphor functions to retain the unknowability of God. Nevertheless, our creation as male and female offers us a peek into some dimension of God's nature.

For many feminists such as Trible, Genesis 1:27 is the foundation of an egalitarian anthropology in which male and female are created to reflect the image of God equally. We must remember, however, that this is but one interpretation of the text. As Anne M. Clifford argues, given the overall patriarchal world view of the P source, such a passage is suspect. In her view it most likely relates to the command to procreate, created male and female in order to continue the species. "Since the Priestly writers probably had no experience of an egalitarian society," Clifford points out, "it is unlikely that *imago Dei* is an explicit claim for women's equality with men."[8] Given the overall tone of the elements of the Pentateuch that are attributed to P, it is difficult to argue, Clifford contends, that such an egalitarian vision of humanity was the intended message of the authors. Nonetheless, Clifford reminds us, this does not mean that the *imago Dei* cannot be used to assert the full humanity of women.

Biblical scholar Phyllis A. Bird offers an interpretation along those same lines. Bird does not interpret the divine image in association with sexual distinction or dominion but instead with fertility in the P account: "*Unlike* God but *like* the other creatures, *adam*, is characterized by sexual differentiation. . . . *Adam* is created *like* (i.e. resembling) God, but *as* creature—and hence male and female. . . . The second statement adds to the first; it does not explicate it."[9] For Bird, "male and female" refers to the procreative function that is shared by all of God's creation. P, Bird notes, would never attribute any form of sexuality to God and would indeed find such distinctions "foreign and repugnant." P understands sexual differentiation as solely procreative. Contrary to Trible, Bird stresses that the idea that human sexuality is in any way revelatory of the divine would be scandalous to the P authors. With Clifford she echoes the procreative intention behind the distinction. Curious, though, is the fact that the command to procreate is bestowed upon sea and winged animals in Genesis 1:22, though they are not distinguished in the text by their sexuality.

As noted by Kristen Kvam, Linda S. Schearing, and Valerie H. Ziegler in their excellent collection of Jewish, Christian, and Muslim interpretations of Genesis, it all boils down to how one interprets the colas (or parts) in 1:27. The three colas of verse 27 are parallel. "The first two are synonymously parallel (they repeat the same idea) and are arranged chiastically (the second reverses the order of the first." The third part ("male and female he created them") is not so easy to decipher. There are two possible interpretations: "If the third cola of v. 27 is *synonymously* parallel to the second—then the image of God may have something to do with sexual differentiation. . . . If the third cola in v. 27 is *synthetically* parallel to the second cola (that is, it adds to the idea in the second cola rather than repeating it)—then 'male and female' may not refer to 'the image of God.'"[10] Some feminist biblical scholars (such as Phyllis Bird) have argued that "male and female" does not refer to the image of God but instead anticipates the fertility statement in verse 28. Others such as Trible claim that "male and female" does refer to the image of God. The "his" in "his image" is also important to mention. The use of a masculine pronoun can be explained by three factors: the grammar of Hebrew for the third person singular; that most metaphors for God in Hebrew scriptures are male, though there are feminine similes; and a denouncement of goddess worship.

My interpretation aligns with Trible, in that I hold that "male and female" does refer to the image of God. While I am sympathetic to Clifford's and Bird's claims, the call for procreation is not exclusive to humanity. As mentioned above, the animals of the air and sea are called to procreate. What is exclusive to humanity is creation as male and female in the image of God. As Chapter 2 demonstrates, this debate has deep historical roots, for humanity's creation in the image of God and what that means has been the subject of intense debate and speculation throughout Christian history. In spite of its prominence within Christian theology, however, creation in the image of God receives little attention in the Hebrew scriptures. Genesis 5:1–5, only a few chapters after the initial mention, is the last reference to male and female created in God's likeness.

Genesis 2:4b-3:24

The creation story found in chapters 2 and 3 of Genesis, referred to as the Fall or the Garden of Eden, offers a radically different account of humanity and the cosmos's creation. Unlike the earlier narrative, in which humanity appears on the sixth day, this account places humanity at the front and center of creation. The human being is formed from the dust in the ground and is placed in the Garden of Eden to care for it, warned against eating from the tree of knowledge of good and evil. God determines that the human being needs companionship, so God puts the human to sleep, removes a rib, and from that rib creates another human being, and male and female are created. With the opening of chapter 3 a new actor enters the narrative, the serpent. The serpent convinces the woman to sample from the tree of knowledge, and she in turn persuades her partner. God enters the garden, finds the two hiding, and realizes what they have done. As a result of their actions, he banishes them from the garden, and the nature of their relationship is forever transformed, with woman destined to be subordinate to man.

My summary of this famous narrative, while brief, highlights the major moments. My analysis of the passage is shaped by two parameters: feminist interpretations of the text and its relevance for the Genesis 1 creation story. Much of my interpretation is influenced again by the work of Phyllis Trible. There are various elements of Trible's analysis that are significant for our purposes. First, the human being is not defined sexually at the beginning of the narrative. "Instead, the earth creature here is precisely and only the human being, so far sexually undifferentiated."[11] Gender differentiation does not occur until the creation of the female. In other words, male and female come to exist at the same moment. Prior to the creation of the female, the human being did not have a distinctive sexuality. Instead, it is only through the creation of the female that the male comes into being. "After God operates on this earth creature, to produce a companion, its identity becomes sexual."[12] There is a simultaneous creation of the sexes.

A second point that is significant to highlight is the use of the word "helper" to describe the creation of woman. As Trible rightfully points out, the Hebrew word ʿēzer is more appropriately translated "companion." Often the term *helper* implies a state of submission that is not found in the original text. The use of "helper" in 2:18 is often cited as a source to justify women's subordination. However, the meaning of these terms remains contested, for a relationship of subordination is not explicitly implied in the Hebrew. In fact, certain translations of the Hebrew can even imply that the helper is in fact superior to the one that he or she helps. Linked to this is the above-mentioned order of creation. "While some assume that this makes woman's creation derivative and secondary, others suggest that the last can be first, and argue for the superiority of woman's creation. If we understand *sela'* as side or if we see in this verse sexual differentiation (the creation of man and woman from a single androgynous being), then we might conclude that this verse describes a simultaneous rather than sequential creation."[13] Categorizations of woman as helper and her emerging "from man" have been erroneously used to subordinate women. Man's naming of woman has also been used to justify her submissiveness, but as Trible reminds us, the Hebrew verb used when man names the animals (implying dominance) is not the same as the one used when he names woman. The text shows us male and female in a relationship of equality and mutuality prior to the Fall.

The depiction of woman prior to her disobedience is the third point I wish to raise. Woman becomes the spokesperson for humanity, for it is she that has a theological discussion with the serpent. It is interesting to note that she does not consult with the man before acting and instead acts on her own accord. In her discussion with the serpent she is presented as far from ignorant or passive. "The response of the woman to the serpent reveals her as intelligent, informed, and perceptive. Theologian, ethicist, hermeneut, rabbi, she speaks with clarity and authority."[14] The man, on the other hand, is passive. He does not speak or theologize. A final insight in Trible's analysis that is significant to highlight is the nature of the consequences of humanity's transgression. Reading the text closely one notes that these are consequences, not punishments. Due to their transgression the egalitarian relationship between man and woman is destroyed, and the man becomes the master of the woman. The Fall results in the end of the intended model of companionship and instead leads to dominion. As Bird points out, "The companion of chap. 2 has become a master. The historical subordination of woman to man is inaugurated—and identified as the paradigm expression of sin and alienation in creation."[15] This was not the intended order of creation. This is a consequence of their actions. Thus the domination of women was not how God intended the relationship between the sexes to be. The hierarchy of the sexes is sealed in verse 20, when man names woman using the same verb that was used when he named the animals. As the story closes the woman narratively disappears, and it is man who is banished from the garden. Although it is actually both man and woman who are banished, her identity and existence have become subsumed into his.

Eve is not mentioned anywhere in the Hebrew scriptures beyond Genesis 5. In addition, nowhere else in the Hebrew scriptures are Adam and Eve cited as examples of disobedience or punishment. Certain aspects of the Fall help us shed light on the manner in which Genesis 1 has been interpreted within Christian theology. Sexist interpretations of the Fall have led (male) theologians to write that woman is created second and is thus inferior to man; woman is to be man's helper; because she comes from man's rib woman is dependent on man and needs him for her existence; woman is responsible for allowing sin to enter into the world; woman is untrustworthy; and God allows man to rule over woman. These stereotypes will fuel theological speculation on the manner in which woman does (or does not) reflect the image of God. Both Genesis accounts are stories, mythic accounts written by a particular community to explain the human condition and humanity's relationship with the divine. Throughout Christian history, however, a patriarchal exegesis of the Genesis accounts has been canonized to legitimize women's secondary status within the Christian tradition.

Paul

The relationship between Genesis and the New Testament writings is seen most directly in the writings of the apostle Paul. In this section I focus on two passages: one found in the letter to the Galatian community, and the other in the first letter written to the Corinthians. While Galatians 3:28 has often been cited as claiming an egalitarian vision of humanity, Corinthians is quoted to argue just the opposite. Therefore, I will briefly examine the two and the tension between them in the Pauline corpus. My findings here are grounded in the work of feminist biblical scholar Lone Fatum. My emphasis on feminist biblical interpretation serves the overall intention of this book, which is to introduce the reader to feminist theology and its contributions to Christianity as a whole.

Galatians 3:27–28 reads: "As many of you as were baptized into Christ have clothed yourselves with Christ. There is no longer Jew or Greek, there is no longer slave or free, there is no longer male and female; for all of you are one in Christ Jesus." This baptismal formula implies that through baptism in Christ the divisions that plague humanity will disappear and that we will be fully restored in the image of God, as was the original intention of our creation. For our study it is the erasure of the distinction between male and female that is most important. Fatum argues that many biblical scholars have examined Galatians 3:28 uncritically, without fully examining the implications of abolishing gender distinctions eschatologically. It is difficult to understand, Fatum points out, what Galatians 3:28c meant for the everyday social life of the Galatian community. In other words, was this a social prescription for one's everyday life or a reality that would only be fully realized in the afterlife?

One cannot understand Galatians 3:28 without relating it to Genesis 1:27. Fatum, (and I disagree here) interprets the sexual differentiation of Genesis 1:27 as an addition to the *imago Dei* and sees this differentiation as functional for procreative reasons. In her interpretation, when Galatians 3:28c speaks of the effacement of sexual differentiation, it is referring to the healing of the human being through Christ, a return to the intended original unity of the *imago Dei*.[16] In other words, Fatum argues that the image of God is free of gender distinctions and that Galatians 3:28c is calling for a return to that original androgyny of the *imago Dei*. Fatum is also quick to remind the reader that Paul's writings always have the male as normative. For Paul, Galatians 3:28 is talking about the annulment of negative aspects in men, not embracing positive ones in women. Through baptism women become "sons" of God and consequently reflect God's image by becoming like men. "He [Paul] accepts that likeness of God is in fact a token of a definite and absolute order of creation reflecting the qualitative difference between man and woman."[17] Galatians 3:28 is an attempt to return to the *imago Dei* as it is meant to be prior to sexual differentiation.

An excerpt from 1 Corinthians 11:3–9 reads:

> But I want you to understand that Christ is the head of every man, and the husband is the head of his wife, and God is the head of Christ. . . . For if a woman will not veil herself, then she should cut off her hair; but if it is disgraceful for a woman to have her hair cut off or to be shaved, she should wear a veil. For a man ought not to have his head veiled, since he is the image and reflection of God; but woman is the reflection of man. Indeed, man was not made from woman, but woman from man. Neither was man created for the sake of woman, but woman for the sake of man.

These verses clearly demonstrate, among other things, the influence of the second creation story on interpretations of humanity as created in the image of God. Paul states in verse 7 that only man is in the image of God and that in relationship to woman he is dominant. Woman depends on man in her relationship with God. For Paul, the image of God is the foundation of man's authority, for woman is secondary:

> Because sexual liberation to Paul is synonymous with an eschatological affirmation of life based on the annulment of sexual differentiation, sexual liberation is in fact liberation from sexuality; and it follows that to Christian women sexual liberation means not only a denial of their female gender and bodies, but practically speaking also, as a direct consequence of Gen 1:27b (LXX), an actual self-denial.[18]

To be liberated as a Christian woman means to reject one's sex and become like a man. Underlying both Galatians and Corinthians is a negative, androcentric view of women.

Unlike many feminist scripture scholars, Fatum does not view the Galatians and Corinthians texts as contradictory:

Either the Christian woman is exempted from her sexuality, i.e. her femaleness, in Christ and given the opportunity to be reckoned among the sons of God like a Christian male, or she remains bound to her body and female gender with the result that she is literally left behind in this world and its sexual hierarchy, belonging to a man before she may be said to belong to Christ, and thus socially as well as theologically of course dependent on the superior male also in her relation to God.[19]

While I am not always in agreement with Fatum's logic, I do agree with her conclusion. Both texts are informed by a patriarchal view of humanity, and Galatians is thus not as "liberating" as it appears at first glance. Both texts imply that woman must be liberated from her sexuality and her body in order to be fully realized as a human being and fully reflect the image of God. These two New Testament texts serve as examples of the beginnings of Christian interpretations of Genesis and the manner in which they began, in the early church, to shape sexist understandings of the subordination of women.

Scripture in Systematic Theology

Before turning to the philosophical foundations of Christian interpretations of Genesis, I include a word about the role of scripture within systematic theology. From the onset one must acknowledge that the Christian scriptures (and Hebrew scriptures, for that matter) are theological documents. As Francis Schüssler Fiorenza indicates: "The Scriptures are not simply sources for theological reflection but themselves are examples of theological reflection. . . . The Christian Scriptures, therefore, are constituted not only by the symbols and testimonies of faith, but also by that theological reflection emerging within those symbols and testimonies."[20] In other words, Christian theology did not begin after New Testament times. Christian theology began *with* the New Testament. The gospels and letters are theological documents. Therefore, to speak of the relationship of scripture within systematic theology is a bit complex, for linguistically it implies that scripture is somehow not theological.

Protestant theologians have always had a strong scriptural foundation in their writings. For Roman Catholic theologians, however, it was only with Vatican II, when a two-source understanding of revelation as scripture and tradition was established, that the Bible came to figure prominently. These sources are parallel and equal. The Magisterium was understood as the servant of scripture. Scripture also became a major source of Catholic spirituality, and Vatican II opened up the Bible for lay Catholics. After an initial enthusiastic response to Vatican II's biblical renaissance for lay Catholics, women became increasingly disenchanted with the patriarchal nature of the Bible and its male-gendered God. As Schneiders points out, "Within a couple of decades of the Council, many Catholic women, as their feminist consciousness developed, moved from enthusiasm for the Bible as a privileged locus of encounter with God to vague discomfort, rising anger, deep alienation, and finally rejection of the Bible as a hopelessly oppressive tool of historical and contemporary patriarchy."[21] Thus for feminist lay women as well as theologians, scripture remains a double-edged sword.

Feminist theologians vary vastly in the manner in which they approach scripture and its function in their theology. Many, such as Rosemary Radford Ruether and Ada María Isasi-Díaz, take a "canon within the canon" approach, determining based on critical feminist principles whether a biblical passage is revelatory or not.[22] Schneiders does not accept the approach that removes texts that are oppressive and deems them un-revelatory. Scripture as a whole must be deemed revelatory or not. She instead proposes a theory that embraces the revelatory nature of the text while being mindful of its human coloring. "Because the text is human language giving voice to human experience of God in Christ, as well as to the experience of the early community in all its weakness and sinfulness, the text, even though it is inspired (written and read under the influence of the Holy Spirit), is as capable of error, distortion, and even sinfulness as the church itself."[23] My approach leans toward Schneiders's approach in that it recognizes the revelatory nature of all scripture while being constantly mindful of the manner in which context and culture shape the text.

Philosophical Foundations

Unlike scripture, the manner in which philosophy has come to influence and shape Christian understandings of humanity, and in fact Christianity as a whole, is much more implicit and unsystematic. As mentioned in the Introduction, philosophy and theology have historically been very closely united, and many would argue that it was only after the Middle Ages that the two became divorced into distinct disciplines. In this section I examine two philosophical voices that have influenced Christian thought substantially. Traces of both Plato and Aristotle, as the rest of this book makes evident, have marked Christian theology throughout its history and continue to thrive in the contemporary era. They are not the only non-Christian philosophical influences, but they are the most significant. While brief, my comments on both thinkers are limited to the task at hand, examining reflections on humanity with special attention to gender roles and biological sex.

Plato

The Greek philosopher Plato (428–355 BCE) is the first in the history of philosophy to develop a substantial understanding of male and female identity. Nonetheless, it must be noted that Plato was not always a systematic thinker, and at times one finds contradictions in his corpus regarding the role of women. He is often pitted against Aristotle and seen as the more "feminist friendly" of the Greeks. The center of Plato's "feminism" is found in the *Republic*, where he argues that women in the upper classes must be assigned social roles similar if not equal to men. Similarly, as Nicholas D. Smith highlights, "The *Meno*, for example, assigns the same virtues to women as to men (73A ff.), and Aristophanes' speech in the *Symposium* provides women with a genetic and biological status equal to that of men (109A ff.), a status never disputed elsewhere in the dialogue."[24] For many feminist philosophers and theologians, Plato's vision of the human, while flawed, is a much more welcome perspective than the Aristotelian logic that later became cemented within Christian theology.

In the simplest terms, Plato's view of the sexes is grounded in his mind-body dualism. The soul or mind is not necessarily reflected in and is distinct from the body. Therefore, with regard to the soul, men and women have similar natures; with regard to their bodies, women are inferior to men. Women's souls are equal to men's, it is only in their bodies that one finds a hierarchy of being. This framework will be later echoed by Augustine of Hippo in the early Christian church. As Prudence Allen describes it, Plato only views women as inferior in their embodied state: "Indeed, he is accepting a cosmic view of sex polarity in the inferior incarnation of woman, while also suggesting a theory of sex unity for the actual lives of women and men in the world."[25] Women are weaker due to their inferior bodies; however, this does not entirely hinder their rationality. Instead, Plato argues, women will have to study harder before gaining the wisdom to become a philosopher. "Plato was the first philosopher in the West to offer extensive arguments for women and men receiving the same education. His rationale for this position was an appeal to the same nature. A person's nature has nothing to do with his or her sex, but simply with the quality of soul."[26] Female identity is grounded in the soul, not the body. It is perspectives such as this that fuel feminist appreciation of Plato's corpus.

One cannot, however, uncritically embrace Plato as a proto-feminist. Plato may have an egalitarian vision of men's and women's souls, but when it comes to embodied existence women are clearly inferior. As he writes in the *Republic:* "There is no pursuit of the administration of a state that belongs to a woman because she is a woman or to a man because he is a man. But the natural capacities are distributed alike among both creatures, and women naturally share in all pursuits and men in all—yet for all woman is weaker than the man."[27] Woman's weakness does not impede her from struggling to attain certain goals, for example, a philosopher guardian of the state: "The women and the men, then, have the same nature in respect to the guardianship of the state, save in so far as the one is weaker, the other stronger."[28] Women will have to work harder than men to attain the same goals.

As Beverly Clack notes, however, many of the egalitarian writings in the *Republic* are tempered by more sexist claims in other places within Plato's corpus:

> At the heart of the case for a "feminist" Plato lies the *Republic*. In Book V, Plato argues that women should receive the same education as men. . . . However, the claim that Plato is feminist has been much disputed. While parts of the *Republic* may suggest an egalitarian Plato, other aspects refute such a claim. The language Plato uses suggests that while in theory women might be leaders of his ideal society, in practice he expects men to take on this role. . . . In other works, Plato argues for the innate inferiority of women. In the *Symposium* he argues that love of man for man is a higher form of love than love of man for woman. The latter form of love is purely connected with procreation; the love of man for man leads to the higher appreciation of the Good. In the *Timaeus*, a hierarchy of creation is advanced, for women are closer to animals than are men.[29]

Clack's hesitancy is echoed by L. D. Derksen, who writes, "Despite his radical view of women in the *Republic*, feminist theorists are not totally convinced that Plato's philosophy as a whole presents a positive image of women." There are confusing and sometimes unflattering references to women. "They do seem to be able to be fitted into a pattern: when women are criticized it is mostly in terms of their lesser capacity for reasoning."[30] Taking a slightly different perspective, Smith highlights recent claims that the status of women in Athens has been "overstated" and that Plato's "slurs" regarding women merely demonstrate how his context shaped him and do not reflect inconsistency in his thought.[31] However one approaches it, with Plato one has an ambiguous legacy. On the one hand, women are given a certain equality with men based on the Platonic belief that souls are not shaped by one's embodied sexuality. In addition, women are given opportunities in education, even to aspire to become philosophers, within the Platonic world view. However, within their embodied existence they are inferior and weaker. In spite of all his attempts to give some sort of equal standing to women, in his world they remain second-class citizens.

Aristotle

The contribution of Aristotle to Christian understandings of humanity cannot be overestimated. His understanding of humanity, grounded in a hierarchical biological framework, continues to influence Christian theology even today. This is most clearly seen in the Vatican's position regarding the sexes, one that will be explored later in this text. Aristotle's influence in Christian theology and philosophy was cemented in the Middle Ages by Thomas Aquinas's appropriation of his thought within his own writings. In addition, Aristotle is the first philosopher to offer a truly systematic account of the sexes. As Allen rightly claims:

Aristotle (384–322 BC) was the first philosopher to develop a completely consistent set of answers to questions about sex identity that previous philosophers had raised.

His theory developed a comprehensive rationale for the theory of sex polarity. That is, Aristotle argued that differences between women and men were philosophically significant and that men were naturally superior to women. . . . Aristotle's description of the female as the privation of the male in the category of opposites, as considered in the area of metaphysics, was the foundation for the devaluation of woman in the area of generation. Further, the theory of the inferior generation of the female fetus offered the rationale for the devaluation of woman under the categories of wisdom and virtue. In this way, Aristotle's drive for consistency led to the first systematic attempt to defend a single theory of sex identity.[32]

As Allen indicates, Aristotle argued that the differences between men and women, ones that made men superior, are philosophically significant. His understanding of the female as a mutilated male, as an incomplete and deprived male, is the foundation of sexist understandings of women as essentially inferior to men. Aristotle devotes a chapter of the *Metaphysics* to the question of male and female, showing the centrality of the issue for him.

Aristotle's philosophical vision is grounded in his reproductive biology. For Aristotle, woman's seed did not contribute to reproduction. She was a passive receptacle. In *On the Generation of Animals*, he makes man the active source of life in reproduction. The female is passive and thus inferior. He writes, "Now of course the female, *qua* female, is passive, and the male, *qua* male, is active—it is that whence the principle of movement comes."[33] Within reproduction, man contributes the energy of creation, while woman contributes the material "stuff" of creation. The semen enters the uterus and mixes with the female secretion (which has potential, not actual parts). Ultimately, this leads to one of his most offensive statements: the female is "a mutilated male." Woman is a deficient man. She is mutilated and lacking.

why did he hold this?

—what is this?

Underlying his biology is Aristotle's theory of contraries. Aristotle held that in a pair of contraries, one is always the privation of the other. Since men and women were a pair of contraries, woman must be inferior to man. She was an imperfect man, a deformity: "The female is as it were a deformed male; and the menstrual discharge is semen though in an impure condition."[34] Woman is associated with matter and passivity, man with form and activity. Aristotle associated woman with matter and man with form, and this was based on his theory of generation. Because form is superior to matter, man is superior to woman. Aristotle's theory cemented the idea that woman was associated with passivity and man with activity.

The implications of Aristotle's thought reach into the political and societal realm. In *Politics* he argues for a patriarchal, hierarchal family, in which the man rules over the woman: "The male is by nature superior, and the female inferior, one rules and the other is ruled; this principle of necessity extends to all mankind."[35] His hierarchical understanding of society is grounded in his view that women are deficient. This vision also includes children and slaves, who, like women, are to be ruled by men: "The freeman rules over the slave after another manner from that in which the male rules over the female, or the man over the child; although the parts of the soul are present in all of them, they are present in different degrees. For the slave has no deliberate faculty at all; the woman has, but it is without authority, and the child has, but it is immature."[36] Grounded in his biology and its underlying philosophy, woman, much like a child, is to be ruled by man and accept his ultimate authority.

Aristotle defines man as more fully human than woman. The man is associated with the animating force in life and with reason. It is this male active force that gives shape to the formless matter that the female offers. One is left with the conclusion that woman is associated with nature and man with reason. The passive female is in opposition to the active, rational male. This even has implications for the nature of philosophy, for as the one who is associated with reason man becomes associated with philosophy:

> He [Aristotle] argued that while women have the same kind of reason as men, in the female the higher power of reason is without authority over the lower or irrational powers. As a consequence, women have an inferior reasoning capacity; they are therefore considered capable only of true opinion and not of knowledge, properly speaking. Consequently, for Aristotle, women cannot be wise in the same way as men. It obviously followed from this that women could not be philosophers. . . . He assumed a similarity between the association of the male with soul and the female with body on the one hand, and the association of the male with the higher reasoning capabilities and the female with the lower on the other. This marked the first time in western philosophy that the concept of woman was directly linked with irrational thought. Therefore, Aristotle's sex polarity brought about a clear shift on the subject of women's relation to wisdom.[37]

Because women are associated with the lower or irrational functions and men with the higher or rational functions, in Aristotle's philosophical system women were deprived of any authority or public voice. Contrary to Plato's view, they are incapable of becoming philosophers. Because of her inferior rationality, woman can become virtuous by obedience to a virtuous man. Woman's nature is to obey, while man's is to rule.

Aristotle undermines Plato's body-soul dualism and instead argues that the soul is the form of the body. In other words, because women's bodies are different from men's, their souls must also be different. Aristotle rejects Plato's notion of the sexless soul and concludes that women are not only weaker in body but that their souls in fact are weaker. This, in turn, leads to an understanding of the differences between men and women as absolute. Ultimately, Aristotle has a more consistent and "scientific" misogyny than Plato, for he elaborates it in a systematic manner across various disciplines. Both philosophers leave a weighty legacy on the history of philosophy and theology. As the following chapter demonstrates, their influence is clearly embedded within the history of Christian thought, where they became key players in the construction of male and female identity. Coupled with an understanding of woman as inferior that is found in the earliest of Christian writings and an interpretation of Genesis 1 that is tainted by a misinterpretation of the Genesis 2—3 account, it is clear that woman's inferior status became cemented early on within Christian theology. The egalitarian vision of women and men found in Genesis 1, as well as the egalitarian impulses of the early Jesus movement, are quickly silenced as male theologians begin their historical crusade to silence and control women's bodies and souls.

Chapter 2

Historical Theology

The doctrine of the *imago Dei* is a central theological theme throughout Christian history. This chapter provides an overview of the key voices and ideas that have created the foundation for theological speculation on the nature of our humanity as created in the image of God. The chapter is in no way exhaustive; as the bibliography attests, entire books have been written on merely one historical era or figure. Nonetheless, the purpose of this chapter is to trace the development of the theological interpretation of the *imago Dei*, not to provide a quintessential history. As always, the emphasis of my study centers on the question of gender and biological sex. Beginning with the church fathers, I move to medieval and Reformation theology. The chapter concludes with an eye toward the modern era, looking at the philosophical impulses that will shape the theologies examined in Chapter 3.

Church Fathers

Reflection on the divine image flourished in the patristic era. This section could be a book in and of itself, for writings on the *imago Dei* were extensive in this era. For the purposes of our study I have limited my scope to three major figures: Irenaeus of Lyons, Gregory of Nyssa, and Augustine of Hippo. My section on Augustine is the lengthiest, because his impact on the history of Christian theology is the most substantial. However, the three taken together reveal the ethos of this era while offering distinctive voices. For many of the church fathers, the *imago Dei* was intimately linked to their understanding of the soul and spirituality. The image was most fully realized in the act of contemplation of God. Human beings do not truly realize themselves unless they go beyond their selves and return to the being in whose image we are created. This is the most profound sense of the patristic theology of the *imago Dei*.[1] The church fathers contend that the *imago Dei* is a dimension of the human soul and mind. For the majority of thinkers, the body does not reflect the image, though for woman it comes to be a factor that hinders the image's expression.

Often the patristic era is celebrated as a heyday for theological speculation on the nature of women. However, the church fathers provide a mixed bag for feminists. A pivotal phrase is Genesis 1:27 and the significance of "male and female" on the image of God. As the previous chapter explored, this continues to be a question for theologians and scripture scholars even today. The point of contention for the church fathers is not the nature of the image, but rather how sexuality relates to it. As Rosemary Radford Ruether points out:

> The crucial biblical text for the creation of man was Genesis 1:27: "God created man in His own image; male and female he created them." If the Fathers could have had the first part of the text without the final phrase, they would have been happier. Indeed they often only quote about the first part of this text without alluding to the second. About the character of the image of God in man they had no doubts. This referred to man's soul or reason.[2]

While the fathers affirm the rationality of woman's mind, because she is symbolically tied to the body, her salvation must be seen as the negation of her nature. Thus many church fathers, such as Augustine, argue that spiritually women share the *imago*

Dei in spite of their bodies. Kari Elisabeth Børreson sees traditional Christian anthropology as beginning with two divergent
beliefs: a female subordination established by God's order, and
a human equality realized through redemption in Christ. Wom-
en are redeemed *in spite of* their femaleness. The *imago Dei*
becomes rational and sexless. However, this does not always
serve in women's favor. "This gender free privilege in man-like
disguise permits *backdating* women's redemptive Christ-like-
ness to the creational level, without affecting their God-given
subservience *qua* females, a split which has been upheld in
theological anthropology until this century."[3] Woman's *imago*
becomes something she lost in the Fall and will fully recover
only in the afterlife. This leads to female subservience in the
here and now.

Irenaeus of Lyons

One cannot overestimate the impact of Irenaeus of Lyons on
the history of theology. This is due to his corpus and his historical era. As Irenaean scholar Mary Ann Donovan points out:
"The second century was *the* century for the construction of
Christian identity. One of the principal architects of that identity was Irenaeus of Lyons. His work shaped the Scriptures, the
exegesis, the theology, the institutions, and the spirituality of
nascent Christianity to such an extent that his imprint is dis-
cernible almost two thousand years later."[4] Irenaeus has been
called the first Christian theologian, and he is the first to use the
terms *image* and *likeness* together. Born between 140 and 160
CE, he is most known for his writings against Gnosticism (especially the figures Valentinus and Marcion). Due to this, many
of his writings are polemical. A key concern for Irenaeus's theology is the question of God's universal salvific will. For
Irenaeus, God is uncreated, humanity is dependent, and God's
power is not diminished in God's creation of us.

The theology of Irenaeus is difficult to approach on the theme
of the divine image due to his conflicting and contradictory

writings on the image and likeness. "Irenaeus lapses into an inconsistent use of these two terms, image and likeness, at times using them synonymously, but more often distinguishing them."[5] To approach Irenaeus's theology, therefore, one must accept these inconsistencies and enter into his corpus aware that he is not a systematic thinker on this topic. At times, for Irenaeus, likeness equals similitude. Man is described as the likeness of God, yet this likeness is lost in the Fall. The Son becomes the archetype of likeness, which is revealed in the incarnation. We humans lost our resemblance, but it is reestablished by the incarnation: "Likeness is revealed in the incarnate Son; humanity shares that likeness with the Son."[6]

Irenaeus's notion of likeness is dynamic. For Irenaeus, likeness has to do with human behavior; it is a soteriological notion. At times Irenaeus also speaks of similitude. Similitude has to do with our similarity to God. Image and similitude are anthropological categories, for they reveal something about human nature. Likeness is a soteriological concept that refers to the human's relationship with God. "The concept of image is tied to that of likeness. This last concept, as we have seen, is tied to the soteriological order: likeness is at the same time the dynamism that transforms man and the goal envisioned by this transformation, certified by God, knowing the realization of his design."[7] Ultimately, one cannot truly unpack Irenaeus's understanding of the human, especially in reference to the *imago Dei,* without turning to his Christology.

Irenaeus does not refute the notion that the Son has always existed with the Father. What is important, however, is the role of the incarnation within salvation history and its implications for our creation in the image and likeness of God. "But when He became incarnate, and was made man, He commenced afresh the long line of human beings, and furnished us, in a brief, comprehensive manner, with salvation; so that what we had lost in Adam—namely to be according to the image and likeness of God—that we might recover in Jesus Christ" (III,18,1).[8] Christ's incarnation was necessary, for human beings could not save themselves from sin; they needed Christ. The manner in which Christ saves is connected with the importance of obedience in Irenaeus's theology. Jesus' obedience did away with Adam's disobedience. Similarly, Mary's obedience did away with the damage inflicted by Eve's disobedience. Eve, "having become disobedient, was made the cause of death, both to herself and to the entire human race; so also did Mary, having a man betrothed [to her], and being nevertheless a virgin, by yielding obedience, become the cause of salvation, both to herself and the whole human race. . . . And thus also it was that the knot of Eve's disobedience was loosed by the obedience of Mary" (III,22,4). Interestingly, as Donovan points out, "Absent here is any suggestion of the impact of sexuality on either Eve's sin or Mary's obedience."⁹ Irenaeus does not place specific blame on Mary or Eve because they are women.

In Irenaeus's thought, Jesus becomes the man Adam was destined to become. There are three elements to the image of Christ and man in his fullness: body, soul, and spirit. "All three elements, as assumed by the humanity of Christ, are essential to man as God made him to be eventually completed."¹⁰ Irenaeus distinguished between a natural person and the perfection of the person. The natural person consisted of a body and soul. The perfected person consisted of a body, soul, and spirit. The spirit is received through God. This spirit is tied to his notion of redemption, a recovery of something lost, our likeness to God. Here we find a moment where Irenaeus distinguishes between image and likeness. Adam never lost his image. His likeness, his similarity to God, is what was lost through Adam's sin. The body, however, always constitutes the image of God. This is a fundamental point that distinguishes Irenaeus's theology. Unlike other church fathers, Irenaeus holds that the body is a reflection of the image. "In the Irenaean schema the image of God in the person is in the flesh. This sense of image corresponds to form, and form inheres only in matter. Both the Gnostics and the later Alexandrian Fathers hold that the image is in the spiritual part of the human being.

Irenaeus rejects this possibility explicitly. Consequently the image of God in the human being must exist in matter, that is, in our very flesh."[11] He elaborates this theme against the teachings of Gnosticism, yet nonetheless, here we find a moment where the image exists not in spite of but within the body.

We are made in the image of God, who is revealed in Jesus Christ. Incarnation is the central point in human history. In Irenaeus, the image refers to the body and soul, while the likeness refers to grace dwelling within us. Before the Fall, Adam possessed the image and was a child in spirit; he was supposed to move on to spiritual maturity. When he sinned, he lost his spirit and thus his likeness to God. Christ restores our spirit through his recapitulation of our communion with God. "In becoming a human being the Son of God 'recapitulates' or sums up the entire creation in himself."[12] Christ creates a new beginning for the human race and undoes Adam's disobedience. In the words of Irenaeus, "When [the Son of God] was made incarnate and made a human being, he recapitulated in himself the long history of humankind, procuring salvation for us in the compendium, that what we lost in Adam, that is to be according to the image and likeness of God, this we would recover in Jesus Christ" (III,18,1). Our salvation is the recovery through Christ of what was lost in Adam, namely the image and likeness of God. The Son reflects the image of God, and we, in turn, are the image of the Son. Until the incarnation the image of God was invisible. Jesus Christ makes visible the invisible God.[13]

Gregory of Nyssa

Gregory of Nyssa (330/335–395/400) is recognized as one of the great theological voices of the early Eastern church. Along with his older brother, Basil of Caesaria, and their friend Gregory of Nazianzus, these three Cappadocian theologians offered a powerful contribution to early Christianity. The three are often studied within the context of the great fourth-century trinitarian debates. Gregory was educated in Athens and influenced by the writings of Plato and Origen. Details of his life are scant, though it is known that he abandoned the secular life as a teacher of rhetoric and became, like his brother, a bishop. He is recognized as one of the great opponents of Arianism, arguing that the one God exists as three hypostases and that person rather than substance is the primary ontological category of God. In this section we explore his theological anthropology, for in the work of Gregory feminists find a kindred spirit; his gender-free notion of the divine image allows men and women to share the *imago* equally.

Gregory locates our greatness in our creation in the image of God, not in our likeness to creation. Sin does not completely destroy the original *imago*. In sharp contrast to Irenaeus, and demonstrating the influence of Plato on his thought, Gregory argues that the image is not found in the body but in the spirit. The *imago Dei* is characterized by our openness to the divine through our intellect and our will. As noted by George A. Maloney, "Man in his intellect and the faculty of love, his will, is made to God's image insofar as man with his highest faculties opens himself 'to behold and to hear' God. God is mirrored forth in His image in man through contemplation. Man's *nous* or *logos* is capable of being divinized by its openness to the Divine Logos."[14] Through our openness to God we reflect the image most authentically. We find in Gregory a spiritualized notion of the image, one that grows through contemplation.

For Gregory, the whole of humanity resembles God's image and bears the image equally. God already understands humanity as created fully in God's image. However, this is God's foreknowledge of the human condition, for Gregory distinguishes between creation in its initial state and its eventual fulfillment. The fulfillment will only occur in the parousia at the end of time. In God's mind, however, we are already fulfilled and actualized. However, in our human reality we must go through time and material space in order to reach fulfillment. "The image of God in man is both at one and the same time in God's mind universally and concretely realized."[15] While we must go through the steps to realize fully the *imago* within us, God's "mind" is not tempered by the constraints of time and space. Image is understood in Gregory's theology as a relationship between God and humanity, where we grow in likeness to Christ. Love is what constitutes the image of God in humanity, and through desire in faith this love grows.

A fundamental text for understanding the *imago Dei* in Gregory's corpus is *On the Making of Man*. In the prologue Gregory establishes that only the soul was created in the image of God and that only humans share in God's image.[16] Humanity lies between two extremes, the heavens and the earth, and thus has a dual nature. "He gives him as foundations the instincts of a two-fold organization, blending the Divine with the earthy, that by means of both he may be naturally and properly disposed to each enjoyment, enjoying God by means of his more divine nature, and the good things of earth by the sense that is akin to them" (II, 2). Humanity was created last, for the dominion of creation had to be established before the arrival of the ruler. The human consists of three elements: "so that man consists of these three: . . . 'body and soul and spirit' . . . using the word 'body' for the nutritive part, and denoting the sensitive by the word 'soul,' and the intellectual by 'spirit'" (IIX, 5). We gather knowledge from the senses, but the mind is working behind that. This is the invisible mind that is incomprehensible to us, for just as God is incomprehensible, since we share in God's image, we will never fully understand ourselves. The soul finds its perfection in the intellectual and rational.

Our glory is found in our being created in the image of God, though this image is something that must be cultivated within humanity. Imitation of God becomes a central dimension of Gregory's notion of the manner in which we image God. If we do not keep up our imitation, we can lose the image within us (XVI, 3). This reaffirms the prominence of contemplation within Gregory's anthropology. The image is not something static that is merely implanted within humanity. Instead, it is something that exists dynamically within us and is intimately tied to our spiritual life. Affirming that the image is purely spiritual and intellectual, Gregory rejects any connection between the image and the body. Humanity is the unity of the divine and brutal nature, with the brutal being associated with bodiliness and sexuality:

> While two natures—the Divine and incorporeal nature, and the irrational life of brutes—are separated from each other as extremes, human nature is the mean between them: for in the compound nature of man we may behold a part of each of the natures that I have mentioned,—of the Divine, rational, and intelligent element, which does not admit the distinction of male and female; of the irrational, our bodily form and structure, divided into male and female: for each of these elements is certainly to be found in all that partakes of human life. (XVI, 9)

Our creation as embodied men and women is solely for procreative reasons. God made us male and female with the foreknowledge that we would need reproduction after the Fall, when our angelic majesty was replaced with animal reproduction. We are a composite of the divine and the irrational. Had we been obedient to God, we would have been immutable, but because of the Fall we are mutable. We would not have procreated but experienced some sort of angelic multiplication. The distinction between male and female is irrational; to increase and multiply thus belongs to our irrational nature. *On the Making of Man* presents humanity divided, struggling between our divine and brutal (bodily, passionate) natures. Sadly, the impulse of sin and the irrational is greater than that of the intellect. Nonetheless, the good and wisdom will prevail; we are in constant motion, progressing toward the good.

Another key text on the *imago Dei* is *On Virginity*.[17] In this text Gregory returns again to the theme of creation in the image of God, though with an eye toward sin. In humanity's first creation we did not have passion or death. Instead, "being the image and the likeness, as has been said, of the Power which rules all things, man kept also in the matter of a Free-Will this likeness to Him whose Will is over all." Humanity chose to turn away from virtue and created evil. Humanity is clouded and soiled by the evil of sin. But, the image is not lost. "The earthly envelopment once removed, the soul's beauty will again appear." However, the uncovering of the image is not attributed to human nature but instead finds its origins in the divine; as humans, we can only go so far without divine assistance. "In fact this likeness to the divine is not our work at all; it is not the achievement of any faculty of man; it is the great gift of God bestowed upon our nature at the very moment of our birth; human efforts can only go so far as to clear away the filth of sin and so cause the buried beauty of the soul to shine forth again." The image is not something alien to our nature, it is just covered up. "The image of our King, not yet hopelessly lost, but hidden beneath the dirt; and this last we must understand the impurities of the flesh, which, being swept and purged away by carefulness of life, leave clear to the view the object of our search." To restore the divine image we must become like Adam before the Fall.

As mentioned above, the distinction between male and female does not belong to our image, since God has no distinct sex. Sex is not sinful; it is part of creation. God foresaw what was going to happen to humanity in the Fall, and our biological sex becomes a means to attain our original perfection. Sexual differentiation does not play into Gregory's idea of the image and likeness. For Gregory of Nyssa, the image is spiritual; in resurrection we will be neither male nor female. Our bodies symbolize our fallen state. As noted by Kari Elisabeth Børreson, Gregory of Nyssa "includes women in God-like humanity by defining creational image of God as presexual privilege." Gender differentiation, femaleness, is caused by primeval sin. There is, in Gregory, a double creation: Genesis 1:26–27a is spiritual creation in God's image; Genesis 1:27b-28, where we are distinguished as male and female, is because of God's foreknowledge of our sin. Male and female embodiment is equally marginalized in Gregory's theology, and the female is not depicted as the weaker sex. "Gregory's twofold anthropology is 'feminist' in the sense that by placing Adam's formation in Gen 2,7 on the *same* secondary level as derived woman in Gen 2,18,21–23, he severs the traditional link between theomorphic humanity and exemplary maleness."[18] Gregory refutes andromorphic God-language, for the divine image in his anthropology excludes both male and female attributes. Feminists can celebrate Gregory's theology, therefore, for not privileging the male over the female. However, in his association of the body with our brutal nature, given the body's historical association with femaleness, he unwittingly contributes to women's marginalization.

Augustine of Hippo

Augustine of Hippo was born in 354 in Thagaste (modern-day Algeria). He is, arguably, the most influential theologian in the history of Christianity. Considered the "father" of the doctrine of original sin, Augustine's monumental corpus covers a variety of themes, including the Trinity, grace, sexual ethics, the nature of the church, and spirituality. Augustine's *Confessions* is considered the first Western spiritual autobiography. He personally encountered and struggled against two of the most significant heresies in the early church: Donatism and Pelegianism. His theology offers a North African contribution, one that is shaped by the concerns of his culture and era. It is difficult to approach Augustine's writings on the *imago Dei*, for as John Edward Sullivan points out, "His teaching about the image does not appear in systematic fashion in any one treatise, but is scattered throughout his letters, his sermons, the exegetical and polemical works, the *Confessions*, the *City of God*, and in the *De Trinitate*, the principal source of his teaching, it is almost inextricably bound up with the trinitarian doctrine."[19] Within this section I limit my reflections to Augustine's writings within the confines of his reflection on the Trinity and his interpretations of the book of Genesis.

De Trinitate is a fundamental text for understanding Augustine's notion of the divine image. In book 7, chapter 12, Augustine gives his trinitarian exegesis of Genesis 1:26: "But *let us make* and *our* are said in the plural, and ought not to be received except in terms of relative names. For it was not that gods might make, or make after the image and likeness of gods, but that the Father, and Son, and Holy Spirit might make after the image of the Father, and Son, and Holy Spirit."[20] For Augustine, the fact that the Genesis account says "let us" with regard to the creation of the human and "let there be" with regard to everything else indicates the involvement of the three Persons of the Trinity in creation. The same sentiment is repeated in *The Literal Meaning of Genesis:* "Because of the three Persons, it is said *to Our image*; because of the one God, it is said *to the image of God*."[21] This leads to an understanding of the *imago Dei* as trinitarian. "Our image" and "to the image of God" indicate that man is made in the trinitarian God's image (not just the image of the Son or the image of the Father).

Book 14 of *De Trinitate* argues that the image of God in the mind is permanent, just defaced: "The mind is God's image *par excellence* in virtue of its capacity for knowing God. . . . The perfection of the divine image in the mind is the divine gift of wisdom, by which the mind becomes aware of God, and is not only 'in' God, but 'with' God, through the revival in it if that 'memory of God' which was never entirely obliterated." Sin damaged but did not destroy the image. Christ's grace restored the image within us, healing our nature. Following a similar vein as Gregory of Nyssa, Augustine also holds that only when contemplating God is human nature in the image of God. "As we said of the nature of the human mind that if as a whole it contemplates the truth, it is in the image of God; and when its functions are divided and something of it is diverted to the handling of temporal things, nevertheless that part which consults the truth is in the image of God, but the other part, which is directed to the handling of inferior things, is not the image of God" (book 12, chap. 7, 10). We are only truly human when we are fully oriented toward God. Augustine's understanding of the image, therefore, comes to be associated with the intellectual capacities of the human being: "Augustine interpreted *image of God* to mean the rational and moral capacities in human nature."[22] For Augustine, the image functions on three levels: that likeness to God in which we were created; the return to that likeness, which was obscured by sin, through the life of grace; and the perfection of that likeness in the kingdom of God.[23] Echoing again the theology of Gregory, we find a notion of the *imago Dei* that is dynamic.

Turning specifically to the function of biological sex in Augustine's anthropology, in his theology woman symbolizes the lower orientation of the mind. Because of their weakened intellectual powers when they are embodied as women, they are incapable of reflecting the image of God. Because of this, technically only men reflect the image of God. Woman in the afterlife, however, will reflect the image fully. As he writes in *De Genesis as Litteram* XI, "Indeed, in the same way women are not excluded from this grace of renewal and of the resurrection, after the image of God—although, in their corporeal sex, it is figured otherwise, in the sense that it is said that man only is the image and glory of God." Woman can only reflect the image in this life when she is united with a man, her husband; alone, she cannot reflect the image. "The woman together with her husband is the image of God, so that the whole substance is one image. But when she is assigned as a helpmate, a function which pertains to her alone, then she is not the image of God, just as fully and completely as when he and the woman are joined together in one."[24] In Augustine's exegesis of 1 Corinthians 11:7, where Paul states that man (as opposed to woman) is the image of God, Augustine argues that this claim is best interpreted in accordance with the distinction suggested above, of the double function, higher and lower, of the rational mind, with woman representing the lower.

Woman as representative of lower reason also explains the role of Eve in the Fall of humanity. As Augustine writes in book 12 of *De Trinitate*:

> The Fall of man is the result of the "lower reason" throwing off the control of the "higher," and devoting itself to the material and temporal. . . . In the story of the forbidden fruit, is symbolized the yielding of the higher reason (Adam) to the solicitations of the lower (Eve), which has already been perverted by the flesh (the serpent), so that sinful desire becomes sinful act. This is a better exegesis than to take the woman as symbolizing the bodily senses which we share with the beasts. (book 12, argument 3)

The human mind is in the image of God when it is contemplating truth. Even when it is distracted by worldly affairs, the mind is always on some level turning toward God. However, the part of the mind, the lower rational function, which is concerned with worldly affairs, is not in the image of God. Woman becomes associated with that lower function in Augustine's theology, thus excluding her from higher rational contemplation. Women symbolize the temporal order, while men symbolize the orientation toward the spiritual.

Continuing with the themes of the relationship between man and woman, book 9 of *The Literal Meaning of Genesis* offers some of Augustine's key thoughts on the relationship between men and women. Woman was created as man's helper for the task of procreation. This is based on Augustine's belief that if God merely wanted to create a companion for Adam, he would have created another male. "How much more agreeably could two male friends, rather than a man and a woman, enjoy companionship and conversation in a life shared together."[25] A woman, in Augustine's eye, would not make a worthy companion; therefore, the only explanation of her creation is for the purposes of procreation. Augustine also argues that the enjoyment of the sexual act is a result of sin. If Adam had not sinned, there would be no passion in procreation. Ultimately, Augustine's understanding of the role of woman in creation can be summed up by his statement that woman "was made for the man from the man" (chap. 11, 19). She is created only to serve man in her procreative function. Clearly, in Augustine's eyes, if God could have created a man with a procreative function, God would have done so.

Following the philosophy of Plato (and the theology of Gregory), Augustine contends that the image does not reside in the body. Because of his belief in the resurrection of the body, however, women's bodies had to be as perfect as men's. This applied only in heaven, not earth. Augustine does not situate his marginalization of women in their embodiment, but instead, as indicated above, in their weakened rationality. Before the Fall men and women were in a state of complementarity. Thus women were called to obey only after the Fall, and it is not in their original nature. Women are not in their nature inferior. However, and here again we hear echoes of Plato, women must overcome their womanhood, become like men, in order to exercise any sort of higher reason. "The female philosopher, when exercising her highest reason, led others to be unmindful of her sex, or to think of her as a man. . . . The differentiation between the sexes disappears and only a neutralized masculinity remains."[26] She must become like a man in order to escape her weakened female state.

Ultimately, Augustine understands the image of God as functioning within men and women on different levels depending on their orientation. In the spiritual realm Augustine has a complementary understanding of the sexes, each having its distinctive yet equal role. In this world, when the mind is oriented toward contemplation of God, men and women share the image equally. Men and women equally reflect the image of God when contemplating God, for they transcend their sexual identity. In this world, when contemplating the temporal world, man reflects the image while woman does not. Nonetheless, woman is always symbolically associated with lower reason.

Also, as Kari Elisabeth Børreson points out, "As regards the *homo interior*, woman possesses the quality of the image of God through her soul, which is identical with that of a man, for souls have no sex. But as regards the *homo exterior*, woman is distinguished from man, formed as she was in second place *(conformatio)*, and taken from the side of man."[27] The image of God is found in the masculine dimension of the soul. The woman is to be oriented toward the earthly realm and receive guidance from the male. While woman possesses the image in her rational soul, on a bodily level she does not reflect the image. There is a duality in woman's *homo exterior* and *homo interior*. Her inferior body prevents her from displaying her rational soul.

With Augustine, like so many of the church fathers, one is left with an ambiguous legacy. Augustine, like Gregory, does not degrade women's bodies or see them as inferior to men's bodies. He also, like Plato, gives women the opportunity to become philosophers. On certain levels women are seen as reflecting the *imago Dei*. Nonetheless, within Augustine's theology men represent the higher intellect and women the inferior level. Intellect, as stated earlier, is fundamental for understanding Augustine's notion of the *imago*. Within his theology, women reflect the image of God in spite of their sexuality, not because of it. "Human female beings are theomorphic *in spite of* their bodily sex, whereas men's spiritual God-likeness, *imago Dei*, corresponds to their exemplary maleness. Exclusion of femaleness at the divine level remains basic in Augustine's God-language."[28] Women must negate their very womanhood in order to reflect their creation in God's image.

Medieval Theology

Thomas Aquinas

The theology of Thomas Aquinas (1225/1227–1274) offers one of the most extensive and influential contributions to

Christian theology. The "Angelic Doctor" has left a stamp on several central ideas within the history of Christian thought, most notably on Christian understandings of the human. In his late teens Aquinas entered the Order of Saint Dominic. In a dramatic turn of events his family protested his decision and kidnapped him from the order, detaining him for two years in an effort to squelch his religious vocation. It was during his captivity that he first encountered the philosophy of Aristotle, which would become one of the great influences on his theology. After eventually being liberated, vocation intact, he returned to the Dominicans, becoming one of the greatest philosophers and theologians in the history of Christianity. He is best known for his *Summa Theologiae*, a systematic exploration of Christian theology and philosophy written over the course of eight years.

My overview of the *imago Dei* in Aquinas's anthropology focuses on two key texts, *The Disputed Questions on Truth* and the *Summa Theologiae*. Beginning with *The Disputed Questions on Truth*, one finds various themes that resonate with the theology of Augustine. Like Augustine, Aquinas locates the image of God in the rational capabilities of the human: "In us the mind designates the highest power of our soul. And since the image of God is in us according to that which is highest in us, that image will belong to the essence of the soul only in so far as mind is its highest power. Thus, mind, as containing the image of God, designates a power of the soul and not its essence" (Question 10, art. 1, p. 6).[29] As representative of the highest capabilities of the human, the mind, for Aquinas, is the locus for the image. Yet it is only when the mind is turned toward higher things that it truly reflects the image. Also echoing Augustine, Aquinas has a trinitarian understanding of the *imago:* "Likeness brings the character of image to completion. . . . There is a likeness of the uncreated Trinity in our soul according to any knowledge which it has of itself, not only of the mind, but also of the sense, as Augustine clearly shows. But we find the image of God only in that knowledge according to which there arises in the mind the fuller likeness of God" (Question 10, art.7, p. 33). We grow in likeness to the image of the Trinity within us as we turn our knowledge toward divine things. As noted by D. Juvenal Merriell, "St. Thomas held that man is the image of the Trinity by virtue of his intellectual nature, inasmuch as by his nature man is inclined to know and love God and is capable of accepting the invitation of grace that the triune God makes when He calls man through Christ to participate in the innermost life of the Trinity."[30] In Aquinas's theology the human possesses three types of knowledge: knowledge of God, knowledge of self, and knowledge of temporal things. We can't express likeness to the Trinity in knowing temporal things. The image of the Trinity is in the mind, as far as it knows God, and in self-knowledge, insofar as we reflect the image of God.

Several of these themes also appear in Aquinas's masterpiece, the *Summa Theologiae*. In Question 93 Aquinas adds the dimension of biological sex to his analysis of the image. For Aquinas, the *imago Dei* exists in humanity in three ways: "First, inasmuch as man possesses a natural aptitude for understanding and loving God; and this aptitude consists in the very nature of the mind, which is common to all men. Secondly, inasmuch as man actually or habitually knows and loves God, though imperfectly; and this image consists in the conformity of grace. Thirdly, inasmuch as man knows God actually and loves Him perfectly; and this image consists in the likeness of glory" (art. 4, p. 890).[31] This threefold understanding of the image reveals its dynamic nature. The image functions on the basic level in which we are created to understand and love God. This is, in a sense, the foundation of the image. Second, through the gift of grace we come to know God imperfectly, thus growing in the image. Finally, we can achieve the final level of knowing and loving God perfectly, reflecting the image in all its glory. Well, some of us can. As the following statement indicates, for Aquinas men and women do not reflect the image equally: "The image of God, in its principal signification, namely the intellectual nature, is found both in man and woman. . . . But in a secondary sense the image of God is found in man, and not in woman, for man is the beginning and end of woman, just as God is the beginning and end of every creature" (art. 4, p. 890). Women are not able to achieve and reflect the image in such an elevated manner as men.

Aquinas's multi-tiered understanding of the image allows him to articulate an ambiguous theology in which women reflect the image on some levels but not on others. The foundation of this belief, one that represents a radical break from the theology of Augustine, is that, for Aquinas, the body reflects the image: "Although the image of God in man is not to be found in his bodily shape, . . . the very shape of the human body represents the image of God in the soul by way of trace" (art. 6, p. 894). This is based on the Aristotelian belief that the body reflects the soul. Woman has the first degree of the image but does not have the second in the same way that man does. This is based on woman's bodily weakness, which represents a weakness of the soul and mind. Ultimately, however, the image dwells in the highest rationality of the human, where there is no distinction between the sexes. However, here on earth woman is inferior to man. As Børreson indicates:

> In her position as helper in the process of procreation, woman is therefore subordinated to man, considered as the superior sex. For Thomas, the distinction of the sexes signifies that woman is different from man. The manner in which the female body was formed is interpreted in this sense of subordination. . . . Further, in Thomas' thought, man's domination over woman is based on the primacy of the male sex, in the sense that it is considered as more perfect.[32]

Aquinas contends that woman's imperfect creation, as expressed in her bodiliness, reveals her inferior status.

Question 92 of the *Summa*, while not specifically addressing the *imago Dei*, reveals Aquinas's thoughts on the different gender roles within the created order. Woman, echoing Augustine, is solely created for the purpose of procreation. "It was necessary for woman to be made, as the Scripture says, as *a helper* of man; not, indeed, as a helpmate in other works, as some say, since man can be more efficiently helped by another man in other works; but as a helper in the work of generation" (art. 1, p. 879). Obviously, since another man would have made a better helper, woman was only created for the act of procreation. In addition, man, unlike woman, is called to the higher life of intellectual speculation. Because of this, "woman is naturally subject to man, because in man the discernment of reason predominates" (art. 1, pp. 880–81). Woman was fittingly made out of man's rib to show that she neither has authority over man (his head) nor is his slave (his feet). Ultimately, Aquinas concludes, echoing the philosophy of Aristotle:

> As regards the individual nature, woman is defective and misbegotten, for the active power in the male seed tends to the production of a perfect likeness according to the masculine sex; while the production of woman comes from defect in the active power, or from some material indisposition. . . . On the other hand, as regards universal human nature, woman is not misbegotten, but is included in nature's intention as directed to the work of generation. (art. 1, p. 880)

In describing woman as a misbegotten male, Aquinas perpetuates an Aristotelian and unbiblical notion of humanity that leaves a mark on Christian theology. This last statement reeks of Aristotelian biology. Here one finds a clear moment when it is non-Christian philosophy, and not the biblical witness, that leads to a profoundly offensive and sexist moment in Christian understandings of the human.

Mirroring Aristotle, for Aquinas, in generation women are the passive impulse and men the active one. Thus Eve had nothing to do with the transmission of original sin. While it may appear good that women have no culpability in generating original sin, it is still a negative view of women. Eve's only role was for procreation. In a sense Eve, like all women, does not count for Aquinas. Eve's lack of participation in the transmission of original sin relates to her lack of worth in Aquinas's theology. Aquinas also follows Aristotle in contending that because women are "weaker minded," they must be ruled and ordered by men. This is grounded in the Aristotelian view that woman has a weaker intellect based in her defective biological state. Obedience (to man) must be cultivated in woman due to her weak state of mind. Aquinas also argues that the misbegotten female is a "natural" mistake that must occur so that the human species can procreate. "Since the father's sperm is what actually produces the child, the child should ideally resemble the father, and hence should always be male. This 'mistake of nature,' however, is necessary because women are needed for reproduction."[33] In spite of this, however, Aquinas contends that in the spiritual realm women are capable of higher reasoning and therefore reflect the image of God.

On the level of nature Aquinas mirrors Aristotle's notion that male and female are distinct and unequal. On the level of grace, however, his theology moves to more of a complementarity understanding of the sexes. This is grounded in Aquinas's belief that there are degrees to the image of God. It is in the body, but it is found most perfectly in the highest activities of the mind. Man reflects the image more perfectly because God directly created him. There is a hierarchy of perfection. On an individual level woman is inferior, yet on the level of procreation she plays a necessary and complementary role to the function of man. The different degrees of the image also allow Aquinas to build on Aristotle's philosophy while adding his own interpretation. As Allen indicates:

By introducing a theory of difference in perfection according to a scale of degrees of perfection, Thomas avoided the ironic Aristotelian pronouncement that woman was in the image of God in the highest part of her intellect, which contained no sex identity, while she was not in the image of God when considered in her temporal existence. For Thomas, woman was always in the image of God, but she reflected this image less perfectly than man. . . . Thomas argued instead that a person necessarily included a material aspect of his or her nature. Therefore, sex identity would always be an essential part of personal identity. . . . For Thomas, grace did not overturn or destroy human nature. He believed instead that grace built on or perfected nature. Therefore, woman was able to achieve the full perfection of her "imperfect" nature.[34]

Ultimately, for Aquinas, woman always reflects the image of God, yet she always reflects it in a manner that is "less perfect" than man. Within his theology she remains a passive defect of nature, one that only came into existence in order to generate the species, a submissive receptacle to the male seed.

Hildegard of Bingen

With the theology of Hildegard of Bingen we find the first woman's contribution examined in this chapter. Sadly, while women have contributed to the history of Christian thought, their voices have been historically marginalized and ignored, minimizing their contribution to Christianity as a whole.[35] This is why we are not exploring more women's contributions in this chapter. While they do exist, they did not substantially influence the construction of Christian anthropology within the history of Christian theology. Before entering into Hildegard's theology, as the only woman examined in this chapter, it would help to situate her in light of medieval women's theology. In spite of all the writings to the contrary, a theological understanding of women as created in God's image in a defective or deficient manner was not necessarily viewed by medieval women as impeding their relationship with God. As noted by Caroline Walker Bynum:

On the contrary, the writing of women mystics is full of
references to being created in God's image. Gertrude the
Great, Margaret of Oingt, Douceline of Marseilles, and
Beatrice of Nazareth all rejoiced in their creation in the
image and likeness of God and saw this image as the basis in which *imitatio* is built. In a vision, Mechtild of
Hackeborn saw Christ place his hands on hers and give
her "the imprint and resemblance like a seal in wax." And
Catherine of Siena wrote, addressing God: "By the light
of understanding within your light I have tasted and seen
your depth, eternal Trinity, and the beauty of your creation. Then when I considered myself in you, I saw that
I am in your image."[36]

Medieval women, Walker Bynum notes, did not understand
themselves as the subordinate factor in a male-female polarity;
they most often embraced an androgynous voice in their writings.

In addition to embracing this androgynous voice, medieval
women also connected the historical association of women
with bodiliness to the incarnation: "If anything, women drew
from the traditional notion of the female as physical an emphasis on their own redemption by a Christ who was supremely
physical because supremely human. . . . To women, the notion
of the female as flesh became an argument for women's *imitatio
Christi* through physicality."[37] Women thus came to symbolize
all of humanity through the incarnation. Catherine of Siena, for
example, places an emphasis on humanity as created in the
image of God as the foundation for our possibility to return to
God. In a sense the image is our humanity, for that is what we
share with Christ. "I [God] gifted you with my image and likeness. And when you lost the life of grace through sin, to restore
it to you I united my nature with you, hiding it in your humanity. I had made you in my image; now I took your image by
assuming human form."[38] Walker Bynum argues that medieval
women did not internalize the idea that they were somehow

inferior to men. Women did not see themselves in a dualistic manner: "Religious women in the later Middle Ages saw in their own female bodies not only a symbol of the humanness of both genders but also a symbol of—and a means to approach to—the humanity of God."[39] Their bodies became a manner to connect themselves with Christ's incarnation, making them a link between God and all of humanity.

Hildegard of Bingen was born in 1098 and died in 1179. She was a sickly child, received little formal education, and entered the Benedictine monastery as a novice at the age of fifteen. At an early age Hildegard began to experience visions of God; as an adult she was instructed to publish them by her spiritual director. Her writings were deemed revelatory, and she became a popular healer and spiritual counselor. While her writings display familiarity with contemporary Christian authors, she always claimed her knowledge came directly from God. "No woman previous to Hildegard revealed such a wide range of knowledge and creative thought. The extraordinary breadth of her writing skills, which ranged from music to drama, to scientific texts on the classification of stones and herbs, to theological speculation, to language games, to the philosophy of psychology, reveal a genius unparalleled by a woman and matched by very few men up to the twelfth century."[40] Hildegard is considered one of the great scholars of the twelfth century, and her writings demonstrate that women indeed offered a learned contribution to Christian theology.

Hildegard argued that womankind symbolizes all of humanity, fallen in Eve yet restored in Mary. Hildegard has a complementary view of the sexes; each needs the other in religious life and procreation. "Repeatedly in her work, Hildegard describes that which is redeemed by Christ—the humanity (including physicality) that comes from Mary—as feminine; and she underlines the association of woman-humanity with fleshiness by arguing that Adam is created from clay but Eve from flesh."[41] Eve's creation becomes parallel to the incarnation. Hildegard viewed Christ's body as the (feminine) church. Thus, while maintaining a male priesthood, she saw its role functioning through the female church. "The image of both sinful *and saved* humanity is the image of woman."[42] Nonetheless, in Hildegard's thought man is associated with divinity, woman with humanity. Her writings are thus a double-edged sword. Woman always symbolizes flesh. Hildegard also argues that Christ received his flesh from woman, Mary. Thus it is female flesh that eventually restores the world. With Hildegard one finds the ambiguous association of woman with Christ through the incarnation, yet woman always symbolizes flesh and man divinity. Woman alone represents the embodied dimension of divinity.

As argued by Allen, Hildegard is the first Christian theologian to understand the sexes in a complementary manner throughout her theology:

> Hildegard of Bingen emerged as the first philosopher to articulate a complete theory of sex complementarity. Although some previous Christian philosophers, such as Augustine, Boethius, and Anselm, had defended sex complementarity in certain isolated categories of thought about woman and man, Hildegard was the first to develop a rationale for this theory.[43]

While not offering a systematic and entirely consistent account of gender complementarity, her work overwhelmingly presents a view of men and women as different but equal. Male and female are equally created in the image of God, for Hildegard understood God as both feminine and masculine. Also, men and women contained both masculine and feminine natures within their souls. Men and women were opposites, yet these polarities were not hierarchical but instead interconnected.

Hildegard also, like Aquinas and Aristotle, kept an integration of the soul and body. Unlike them, she did not devalue women. The *imago Dei* was closely identified with the body, and woman more closely connected to the incarnation. For procreation and the incarnation one needed woman. "Only woman could give to human beings their participation in the divine image."[44] Given the complementary vision of her anthropology, Hildegard does fall into gender stereotypes. Men are associated with strength, courage, and justice, while women are linked to mercy, grace, and penance. She believed that members of each sex should try to cultivate the opposite sex's attributes within themselves and that each was equally important. A strong current in Hildegard's thought is the integration of the body and the soul. For this she is to be celebrated. However, as Chapter 5 of this book indicates, in embracing a complementary understanding of the sexes Hildegard embraces a position that many feminists will argue ultimately leads to the subordination of women. While Hildegard strove to maintain an egalitarian vision of the sexes, her separate but equal reasoning is situated in a broader tradition where that which is associated with the female is ultimately deemed inferior to male qualities.

Reformation

Martin Luther

Former Roman Catholic monk Martin Luther is known as one of the fathers of the Protestant Reformation. His critique of church corruption, especially through the selling of indulgences, triggered the greatest historical upheaval in the history of Christianity. Two themes mark his theology: the cross, where God must be understood through Jesus' crucifixion; and justification. For Luther, the precondition of our salvation is the gift of God's grace, not human works. Even our faith is a gift of grace. Thus, for Luther, our justification is *by* grace *through* faith. We receive God's grace through faith, but God meets the precondition for our justification. God becomes the sole source of our salvation, even of the faith that allows for it.

This theological view emerges in part from Luther's critique of the Catholic church and his view of humanity's corruption after the Fall.

With the theology of Luther we find a radically different approach and theology surrounding the *imago Dei*. For example, contrary to Augustine and Aquinas, Luther is not sure how useful trinitarian understandings of the image are. Thus one does not find a heavy trinitarian emphasis in his anthropological reflections. As Anthony O. Erhueh emphasizes: "Martin Luther's *imago dei* doctrine is radically different from any previous positions. He maintains that both the *imago* and the *similitudo* were completely destroyed by the Fall."[45] The image only appears when one lives a life that reflects the will of God. Both Luther and Calvin broke with the Scholastic tradition and returned to the theology of Augustine. While not following Augustine's trinitarian lead, with Augustine Luther understands the image as the ability to have true knowledge of God. This knowledge is lost in the Fall, yet traces of it remain. In opposition to the Scholastics, who maintained that the image of God always remains part of human nature, Luther argued that Adam's image and likeness (which he saw as one in the same) was destroyed by his sin. This is also the fate of Adam's descendants, who are left with a depraved human nature. Our original righteousness is lost. This creates a bit of an ambiguity in Luther, for he strongly emphasizes the loss of the image while maintaining that a trace of it remains, allowing knowledge of God on certain levels.

In his "Lectures on Genesis" Luther connects his reflections on the *imago Dei* with his account of the second creation story. For Luther, one cannot understand the image and how it exists within us without connecting it to the Fall. We cannot truly understand or know the divine image within us, for it has been seriously damaged in the Fall. It exists within us today in a deficient manner: "Therefore the image of God, according to which Adam was created, was something far more distinguished and excellent, since obviously no leprosy or sin adhered either to his reason or his will. . . . But after the Fall death crept like leprosy into all our perceptive powers, so that with our intellect we cannot even understand that image."[46] The image begins to be restored in this life through God's grace, though it is never fully restored until the afterlife. Pending that, we cannot adequately know the original image that was lost in sin, for the image that remains is so corrupt we cannot even grasp it with our intellect.

Before the Fall, Adam and Eve had perfect knowledge of God, both in the same degree. Now we only have remnants of this knowledge, and other animals have always completely lacked it. Women hold an ambiguous position in Luther's theology, for they both reflect the image in an equal manner as men yet are weaker in nature:

> The woman appears to be a somewhat different being from the man, having different members and a much weaker nature. Although Eve was a most extraordinary creature—similar to Adam so far as the image of God is concerned, that is, in justice, wisdom, and happiness—she was nevertheless a woman. For as the sun is more excellent than the moon (although the moon, too, is a very excellent body), so the woman, although she was a most beautiful work of God, nevertheless was not equal of the man in glory and prestige. . . . Let us note from this passage that it is written that this sex may not be excluded from any glory of the human creature, although it is inferior to the male sex.[47]

Woman is never fully equal to man in Luther's eyes. Her nature forces her into a position of weakness. "Female subjection to men is punishment for the fall."[48] Nonetheless, Luther contends, had Eve not sinned, she would have been entirely equal to Adam. Her punishment is to be subject to man.

Because of Adam and Eve's sin, the image has been significantly lost and weakened. The image will only be fully renewed in the kingdom of God. Refuting tradition, Luther argues that Eve had dominion equally with Adam, yet ambivalently Luther affirms both Eve's equality and her inferiority to Adam. Luther argues that prior to the Fall, Adam and Eve had an egalitarian relationship and were meant to rule together. After the Fall everything changed and women became subject to patriarchal marriage. The effects of the Fall were so devastating that even Christ could not transform patriarchal rule of the husband over the wife. Though they were "equally righteous," the serpent approached Eve because she is the weak part of human nature. Ultimately, Luther's intention is to provide a more biblically based account of the image, for he holds that theology has grown to rely too heavily on Greek philosophy.

As Dempsey Douglass highlights, Luther gives feminists an ambiguous legacy:

> Insofar as Luther places the beginning of women's subor-
> dination after the fall, as the result of sin, he contributes
> to genuine reform in theology, stressing a full equality
> between women and men as intended by God at creation.
> . . . By giving women's inferior place in society the full
> weight of God's command, Luther effectively eliminates
> any possible practical consequences flowing from the
> creational equality of women with men for the earthly
> lives of real women.[49]

For Luther, the only manner in which we can recover the image in any way is through Christ: "For man was created in the image of God, in the image of righteousness, of course, of divine holiness and truth, but in such a way that he could lose it, as he did lose it, moreover, in paradise and has now recovered it through Christ."[50] Both men and women were created equally, however, since this was lost in the Fall, ultimately women in Luther's theology are condemned to a life of subordination.

Transition to the Modern Era

This final section indicates impulses that shape many of the questions and concerns of modern theology. I begin with a brief nod toward the philosophy of René Descartes, considered by many to be the father of modern philosophy. I follow with a more substantial analysis of the philosophy of Immanuel Kant. As always, my emphasis remains the impact these thinkers have had on Christian notions of the human, with special attention to gender. Both Descartes and Kant, I contend, shifted the focus of Western European philosophy in such a manner that it has had significant implications for both philosophy and theology. Indeed, after the two of them the history of philosophy, and our notions of humanity, have been forever transformed.

René Descartes

René Descartes (1596–1650), a native of France, is one of the most important figures in the history of philosophy. In spite of his Jesuit education Descartes' philosophy is marked by a distinct separation between matters of reason and of faith. Though he was a devout Catholic, Descartes rejected the church's authority on matters of reason and was influenced by the Reformation's questioning of ecclesial authority. His method is marked by his rejection of the Aristotelian and Scholastic approach and his attempt to integrate philosophy with his interest in the sciences. For Descartes, the question of doubt and certainty is a clear hallmark for his philosophy. Descartes strove in his corpus to elaborate philosophical statements that were certain. Ultimately this led him to state that the only statement that one can make without doubt is to affirm one's own existence. Our ability to doubt reveals that we exist, informing his famous statement, "I think therefore I am." This claim leads to a radial devaluing of the body and places rational thought as the center of philosophical speculation.

Feminist scholars have noted the double-edged sword of Cartesian philosophy with regard to the body and women. On one level, as Beverly Clack notes, "by claiming that the life of reason, the life of the philosopher, could take place anywhere, Descartes opened up the traditional realm of women to the same intellectual status as the academy."[51] Descartes opens up an egalitarian understanding of the rational. His philosophy does not hold the traditional negative picture of women we find in most Western philosophers, and he does not claim that men embody reason and women the body. Unfortunately, however, Descartes argues that the body is secondary, something that is historically linked with women. His method leads to the radical separation of mind and body, which had unintended implications for women. "In the context of associations already existing between gender and Reason, his version of the mind-body relationship produced stark polarizations of previously existing contrasts."[52] Thus Descartes becomes an unwitting contributor in the devaluation of women's intellectual capabilities.

Descartes' contention that reason is an abstract mode of thought, separate from the emotional and the everyday, also has implications for philosophical assumptions about women. "And the sharpness of his separation of the ultimate requirements of truth-seeking from the practical affairs of everyday life reinforced already existing distinctions between male and female roles, opening the way to the idea of distinctive male and female consciousness."[53] The emotional and daily or private were the very areas of life with which women were associated. Descartes' abstract, disembodied reason continued the philosophical trend of dividing the human's rational functions from the sensual, affirming a false dualistic understanding of human identity. Though Descartes did not encourage the marginalization of women to the sensual in his writings, his philosophical milieu contributed to a reading of his work that cemented women's symbolic embodiment and consequent irrationality.

His philosophy cements the distinction between mind and body, a dualism that, as we have seen, fuels the subordination of women.

Immanuel Kant

As we have seen throughout the chapter, medieval, patristic, and Reformation understandings of the human describe us as created in the image of God and thus in relationship with God. In the patristic era this image is defined, until Augustine, as the image in terms of Christ. With Augustine begins an understanding of the image as trinitarian. With the end of the Middle Ages and the explosion of the scientific revolution, a devaluation of humanity as created and an emphasis on the human as autonomous enters into philosophy, with direct consequences for theological reflection. As Louis Dupré notes:

> At the end of the Middle Ages, however, nominalist theology effectively removed God from creation. . . . The divine became relegated to a supernatural sphere separate from nature, with which it retained no more than casual, external link. . . . Whereas previously meaning had been established in the very act of creation by a wise God, it now fell upon the human mind to interpret a cosmos, the structure of which had ceased to be given as intelligible. Instead of being an integral part of the cosmos, the person became its source of meaning.[54]

Beginning with Descartes and culminating with the great masters of suspicion, such as Freud and Marx, the human becomes defined more and more autonomously, not in relation to God. This is clearly exemplified by the lack of writings surrounding the *imago Dei*. After the Reformation this topic is of little importance to theology until the twentieth century.

The philosophy of Immanuel Kant (1724–1804) is exemplary of the historical period of the Enlightenment and the nineteenth century. Kant is considered by many to be the greatest philosopher since Plato and Aristotle, and while modern philosophy is not necessarily Kantian, his influence on the history of modern philosophy is profound. His corpus covers the areas of metaphysics, epistemology, aesthetics, ethics, and politics. His early work is influenced by Rationalist philosophy, and he is later influenced by Empiricism and Skepticism. He eventually developed his own philosophical method, characterized as critical or transcendental philosophy. This new philosophy was best exemplified in his three critiques: *Critique of Pure Reason*, *Critique of Practical Reason*, and *The Critique of Judgment* (corresponding to metaphysics, ethics, and aesthetics). My emphasis is on the function of gender in his thought. As we shall see, in this area Kant does little more than build on the androcentric and patriarchal scholarship of his predecessors.

Kant's writings on morality are directly linked to his work on gender. For Kant, a truly moral action arises from commitment to duty not from personal inclination. This point plays an important role in his writings on men and women. Kant maintains the complementary understanding of the sexes that has plagued much of Western philosophy. As Beverly Clack notes:

> He denies that men and women share a common nature; rather, male and female characteristics are understood to complement each other. Men have a potential to embody masculine qualities, women to embody feminine qualities. Included in the masculine qualities are nobility, depth, reflectiveness, learning, profundity, and the ability to be principled. The feminine qualities to which women can aspire include beauty, delicacy, modesty, compassion, sympathy, and feeling.[55]

In *Grounding for the Metaphysics of Morals,* Kant equates masculine values for those necessary for moral action. Actions that are motivated by emotion are of no moral worth. Thus we are led to believe that woman, as emotive, cannot truly act in a moral fashion.

Kant's aesthetics also contains a complementary understanding of the two sexes. Women are seen as representing the beautiful, while men represent that which is nobler. In fact, the role of woman is to be beautiful; she should not worry herself over her ignorance:

> A woman is embarrassed little that she does not possess certain high insights, that she is timid, and not fit for serious employments, and so forth; she is beautiful and captivates, and that is enough. On the other hand, she demands all these qualities in a man, and the sublimity of her soul shows itself only in that she knows to treasure these noble qualities so far as they are found in him. How else indeed would it be possible that so many grotesque male faces, whatever merits they may possess, could gain such well-bred and fine wives! Man on the other hand is much more delicate in respect to the beautiful charms of woman. By their fine figure, merry naïveté, and charming friendliness he is sufficiently repaid for the lack of book learning and for other deficiencies that he must supply by his own talents.[56]

For Kant, women are objects to be admired. Not only should women not worry their "pretty little heads" over their ignorance, but also they are seen as less moral and rational than men. Kant's moral philosophy distinguishes between actions performed for "feeling" and those performed for "duty." Women are always linked to feeling and thus operate on the level of emotion. Epistemologically, for Kant, women represent the beautiful and men the sublime. The female is directed epistemologically toward the pretty and concrete; the male is directed toward the theoretical and abstract. This leads to Kant seriously belittling any sort of intellectual aspiration in women. "He mockingly describes the scholarly women who, 'use their books somewhat like a watch, that is, they wear the watch so it can be noticed that they have one, although it is usually broken or does not show the correct time.'"[57] The scholarly woman is an object of ridicule within Kantian philosophy.

Despite the Kantian revolution in philosophy, with regard to gender we find in Kant more of the same androcentric subordination. Kant only continues the same line of thought we have seen throughout the centuries. When one looks at his anthropology and writings on religion as a whole, however, we see a sharp contrast to medieval authors. In Kant's world God is not related to the world and humanity in any vital way. God has been pushed out of the center, onto the margins. Humanity ceases to be understood in the image of God. Thus Kant exemplifies his era. Scholastic theology was characterized by an understanding of the human as imprinted with the image of the divine. For the Enlightenment and the nineteenth century, this very language becomes foreign to the understandings of the human. What does remain a constant, however, is a dualistic construction of male and female, where men and women are seen as sharing a common human nature yet in different capacities. However, even when these anthropologies attempt an egalitarian, complementary understanding of humanity, where male and female are seen as separate but equal, given the overall devaluation of attributes associated with women, they remain secondary and subordinate. With the dawn of the twentieth century a lengthy and weighty historical tradition is inherited by modern Christian theology, one that devalues women and limits their ability truly to reflect their creation in the image of God.

Chapter 3

Twentieth-Century Theology

Prior to the explosion of feminist, US minority, and third-world voices, the theological arena was dominated by European figures. Karl Barth, Karl Rahner, Paul Tillich, and Hans Urs von Balthasar are, arguably, the most significant voices in their era, and their writings represent fundamental theological impulses that marked the twentieth century. The theological landscape did not change dramatically until the late 1960s. One could ask, nonetheless, why I do not include a more diverse picture of twentieth-century theology. For better or worse, I contend that this century remains marked by the European theological tradition. While theologians such as James H. Cone, Gustavo Gutiérrez, Virgilio Elizondo, Rosemary Radford Ruether, and Aloysius Pieris have offered significant and in fact revolutionary contributions to Christian theology, their work has yet to influence this discourse to the extent of these four. Barth, Rahner, Tillich, and Balthasar also represent attempts to articulate a theological anthropology in a climate of growing skepticism surrounding the validity and value of theological claims. As the previous chapter concluded, with the birth and growth of Enlightenment philosophy, a theological understanding of the human faded in prominence in the intellectual arena. These four theologies represent a revival of theological anthropology and an attempt to situate Christian theology in

61

light of its contemporary cultural questions and debates, albeit with varying perspectives.

Christocentric Anthropology: Karl Barth

The theology of Swiss pastor Karl Barth is considered the starting point of twentieth-century theology. His 1919 commentary on Romans was a bomb dropped on the European theological scene. Beginning his training with liberal theologian Adolf von Harnack, Barth quickly became disillusioned with liberal theology and Harnack's submission of Christianity to Enlightenment thought. In particular, Barth critiques liberal theology's optimistic attitude and its focus on the human. Theology, Barth argues, is not done in response to the human condition but to the word of God. Barth is one of the founders of the Confessional church that sought to prevent the unification of Christianity and Nazism. One also sees his anti-Nazi efforts in his contribution to the Barmen Declaration, which stated that God was the church's only *führer*. Barth was forced to flee Germany in 1935 after refusing to take a loyalty oath to Nazism. Heavily influenced by his pastoral life, Barth is extremely critical of the academic nature of theology, whose center of accountability and dialogue is at the university and not the church. He believes that theology should be at the service of the church, not the academy. This pastoral stamp reflects the manner in which Barth integrated his pastoral life with his academic training. For Barth, God, not humanity, is the starting point of theology. God seeks us; we do not seek God. We do not look inside ourselves to find God; we respond to the manner in which God touches our lives.

The starting point of Barth's theology is the Word of God revealed in Jesus Christ. His work is often described as transcendent (top down) or revelatory theology. Barth is critical of the subjective and individualistic nature of theology, arguing that the discipline must return to a theocentric rather than an anthropocentric emphasis. Two labels or movements are often associated with Barth's theology: dialectical theology and neo-orthodoxy. Dialectical theology emphasizes the discontinuity between humanity and God—the gospel and culture—and God as wholly Other. In other words, dialectical theology emphasizes our dissimilarity to God. While we are created in the image of God, our dissimilarity to God is greater than our similarity to our Creator. This dimension of Barth's theology is best seen in his earlier work on Romans: "God and humanity are not on a continuum but only related obliquely like a tangent striking a circle. . . . Barth wanted to stress the freedom and primacy of God, and *God's* initiative and grace toward humanity in Jesus Christ."[1] Barth's strong emphasis on God's initiative in human life and the difference between the gospel and culture is in great part a reaction to what he interprets as Protestant theology's heavy alignment with contemporary secular cultural movements. In a sense, Barth accuses Christian theology of "selling out" to contemporary culture.

A second theological movement closely associated with Barth is neo-orthodox theology. Neo-orthodoxy is a response to the developing crisis in the world (and is sometimes referred to as crisis theology), especially as a result of two world wars. This theology draws from the theological concerns and sources of Reformation theology. Again we find an emphasis on the separation of Christianity and culture as a critical response to liberalism. As opposed to liberalism's emphasis on an immanent God in nature and culture, neo-orthodoxy emphasizes God's transcendence; in response to liberalism's view of humanity as good, neo-orthodoxy emphasizes our need for salvation from beyond. Neo-orthodox theology is also critical of natural theology, a theology rooted in reason that allows for possibility of knowledge of God outside of faith. For Barth there is no unthematic, innate knowledge of God in human nature. We only know God through God's self-revelation in Jesus Christ.

Christology is the keystone of Barth's theology. For Barth, every teaching of Christian theology begins and ends with Jesus

Christ.[2] To approach Barth's anthropology one must enter
through his Christology. Barth's is a Christocentric, kerygmatic
theology. Jesus sets the terms to recognize God's revelation.
There is no unthematic knowledge of God; only in Jesus Christ
do we know God. Our true humanity is revealed in Jesus of
Nazareth. Jesus is God's being-for-humanity and is God's co-
humanity. This is the basis for defining our humanity as co-
humanity: to be human is to be in community and to be for one
another. Our *imago Dei* is our co-humanity. Jesus reveals that
it is in God's very being to be there for us (co-humanity). This
being-for-others, or co-humanity, is the foundation of the
imago Dei. Echoing the early church fathers Barth understands
the image of God as the image of Christ. Because God does not
choose to be God apart from Jesus Christ, we only know God
through Christ, and we can only understand the image of God
within us as the image of Christ. God's revelation in Jesus
Christ is the exclusive starting point of anthropology. Barth's
notion of the *imago Dei* is relational. To be human is to be in
community with God and with ourselves. Jesus reveals that
God's true nature is to accompany us. Jesus as our companion
teaches us that we must be companions. "Since God in Jesus
Christ is a God of pro-humanity and co-humanity, so human
life is essentially co-humanity and mutuality. . . . The image of
God is not some individually possessed quality, such as reason,
which likens a human being to God; rather, our likeness to God
is our co-humanity. . . . The life of women and men is life with
and for others; it is not isolated, self-sufficient and self-serving,
but life with and for others, co-humanity in community."[3]

   Turning specifically to the themes of gender and biological
sex in Barth's theology, Barth offers an exegesis of the Genesis
creation accounts.[4] He understands humanity as created male
and female in the image of God as a differentiated unity. Our
creation as covenant partner with God reveals that humanity is
created to exist in relationship. While not denying the full humanity of men and women, male and female have a functional
distinction in Barth's theology that fuels his anthropological

understanding of gender complementarity. Humanity can never free itself from its sexual determination, always embodied as either male or female. "Nor can he wish to liberate himself from the relationship and be man without woman or woman apart from man; for in all that characterizes him as man he will be thrown back upon woman, or as woman upon man, both man and woman being referred to this encounter and co-existence."[5] God created humanity in mutual relation and differentiation.

Contrary to what he labels as typologies that tell men and women their proper place in society, Barth argues that "the command of God comes to man and woman in the relationship and order in which God created them to be together as His image, as the likeness of his covenant of grace, in the male and female existence which they gain in His eyes within the framework of their character as likeness and image."[6] Barth rejects the systematization of gender roles. However, he paradoxically asserts that God calls male and female to specific roles based on their sex, where their relationship is complementary. Citing 1 Corinthians 11, Barth highlights that this text serves to put women "in their place" and is in no way in contention with Galatians 3:28:

> The command of the Lord does not put anyone, man or woman, in a humiliating, dishonourable or unworthy position. It puts both man and woman in their proper place. . . . The essential point is that woman must always and in all circumstances be woman; that she must feel and conduct herself as such and not as a man; that the command of the Lord, which is for all eternity, directs both man and woman to their own proper sacred place and forbids all attempts to violate this order.[7]

One can never have a neutral humanity free from sexual differentiation; humanity is created male and female in the image and likeness of God. God requires fidelity to one's sex, honoring the sexual polarity in which we are created.

Barth argues that authentic humanity is co-humanity, always maintaining the appropriate roles as male and female. Male and female are equal, yet equal in their complementary mutuality. However, male is A and female B. "A precedes B and B follows A. Order means succession. It means preceding and following. It means super- and sub-ordination."[8] This model, Barth claims, does not perpetuate or support any inequality. It points man to the position that he must humbly occupy as leader and inspirer of woman. "She, too, has to realize that she is ordered, related and directed toward man and has thus to follow the initiative which he must take. . . . Properly speaking, the business of woman, her task and function, is to actualize the fellowship, in which matter man can only precede her, stimulating, leading and inspiring."[9] This is the divine command, the order of creation. Woman must be mature enough to accept her place as obedient. She must stay true to the order of creation. Barth contends that woman as the complement of man is symbolized in her creation from man's rib. Because woman "marks the completion of his creation, it is not problematic but self-evident for her to be ordained for man and to be for man in her whole existence."[10]

Because of his monumental impact on modern Christian theology, Barth's theology has been critiqued on various fronts. On one level, many ask, can we really separate Christianity from culture? Along those same lines, many claim that Barth, with his heavy ecclesial emphasis, argues for a privatization of theology that is unrealistic given the growing interdisciplinary nature of the academy (and theology, whether Barth likes it or not, is an academic discipline). Theology is autonomous in Barth's system, yet isolated. Liberationists point out that even with all of his talk of a Christocentric theology, Barth ignores the liberative message of Jesus. From a feminist perspective his theological anthropology offers a narrow view of male and female roles, limiting the fullness of humanity by parceling out certain attributes to each sex in a complementary model. Barth's model of humanity is a patriarchal anthropology that

legitimizes itself as the divine order of creation. As Rosemary
Radford Ruether points out:

> For Barth, this established, created order of male over
> female reflects the covenant of creation. God as Creator
> is sovereign over his Creation. The covenant of nature has
> not been annulled but reestablished in the covenant of
> grace by which Christ as head rules his people as obedi-
> ent servants. Male and female, then, are necessarily or-
> dered in a relation of those who lead and those who fol-
> low. Men and women should accept their place in this
> order, the man humbly and the woman willingly. Man is
> not exalted, thereby, nor is woman debased, but they ful-
> fill their own place in the divinely decreed scheme of
> things only by accepting this proper order. . . . Any effort
> to change this order and give woman equality with man
> would itself be a sinful rebellion against God's divinely
> enacted ordinances of creation and redemption.[11]

As Ruether indicates, Barth's theology divinizes patriarchal
anthropology and makes any attempts to vary from "the order
of creation" sinful. While he claims to offer an egalitarian
model, it is one in which women must become submissive followers of men, for if they do not, they fall into the sinful state
of challenging God's order of creation.

Transcendental Anthropology: Karl Rahner

For many Roman Catholic theologians, the work of the Jesuit priest Karl Rahner remains the greatest and most significant theological achievement of the twentieth century. "Even
before his death at Innsbruck on March 30, 1984, Karl Rahner
had been hailed as *the* religious thinker who had contributed
more than any other to the renewal of Catholic theology in the
twentieth century."[12] Rahner is a student of Scholastic and
modern German philosophy and is extremely influenced by the

spirituality of Ignatius of Loyola. While not taking it to the same extreme as Barth, Rahner considers the church a significant audience for theology. Rahner believes theology must serve the church and be its voice in the contemporary context. While not a dogmatic theologian, Rahner argues that academic theology must always remain connected to pastoral theology. Rahner ran into several problems with the Vatican throughout his career. His text on Mariology, for example, was prohibited from publication and remains unpublished even today. Vatican II, however, vindicated him. His theology marks the spirit of the council, and his openness to world religions and the world in general is a clear stamp of his theology.

Before examining Rahner's anthropology it is helpful to say a word about his theological method. Rahner builds a theology based on the human experience of self-transcendence. In direct contrast to Barth, Rahner affirms the existence of unthematic or "natural" human thought about God. For Rahner, the human life is utterly saturated with the experience of grace, and this makes such natural reflection on God possible. "The internal coherence of Rahner's theology rests less on his espousal of a unitary system or methodology than on a vision of the human reality as being completely embraced and irreversibly transformed by divine grace."[13] Rahner's theology is often described as a transcendental method that looks at the a priori conditions within the believer for knowledge of faith—striving to grasp the whole of reality. His work is also referred to as transcendental Thomism, for it integrates neo-Scholasticism with post-Kantian philosophical impulses. Philosophical analysis plays a key role in his theology, especially German idealism and existentialism. Rahner is related to a movement in twentieth-century Roman Catholic theology known as *ressourcement,* a retrieval of pre-Scholastic sources in order to revive contemporary theology.

Rahner's method is based on the assertion that through acts of knowledge and freedom we transcend ourselves. We experience ourselves as finite with unlimited questions. Because God appeared in history through Jesus Christ, we place our hope for our salvation in human history. Since we exist in history, we search for God within our limited human context. Christ stamps all of creation, and Christology grounds anthropology. Humans are created to be saved and are oriented toward God. Nature is bound by grace; the ground for grace has been prepared in the structure of the human (the possibility of grace is in our nature). Christ shows us the realization of God's promise in human life; Jesus is the fulfillment of humanity. Rahner understands God as absolute Mystery. Our human lives are unintelligible without the transcendent God that is Mystery, yet that Mystery must be encountered in our daily lives. Rahner's book on the Trinity restored the Trinity to the center of Christian faith. He argues that the immanent Trinity equals the economic Trinity. The distinction between the two is not ontological; there is only one Trinity. In other words, God as God revealed to us (the economic Trinity) is really God's intradivine nature (the immanent Trinity). God's actions in salvation history reveal the nature of God's inner life. While this statement may seem logical, it implies that human beings, with their limited capabilities, can know God in God's fullness.

For Rahner, the starting point of theology is anthropology. Contrary to Barth, the foundation of Rahner's theology is the human being who is the hearer of God's message. Geffrey B. Kelly links the fundamental insight of Rahner's theology to his anthropological insights: "Rahner's genius was to link the human search for fulfillment with the restlessness implanted in the individual's heart by God and to correlate God's Trinitarian presence in historical, somatic reality with what he affirmed to be signs of God's grace investing human life with dignity and beatific destiny."[14] The human is by nature open to receive revelation; we are recipients of God's gracious self-communication. In other words, we are created to be saved. Rahner argues that we are oriented toward the horizon that we know as God and that the ground for the reception of grace is in the structure of the human. Within us is the experience of grace, and only in grounding our self-reflection of that experience of transcendence will we truly understand ourselves. We have a restlessness in our hearts that is only satisfied by God. It is in human nature to be open to the unlimited quest for meaning. "The horizon of the human spirit as the infinite question is fulfilled by this ineffable self-communication of God with the believing trust that this infinite question is answered by God with the infinite answer which God is, it follows that through this grace the event of free grace and of God's self-communication is already given at all times."[15] We become conscious of ourselves as selves through radical questioning. This is the transcendent present in ordinary experience. The foundation of our everyday thinking is this unthematic deeper consciousness of which we are not consciously aware.

Due to the transcendent nature of the human, theology is essential to anthropology. As "hearers of the word" humanity is the starting point of theology. For Rahner, humanity is able to understand that which is incomprehensible and be seized by that which is beyond the intellect's capabilities:

> Hence the original knowledge of God is not the kind of knowledge in which one grasps an object which happens to present itself directly or indirectly from outside. It has rather the character of a transcendental experience. Insofar as this subjective, non-objective luminosity of the subject in its transcendence is always oriented towards the holy mystery, the knowledge of God is always present unthematically and without name, and not just when we begin to speak of it.[16]

These unthematized, unsystematic experiences (and knowledge)—that which we experience yet can never fully articulate—are the subject matter of theology. "The effort to grasp and to thematize this reality is what Rahner calls the function of theological anthropology."[17] What Rahner names the *potentia oboedientialis* is the obediential potency for a possible revelation, our openness to God. In all our transcendental acts of knowledge we know God implicitly. Another key term in Rahner's anthropology is *supernatural existential*. This refers to our orientation to God's intended transformation through grace. If God intended us for a life of grace, Rahner argues, then the possibility of grace must be in our nature. "Creation is intrinsically ordered to the supernatural life of grace as its deepest dynamism and final goal. The offer of this grace, then, is an existential, an intrinsic component of human existence and part of the very definition of the human in its historical existence."[18] The supernatural existential is ultimately humanity's orientation to God's intended supernatural transformation through grace.

For Rahner, our ordering toward God leads to an endless search for meaning. As we become aware of ourselves, we are open to everything, though nothing is completely satisfying. Our spirits are open to the unlimited quest for meaning. Rahner's anthropology has been described as an anthropology open to the transcendent. Based on the Thomistic understanding that we can know beyond the senses yet answering to the Kantian claim that all knowledge is rooted in the sensory, Rahner posits God as the principle of human knowledge. Rahner will always say, however, that we have the freedom to say yes or no to God. God is the ground of the very freedom to reject God. "God's self-communication as offer is also the necessary condition which makes its acceptance possible."[19] The supernatural existential does not require us to accept God in our lives; it makes us capable of accepting God's invitation. In his analysis of Rahner's anthropology, Miguel Díaz highlights that, for Rahner, all human experience is an experience of grace. Religious activity, Rahner writes, merely makes "explicit for ourselves what we already know implicitly about ourselves in the depths of our personal self-realization."[20] In his depiction of Rahner's anthropology Díaz emphasizes the importance of the everyday in his theology, for Rahner situated the experience of grace in everyday experiences. Díaz interprets this, and Rahner's positive interpretation of popular religious practices, as a precursor to contextual theologies.[21]

Rahner's theology has not been the direct focus of substantial feminist critique. In fact, various prominent Roman Catholic feminist theologians, including Elizabeth Johnson and Anne Carr, have used Rahner's theology as a starting point for their feminist anthropologies. Nonetheless, Rahner is not immune to critical engagement. In attempting to articulate a theological anthropology that describes human experience as a whole, Rahner pays little attention to the contextual nature of human experience. He attempts to speak of universal experience, an endeavor that today is clouded with serious suspicion. Ultimately, Rahner takes the human experience that emerges from his cultural, intellectual, and social milieu and applies it to all of humanity. This, in spite of the fact—and here feminists would celebrate Rahner—that he privileges the everyday and the popular as sources of theology. Rahner does not write extensively on the question of biological sex. On one level he is to be celebrated for not containing a hierarchy of male over female within his theology. Nonetheless, Rahner ignores the vital dimension of our embodied humanity. Indeed, embodiment is not a concern for him. Rahner's theology, and in particular his anthropology, has had a profound impact on contemporary theology, one whose traces we find in the exploration of feminist anthropologies in Chapter 5.

Existential Anthropology: Paul Tillich

Paul Tillich, the son of a pastor, served as a chaplain in the German army during World War I. His firsthand experience of war marked him and his theology in a profound manner. He later became a theology professor in Germany. Due to his opposition to Hitler, Tillich was dismissed from his university position and forced to flee Germany in 1933. Living the rest of his life in the United States, Tillich became an extremely popular college professor and one of the most widely known theologians in recent history. Tillich achieved a certain national recognition in the United States that few theologians in the contemporary era have attained.

Tillich's corpus is marked by his desire to articulate a theology accessible to the contemporary Christian, which contributed to the accessibility and reception of his work by a broader audience. As noted by David H. Kelsey, "Paul Tillich's principal goal was to make Christianity understandable and persuasive to religiously skeptical people, modern in culture and secular in sensibility."[22]

While this section focuses on Tillich's anthropology, the greatest legacy Tillich left for contemporary theology, we begin with a brief word about his method. Tillich defined religion as a person's ultimate concern. "We are those curious beings who have the capacity to look beyond our immediate preliminary interests to those concerns that undergird and give meaning to existence."[23] This ultimate concern is the subject matter of theology. Tillich's theological approach is characterized as a method of correlation. The function of theology, Tillich contends, is to correlate the questions implied in the cultural situation with the answers implied in the Christian message, existential questions and theological answers in mutual interdependence: "After the central theological answer is given to any question, there is always a return to the existential question as the context in which a theological answer is again given."[24] The questions theologians must address arise from the contemporary situation. The answers, however, must always emerge from Christian revelation:

> The existential question, namely, man himself in the conflicts of his existential situation, is not the source for the revelatory answer formulated by theology. . . . Man is the question, not the answer. It is equally wrong to derive the question implied in human existence from the revelatory answer. This is impossible because the revelatory answer is meaningless if there is no question to which it is the answer.[25]

In Tillich's theology there are two poles: the Christian message, and the cultural situation.

Tillich's theological method presupposes common ground between the Christian message and contemporary culture. In radical contrast to Barth he embraces and dialogues with secular disciplines. He is known, for example, for his use of existentialist philosophy within his theology. Tillich holds that every generation must reinterpret the Christian message. Because it belongs to the pole from which questions arise, experience is a medium not a source for theology. Given the contemporary context, Tillich defines theology as apologetic: rendering faith intelligible among a "culture of despisers." The task of theology is to speak to the modern mind on the boundary of the church and secular culture. Tillich's theology strives to be what he described as "theonomous." Rejecting heteronomy (the imposition of law on humanity from outside, religion as dictator) and autonomy (the rule of self by self), theonomy asserts a rule grounded in God, that is, God calls us to be what we are meant to be. Tillich understands God as the creative ground of everything, not alongside or above creation. God is being itself, which is, for Tillich, the only nonsymbolic thing you can say about God. God is the ground and power of all being. Tillich has an immanental understanding of transcendence: God is beneath and within everything, yet transcending the world. "He stands *against* the world, in so far as the world stands against him, and he stands *for* the world, thereby causing it to stand for him."[26] All our God-language is symbolic, for God is not a thing. Tillich does not have a very trinitarian understanding of God, though he highlights God as creative power, saving love, and ecstatic transformation. Essentially, for Tillich, God is the name of our ultimate concern.

Tillich's anthropology characterizes the human condition as one of estrangement and angst. Underlying his view of the human is his metaphysics. Tillich contends that reality must be differentiated into two realms: essence (potential perfection of things), and existence (actual, fallen from essence). Existence is finite and fallen, cut off from its true being. To exist is to stand out. We stand out of nonbeing in our very existence. "For

Tillich, the 'non-being' out of which each of us stands is our potentiality which, until it is realized, is simply a possibility. It is our essential nature. To exist is to be distanced, standing out from our essence."[27] Regardless of something's existence, everything participates in being, in a state of potential being, which precedes actual being. While standing out on nonbeing, we also remain in it, and this is our finitude. This ties back to the two levels of existence: essential and existential.

> True being is essential being and is present in the realm of eternal ideas, i.e. in essences. In order to reach essential being, man must rise above existence. He must return to the essential realm from which he fell into existence. In this way man's existence, his standing out of potentiality, is judged as a fall from what he essentially is. The potential is the essential, and to exist, i.e., to stand out of potentiality, is the loss of true essentiality. . . . In this sense "standing out" has a meaning precisely opposite that of the usual English usage. It means a falling away from what man essentially is.[28]

Humans literally fall into existence. When we come into existence, we become estranged from our essence. When we come to be, we become alienated from our true essence.

Christianity uses the symbols of the Fall and sin to address the alienation of the human condition. Within Tillich's anthropology, therefore, the Fall becomes a symbol of the human condition, not a story about something that happened in the past. It represents our transition from essence to existence. The creation stories demonstrate our awareness of our existential estrangement. Our finite freedom creates the possibility for us to fall into existence: "But the freedom of turning away from God is a quality of the structure of freedom as such. The possibility of the Fall is dependent on all the qualities of human freedom taken in their unity. Symbolically speaking, it is the image of God in man which gives the possibility of the Fall.

Only he who is the image of God has the power of separating himself from God. His greatness and his weakness are identical."[29] Our freedom to reject God is part of the order of creation. For Tillich, that freedom is the *imago Dei*, and ironically, it is that image which allows us to reject God. The very thing that constitutes our *imago Dei* is that which gives us the freedom to turn away from God.

We are aware of our finitude, and this awareness creates angst in the human. Our freedom creates anxiety. The human condition is marked by finitude, the falling into existence, this transition from essence to existence. The divine prohibition in the story of the Fall reveals the separation between Creator and creature and the test of obedience. "This cleavage is the most important point in the interpretation of the Fall. For it presupposes a sin which is not yet sin but which is also no longer innocence. It is the desire to sin." Tillich describes this state as "aroused freedom." Prior to the Fall humans were in a state of "dreaming innocence," where freedom and destiny were in harmony but neither of them was actualized. This is the essential and infinite state. However, this state of dreaming innocence is open to disruption. "The tension occurs in the moment in which finite freedom becomes conscious of itself and tends to become actual. This could be called the moment of aroused freedom. . . . Man is caught between the desire to actualize his freedom and the demand to preserve his dreaming innocence. In the power of his finite freedom, he decides for actualization."[30] Dreaming innocence is not a state of perfection or sinlessness. Because we are aware of our finite freedom, we enter into a state of anxiety, and this leads to the temptation to actualize ourselves. This is symbolized in the Fall by the prohibition on eating from the tree of knowledge. The universal destiny of humanity is this act of existential estrangement. There is no utopia of the past; estranged existence is actualized creation.

Sin is the personal dimension of estrangement. "Sin is estrangement; grace is reconciliation."[31] Tillich emphasizes that sin causes our radical existential estrangement from God. We are never entirely estranged from God, because through our participation in being we know God. Sin is a personal choice to manifest estrangement; sin necessarily follows estrangement. Tillich understood evil as an aspect of finite being. Human fallenness is not merely the result of choices but an aspect of the human condition. Tillich's anthropology, while seemingly positive in our anthropological capacity to know God and our culture as a medium of revelation, actually sees humans as ultimately estranged from God in the actualization of our freedom. Our destiny is tragic. Ironically, when one compares Tillich to Barth, who seems pessimistic in his denial of human natural knowledge of God, Barth actually articulates a more positive view of the human condition. Barth holds that the old human has been replaced by a new one in Christ. We are not estranged; we are chosen by God.

Tillich's anthropology, with humanity in this state of angst, is not his last word. For that, one must turn to his Christology. Tillich understands Jesus as the New Being; that is, God-humanity appearing under the circumstances of existence without being consumed by it. The New Being appears in Jesus the Christ. Tillich does not use hypostatic union language in his Christology but instead uses adoptionist language. The New Being transforms our estrangement from our essential being and our sense of meaninglessness. This New Being reunites self and world, essence and existence. Salvation for Tillich is the transformation of estrangement; it is a healing and reunion through the New Being. Jesus manifests a new order of being, essential humanity under the conditions of existence having conquered estrangement. "For Tillich, the humanity of the New Being seen in Jesus as the Christ is not merely idealized essentiality, but realizes within existence the eternal unity of God and man; thus the New Being transforms man's existence and makes it really new."[32] Christ's estrangement is symbolized by the cross (God sharing in human estrangement) and his conquest by the resurrection. The divine enters into our estrangement with a profound love that transforms us.

Tillich stands as a bit of an anomaly in this chapter, for his apologetic stance fuels a theology that is articulated in non-theological language. While the language of the *imago Dei* and gender are not the center of his theology, they appear under different guises. His theology has also been the subject of substantial study by feminist theologians, most notably in Judith Plaskow's critical examination of Tillich's notions of sin and grace in light of the category of women's experience.[33] His method of correlation has left a stamp on modern Christian theology, shaping the work of various theological voices, including those of feminist theologians. Tillich's limitations are grounded in his application of his particular experience as a representation of universal human experience. To incorporate women's experience into his theology, Plaskow argues, would entail a radical rewriting of various dimensions of his theology. Nonetheless, feminist theologians are indebted to Tillich's methodology, which takes seriously the culture and context from which theological reflection emerges.

Hans Urs von Balthasar

Often, when one hears the name Hans Urs von Balthasar in theological circles, two things come to mind: the conservative nature of his work, and his theological aesthetics. One of the greatest theologians of the twentieth century, he has, until recently, been caricatured as an extremely conservative and therefore to many an unappealing theologian. This is a result, in part, of two interrelated factors. First, there is a tendency to judge Balthasar by his shorter, more polemical writings. These concern popular issues such as women's ordination and the celibacy of the clergy. Second, and directly related to the former, is the fact that it is only in the past few decades that the majority of Balthasar's corpus has been translated into the English language.

The second great trademark of Balthasar's work is his theological aesthetics, which culminates in the seven-volume *Glory*

of the Lord. It is considered by many to be one of the twentieth-century's greatest achievements within theology.[34] Situated
as the first part of Balthasar's enormous trilogy, his aesthetics
seeks to recover the aesthetic form of theology. The trilogy itself is based on the three transcendentals of being: the Beautiful, the Good, and the True. The order of the trilogy is not ar-
bitrary. The manifestation, or theophany, of the aesthetics leads
to the encounter of the dramatics. As Balthasar writes, "God
does not want to be just 'contemplated' and 'perceived' by us,
like a solitary actor by his public; no, from the beginning he has
provided for a play in which we all must share."[35] The theo-
drama is followed by the theo-logic, which treats the human
articulation of the dramatic event.

Perhaps one of the more creative aspects of Balthasar's theology is found in the fact that gender is not merely an anthropological category. In addition to revealing something about
human nature, as Lucy Gardner and David Moss highlight,
"there is another critical role which sexual difference is asked
to perform in Balthasar's theology. It is also presented as *ana-
logical* to the difference between the world and God—a difference we shall name *theological difference*."[36] In other words,
gender functions in his concept of God and Christology. However, I would push the point further and affirm that gender per-
meates every aspect of Balthasar's theology.[37] Unlike in the
works of many of his contemporary Western European coun-
terparts, gender is a central analytic category in Balthasar's
work. Balthasar's model of humanity is based on an understanding of the female as primarily receptive and the male as
active (à la Aristotle and Aquinas). Balthasar models human
sexuality in very clear terms of activity and receptivity. This
giving and receiving is constitutive of the Trinity and also is
linked to Balthasar's kenotic Christology and concept of God.
The self-giving and pouring out that is manifested on the cross
and on Holy Saturday is identical to the inner-trinitarian relations of giving and receiving. God's nature is relational and constituted by action. This in turn leads to a Christology that un-

derstands Jesus Christ, and consequently humanity, as constituted *in relation*. Relationship and action are foundational to
our understanding of God and of humanity.

Angelo Scola notes that, for Balthasar, humanity's self-con-
sciousness "is constituted by two factors: the experience of self-
possession, and universal openness, the necessity of recognizing the coexistence of men and things. . . . In virtue of the first
pole, freedom is the capacity for self-movement, for responsibility, and for choice; by virtue of the second it is the capacity
for assent, for acceptance, and for obedience."[38] The first pole,
self-possession, is characterized by autonomy. The second pole
of freedom is relationships with others. For Balthasar, humans
have a seemingly contradictory awareness of their freedom. It
is contradictory because it is a freedom that is limited.[39] While
humans are free, we have an awareness that this freedom is a
gift; we are free yet dependent on God who has given us the gift
of freedom. This paradox of the human is understood, for
Balthasar, in terms of three polarities: spirit and body, man and
woman, individual and community.[40] We are always struggling
within these polarities to find a sense of our humanity.

While Balthasar always argues for the equality of the polarities, in terms of gender the male has priority. This position has
a christological foundation, for Balthasar argues that based on
man's natural priority Christ was incarnate in male flesh.[41]
Balthasar's understanding of the feminine as receptivity and
response naturally leads to an ontological priority of the male.
While Balthasar wants to maintain the equality of the sexes, it
is arguable, as the following passage demonstrates, whether he
succeeds:

> Man and woman are face to face. Here their equal rank
> is given even more emphasis: man looks around him and
> meets with an answering gaze that turns the one-who-sees
> into the one-who-is-seen. . . . Thus the woman, who is
> both "answer" and "face," is not only man's delight: she
> is the help, the security, the home man needs; she is the

vessel of fulfillment specially designed for him. Nor is she simply the vessel of *his* fruitfulness: she is equipped with her own explicit fruitfulness. Yet her fruitfulness is not a primary fruitfulness: it is an answering fruitfulness, designed to receive man's fruitfulness (which, in itself, is helpless) and bring it to its "fullness."[42]

Three points should be highlighted. First, for Balthasar, feminine receptivity is an active receptivity, not a passive one; women are actively responsive. Second, there is a tension in wanting to depict both sexes as equal yet giving the male primary status. Last, it is important to note that in their relationship to God, all humans are feminine, for they all respond to God's action. The human as the created feminine creature remains responsive and receptive to God's revelation, while women take on this role with regard to men in human relations. This leads, inevitably, to masculine activity becoming equated with divine agency. Gerard Loughlin points out the inconsistency of this: "Balthasar wants equality of male and female but the text displays the priority of the male; he wants the priority of the male but the text insinuates an equality with the female, so we have the 'relative priority of the man,' which only whispers the relative equality of the woman."[43] There is an ambiguous understanding of gender that is simultaneously egalitarian and hierarchical in Balthasar's theology.

Balthasar understands the distinction between the sexes as reflective of their *imago Dei*, and fruitfulness plays a central role, for it mirrors the eternal fecundity of the Trinity. By positing gender in the *imago Dei*, Balthasar understands the distinction between the sexes as embedded in humanity's spirit in such a way that "the physical difference appears insignificant in comparison."[44] The two sexes image the kenotic self-giving and receiving of the trinitarian relationships:

Since it is women's essential vocation to receive man's fruitfulness into her own fruitfulness, thus uniting in herself

the fruitfulness of both, it follows that she is actually the
fruit-bearing principle in the creaturely realm. . . . In the
most general terms, this means that the woman does not
merely give back to man what she has received from him:
she gives him something new, something that integrates
the gift he gave her but that "faces" him in a totally new
and unexpected form. . . . She responds through reproduction.[45]

Moss and Gardner argue that in this passage woman is constructed as oriented toward man; her vocation is understood in
terms of serving him. By constructing woman's response in
terms of reproduction, Balthasar also describes her activity as
returning something to the man, defining her activity in terms
of the male.[46] Though women's receptivity is defined as an active fruitfulness, Balthasar nonetheless maintains a biological
framework for the relationship between men and women. This
generative model orients the female toward the male as active
generative recipient.

For Balthasar, the responsive human is secondary in relationship to God. "We have already indicated that the creature can
only be secondary, responsive, 'feminine' vis-à-vis God. . . .
However, insofar as every creature—be it male or female in the
natural order—is originally the fruit of the primary, absolute,
self-giving divine love, there is a clear analogy to the female
principle in the world."[47] The human is secondary with regard
to God, the female with regard to the male. Therefore, woman
is doubly secondary in Balthasar's theology. This is grounded
in Balthasar's definition of the human as essentially feminine
with regard to God. However, in relationship with each other,
men have an added masculine principle that is not present in
women.

Linked to this theme is Balthasar's understanding of woman
as answer. Once again, returning to an earlier citation, Balthasar defines man and woman as equal, though woman is
understood as man's answer. She is "designed for him"; while

her receptivity is active, it is understood as a responsive active receptivity. Balthasar's construction of woman as answer leads to an understanding of woman as constituted by her relationship to man. Her sense of self is defined in terms of the male and is secondary.[48] In the original German-language text of Balthasar's writings the male-female pair is *Wort-Antwort*. The complementarity Balthasar envisions is more obvious in the original language, yet as *Antwort* to the male *Wort*, the primacy of the male is reinforced. One cannot answer unless spoken to. Woman is constructed as responsive to the man.

While feminists may find what Balthasar writes about gender problematic, he must nonetheless be commended for attempting to understand the human person in light of his or her embodied sexuality. Balthasar constructs gender *theologically*. Also, as one of numerous theologians who contributed to the project of *ressourcement* in twentieth-century Roman Catholic theology, Balthasar's retrieval of "church mothers" is consonant with feminist historical scholarship.[49] While Balthasar's motivations for historical recovery differ from feminists', they still share this tenet in their work. Nevertheless, his theological anthropology is saturated with the language of gender complementarity that the overwhelming majority of feminist theologians abhor. Balthasar, in a similar manner to the historical theologians explored in the previous chapter and Karl Barth in the present one, constructs an anthropology, one that is divinely sanctioned, for it is grounded in the inner-trinitarian life, and one that places women and men in limited roles in which they are incapable of individually expressing humanity in its fullness and in which the male is privileged over the female.

The four theologians explored in this chapter offer four different understandings of the human as created in the image of God. The *imago Dei* functions more prominently for some than for others. Their work both builds and transforms the inherited theological tradition explored in the previous chapters. They share some similarities and differences. Both Tillich and Rahner argue that humanity has a natural ability to understand the

divine, a perspective that Barth rejects. Both Barth and Balthasar specifically address biological sex in their theologies,
constructing theological anthropologies based on gender
complementarity. This is not a direct concern for Tillich and
Rahner, though gender functions in subtle ways within their
theologies. Ultimately, the four create the theological starting
point from which contemporary feminist theology emerges. As
the following chapter explores, the basis for feminist theology
was its reaction to the patriarchal nature of the Christian tradition and the contemporary milieu of theological reflection.

Chapter 4

Feminist Theology

This book traces Christian understandings of the human with special attention to the distinctive categorization of male and female as created in the image of God. Beginning with the scriptural passage that is the foundation for the belief in the *imago Dei*, we moved through different historical eras in order to uncover the central Christian interpretations of the notion that humanity reflects God's image in some manner. Most often the image is associated with the spiritual or rational dimension of the human in contrast to the body. The divine image is also associated with Jesus Christ, so that the image of God becomes equivalent to the image of Christ. The trinitarian nature of the divine also plays into notions of the *imago Dei*, leading to relationship and community as central features of humanity's ability to reflect the divine.

The focal point of our exploration of the *imago Dei* has been the role of gender and biological sex. Far from being a recent concern raised by contemporary feminist thinkers, theological notions of male and female have functioned within Christian theology since its inception. In fact, specific attention to male and female and their distinctiveness has been a central concern for theologians throughout the history of Christianity. Unfortunately, too often Christian understandings of the sexes are grounded in a hierarchy that values men over women. As noted by Daphne Hampson, historically the construction of woman within Christianity has been a composite of those attributes that men have rejected or deemed lesser in humanity: "Though they have been the dominant sex (perhaps because they have been the dominant sex) men, it must often seem, lack a centeredness (in the right sense of that term) in themselves. . . . Woman is then placed in the role of supposedly 'complementing' a man. . . . Hence man's construal of 'woman' as a being on to whom he can project all those qualities which seem to him unmanly."[1] Women are associated with everything that is lesser, most often the body, sensuality, and emotion. Men, in contrast, are associated with rationality and spirituality. Given that the image of God becomes more closely linked to those attributes that are connected to men, women are seen as reflecting the image of God in a deficient or defective manner. Their bodies, in particular, come to be linked to that which impedes the fullness of the image within them.

This sexist understanding of the human, grounded in an androcentric world view that values men over women, and the resulting institutional devaluation of women become the impetus that spurs Christian feminist theology. Exploding onto the theological arena in the 1960s, feminist theology is one of the most widespread and controversial contemporary Christian theological movements. Its birth and growth parallels the feminist movement that swept across the academy and the broader culture. A central source and often norm in feminist theology is women's experience. Feminist theologians argue that what has been deemed human experience in Christian theology is actually male experience, and that in order to have a true vision of the human women's experience must be included. In fact, feminists argue, due to its historical marginalization, women's experience is privileged. Often, feminist theology is critiqued for the centrality of women's experience, arguing that it hampers the objectivity of the discipline. Rosemary Radford Ruether retorts that such statements imply that classical theology is in some way objective. Instead, Ruether argues, those elements that have been canonized as objective sources of

Christian theology—for example, scripture and tradition—are in fact products of human experience. "The uniqueness of feminist theology lies not in its use of the criterion of experience but rather in its use of *women's* experience, which has been almost entirely shut out of theological reflection in the past."[2] Feminist theology is unique in its use of women's experience. A stronger critique regarding feminist theology's use of women's experience, one that we explore in this chapter, is the category of woman within feminist theology. While critiquing the limited notion of woman operating in the Christian theological tradition, feminist theologians, some argue, have created an equally limiting and essentialized understanding of woman's identity and experience.

This chapter examines the category of woman functioning within feminist theology. It is an introduction to Chapter 5, which explores feminist theological anthropologies specifically. I begin by surveying the methodology that shapes contemporary feminist theology. The second section accents the question of diversity within feminist theologies, setting the stage for the rest of the chapter. I then turn to the question of identity, specifically women's experience, as a starting point and site of tension within feminist theology. Feminist theology emerged, for the most part, in response to the patriarchal construction of women's identity explored in Chapters 1 and 2 of this study. As noted by Mary Ann Hinsdale, a critique of androcentric, patriarchal understandings of the human has accompanied feminist theology since its inception in the 1960s.[3] As early as 1960 Valerie Saiving mused, "I am no longer certain as I once was that, when theologians speak of 'man,' they are using the word in its generic sense."[4] The category of women's experience is one of the most significant and contested contributions of feminist theology. While an indispensable dimension of feminist scholarship, one must ask whether the essentialized and abstract notion of woman fares much better than the patriarchal construction of woman in traditional Christian theology. The chapter concludes by examining those voices within feminist theology that are attempting to articulate a notion of women's identity and experience that leaves room for diversity while not erasing the possibility of speaking of women as a collective in a meaningful manner.

Theological Method

Feminist theology is characterized by a tripartite method: a hermeneutics of suspicion (critique and deconstruction of historical Christianity), a hermeneutics of retrieval (recovery of the lost history of women), and reconstruction (revision of Christian categories). Its methodology includes a critique of androcentric, patriarchal scholarship and church life. This leads to a revisioning of the entire Christian tradition for both men and women. Elizabeth Johnson describes feminist theology's threefold method in this manner: "Feminist theology engages in at least three interrelated tasks: it critically analyzes inherited oppressions, searches for alternative wisdom and suppressed history, and risks new interpretations of the tradition in conversation with women's lives."[5] Johnson emphasizes the critical lens of feminist theology and the historical dimension of feminist theological projects. Elisabeth Schüssler Fiorenza echoes, "Feminist scholarship unveils the patriarchal functions of the intellectual and scientific frameworks generated and perpetuated by male-centered scholarship that makes women invisible or peripheral in what we know about the world, human life, and cultural or religious history."[6] The first task in feminist theology is to be mindful of the function of power and marginalization in inherited and current theological discourses. Feminist theologians argue that women's contributions to Christian theology have been intentionally sidelined and undermined.

The second task of feminist theology is dominated by historical research. Through this work the lost women's voices of Christian traditions are recovered through scriptural and historical scholarship. Part of this task is unearthing the role of silence that led to the marginalization of these women's voices. Schüssler Fiorenza highlights the importance of this step, for a feminist critical analysis must be accompanied by knowledge of women's intellectual contributions throughout the centuries:

> Although women have questioned these explanations and internalizations throughout the centuries, we remain ignorant of our own intellectual traditions and foremothers. All "great" philosophers, scientists, theologians, poets, politicians, artists, and religious leaders seem to have been men who have for centuries been writing and talking to each other in order to define God, the world, human community and existence as "they saw it." However that does not mean that women have not been "great" thinkers and leaders. Yet their thoughts and works have not been transmitted and become classics of our culture and religion because patriarchy requires that in any conceptualization of the world men and their power have to be central.[7]

One should not, however, limit the subject matter of this task to the scholarship of women. Part of this second step includes unearthing the male voices that also have been silenced, misinterpreted, or ignored. The third task of feminist theology creates new theological constructions in light of the prior two steps. This third step is perhaps the most vital, for here feminists offer constructive proposals that provide an alternative vision of Christian theological notions informed by a broader and critical appreciation of the Christian tradition. The following chapter provides an overview of feminist constructive work in one area of Christian theology, namely, theological anthropology. In Chapter 6 I offer my own contribution.

The normative principle within the work of an overwhelming number of feminist theologians is the full humanity of women. A Christian theological passage or movement is deemed revelatory if it promotes the full humanity of women in contrast to a sexist construction or practice. For Schüssler

Fiorenza, "feminist theology begins with the experiences of women, of women-church."[8] Women-church becomes the center of feminist biblical interpretation. She defines women-church as "the movement of self-identified women and women-identified men in biblical religion."[9] Within Schüssler Fiorenza's theology the radical nature of feminist theology is in its accountability to women in churches and not to *the* church. Because the church has historically been an institution that denies the full humanity of women, feminist theology does not answer to it. Instead, feminist theology is accountable to women who have remained committed to Christianity in spite of their marginalization. Women's experiences in the struggle for liberation become the starting point of Schüssler Fiorenza's biblical interpretation. Since the Bible is contaminated by patriarchy, it cannot be normative in and of itself. As seen in Chapter 1, this approach to the Bible is seen as problematic by some because it creates a norm for Christianity that is applied externally to the tradition. For Schüssler Fiorenza, however, the promotion of the full humanity of women is a normative principle that determines whether or nor a biblical passage is revelatory.

Schüssler Fiorenza is not alone. According to Ruether, "The critical principle of feminist theology is the promotion of the full humanity of women."[10] Ruether argues that the Christian tradition must be weighed against whether or not a given doctrine, practice, or belief promotes women's full humanity. Whatever denies women's full humanity is not redemptive; what promotes it is holy. In a similar vein Johnson defines the criterion of feminist theology as "the emancipation of women toward human flourishing."[11] Underlying the need for this principle is a critical engagement of the Christian tradition, one which argues that the Christian tradition has not historically promoted the full humanity of women and that it needs to be critically engaged in light of this new hermeneutic.

A quick glance at the authors explored in Chapter 2, grounded in the feminist critical principle of the promotion of the full humanity of women, reveals that historically Christian theology has denied the full humanity of woman as created in the image of God. Gregory of Nyssa, for example, while not privileging male over female, links the body with humanity's brutal nature. The body, in turn, has been historically associated with women. Within Augustine's theology women represent the inferior intellect and only reflect the image of God in spite of their bodies. Aquinas depicts women as misbegotten men, a necessary mistake of nature created solely for procreation. Women reflect the image less perfectly than men. The analysis could continue. What is clear is that when judged based on the critical principle of feminist theology, traditional understandings of the human do not fare well. Therefore, feminist theologians argue, one needs the threefold methodology in order to uncover the authentic Christian understanding of the human, drawing from marginalized and often forgotten elements of Christian tradition.

Feminist Theologies

The first generation of feminist theologians consisted overwhelmingly of white European and European American women. This paralleled the development of feminist theory as a whole and leadership within the feminist movement. Because of this, early feminist scholarship is marked by its limited focus and cultural biases. Women of color were quick to point out that while feminist theology contained a sustained and significant analysis of the function of sexism within the contemporary and historical Christian context, it did not explore the other dimensions of oppression, such as racism, classism, and ethnic prejudice. "Women of color have been critical of white feminists for universalizing their experience and thereby ignoring the experiences unique to them. Social location plays a significant role in the liberation of women. No true liberation exists unless the difference of race, class, age, and sexual orientation make in people's daily lives is heeded."[12] Some feminists of color contend that by ignoring these oppressive elements feminist theologians inadvertently perpetuated them within their work. The second wave of contemporary feminist scholarship is marked by attention to diversity and difference.

Feminists of color from around the globe began to articulate their own theological perspectives grounded in their particular social location. For African American feminist theologians, womanist theology became an avenue for expressing their distinctive voice in contrast to yet in collaboration with what they described as white feminist theology. As noted by Stephanie Y. Mitchem, womanist theology emerged in part as a response to white feminism's exclusive emphasis on gender oppression: "This focus only met the needs of white women, with their histories, and limited the relevance of feminism for black women in the United States who had different experiences of domination."[13] As a black feminist theological voice, womanist theology combines a threefold analysis of racism, sexism, and classism in order to explore the manifold ways in which oppression manifests itself in the African American community in the United States. The starting point of womanist theology is African American women's experiences. Jacquelyn Grant writes: "Womanist theology begins with the experiences of Black women as its point of departure. . . . This perspective in theology which I am calling womanist theology draws upon the life and experiences of some Black women who have created meaningful interpretations of the Christian faith."[14] Womanist theology echoes the methodological starting point of white, European American feminist theologies, with its only qualification being its attention to black women's experiences. Nonetheless, the methodological starting point of women's experience remains the same.

Ada María Isasi-Díaz's *mujerista* theology also shares women's experience as a starting point; however like womanist theologians, she qualifies the women who are the sources of her theology as Latinas:

The goals of *mujerista* theology have always been these: to provide a platform for the voices of Latin grassroots women; to develop a theological method that takes seriously the religious understandings and practices of Latinas as a source for theology; to challenge theological understandings, church teachings, and religious practices that oppress Latina women, that are not life-giving, and, therefore, cannot be theologically correct.[15]

Mujerista theology is a Latina feminist theological voice distinct from Euro-American feminism. In an early definition of *mujerista* she writes, "A *mujerista* is a Latina who makes a preferential option for herself and her Hispanic sisters, understanding that our struggle for liberation has to take into consideration how racism/ethnic prejudice, economic oppression, and sexism work together and reinforce each other."[16] Rejecting the term *feminist hispana*, she argues that, for many Latinas, feminism is viewed as an Anglo creation that marginalizes their concerns. Isasi-Díaz also highlights the painful history and marginalization of Latinas within the White, Euro-American feminist community.[17] These factors contribute to her rejection of *feminist* as an appropriate term to designate Latinas concerned about sexist oppression. Latina feminist theologian María Pilar Aquino, on the other hand, embraces the term *feminism* as an "indigenous" movement within Latin America, yet she qualifies her work as Latina feminism in order to acknowledge its particular cultural context.[18] In spite of womanist, *mujerista*, and other US minority women's critiques of white European American feminist theology, these US scholars remain united in their distinctive efforts to undermine patriarchal understandings of Christianity. They also remain tied in terms of methodology and the use of women's experiences as a starting point for their theologies.

Within third-world feminist theology one also finds an ambiguous relationship with the category of feminism. As noted by Kwok Pui-lan in her introduction to Asian feminist theology, to speak of Asian feminist theology is not without contention. For many Asian women, the term *feminism* is too strongly associated with Europe and the United States. "Women theologians in Asia have not conjured up another name for the kind of liberation theology they are doing because there is no common language or concept they can use together."[19] For Kwok, however, *Asian feminist theology* is a viable term that speaks to the academic and political efforts both in church and society to struggle for Asian women's full humanity. What characterizes Asian feminist theology, among other things, is first of all its context. Unlike Western feminist theologies, Asian feminist theology emerges from a context in which Christianity is a minority religion (except in the Philippines and South Korea). Second, the particularity of Asian women's experiences does not fall neatly into the universalized construction of Western feminist theologies. Third, a mere analysis of sexism is not enough to describe the context of Asian women (one also needs, for example, an analysis of colonialism). Fourth is the enthnocentrism and racism of Western feminism. Asian women must claim their voices as authors and subjects of Christian theology. Kwok notes that the contested nature of the category of women's experience is not new to Asian feminist theologians, given the diversity of Asian women's experiences. Therefore, she emphasizes the nature of this category as socially constructed. In order to access the diversity of Asian women's experiences, storytelling and social analysis are key, as well as aesthetic and liturgical sources. One shared theme is the reality of colonialism. In its early incarnations Asian feminist theologians emphasized the commonalities among Asian women. This was due, in part, to their efforts to articulate a particularly Asian voice in response to Western feminism. However, in the past decade Asian feminist theologians have emphasized the particularity and diversity of Asian women's experiences.

While an essentialized notion of women's experience is contested by feminists of color, the primacy of women's experience within the methodology of feminist theologies remains. In addition to a growing awareness of the need for distinctive feminist theologies collaborating while remaining grounded in their own particular context, another mark of more recent feminist theology is attention to feminist theory. With scholarship informed by feminist theoreticians, feminist theologians approach the question of difference and essentialism. Serene Jones defines feminist theory as "a collection of feminist texts with shared goals, practices, and assumptions." Jones emphasizes that feminist theory is not merely textual, but also embodies the conversations that inform these texts. It is an interdisciplinary project: "Feminist theorizing is not limited to a particular discipline but takes place in almost every department of the university."[20] When feminist theorists turn to the question of identity, a key emphasis is its constructed nature, including a strong critique of essentialist constructions of gender identity and of knowledge.[21] In an excellent article examining the role of critical theory in feminist theology Rebecca Chopp thoughtfully points out that "the refusal to continue foundationalism does not let us beg off the metaphysical question."[22] In other words, attention to the contextual nature of all knowledge, as feminist theorists readily point out, does not eliminate the possibility of saying something meaningful beyond one's context. Chopp's definition of feminist theology is grounded in her understanding of critical theory:

A critical theory uses theoretical discourse to name the struggles of the day and to identify future possibilities. Critical theories, like the emancipatory and progressive movements out of which they arise, are oriented not to the past, but to the future. Critical theories are those theories which address the relations amongst interest, power and knowledge and thus understand knowledge as historical.[23]

Feminist theology, for Chopp, is a critical theory operating within the cultural movement and emancipatory praxis of

feminist liberationist Christianity. "Feminist theology, then, is
the ongoing construction of the symbolic content of emancipatory praxis. This symbolic content relates to how we interpret the world, how we experience the world in our spirituality, and how we work for change and transformation."[24] The
goal of feminist theology is to undermine, identify, and transform patriarchal Christianity. Chopp's definition of feminist
theology attempts to balance the more abstract, theoretical concerns of the discipline with the everyday struggles of women.

The challenge of articulating a theological perspective that
gives voice to women, while not unintentionally silencing some
women through a limited notion of women's identity, is a challenge that feminist theologians will continue to face in years to
come. Also, one must add, while this question is vital, it cannot hamper further constructive feminist theological work. In
their strong emphasis on the politics of identity and articulating a theological voice from a specific context, US minority,
third-world, and theoretically minded feminist theologians
must heed a word of caution, for much of their work remains
at the level of critical analysis and not of constructive work.
While it is vital that these theologies name the various particularities that shape and marginalize their communities and that
they contest an essentialized notion of woman's identity, the
lack of constructive work hampers their contribution to Christian theology. My contribution in Chapter 6 attempts to address this question by offering a constructive proposal for a
theological anthropology emerging from, though not limited
to, the Latina context. In spite of one's specific context, however, what remains clear is the significance of women's experience for feminist theology. What remains contested is the nature of that experience.

Women's Experience

Over fifty years ago Simone de Beauvoir wrote, "One is not
born, but rather becomes, a woman."[25] With this statement

Beauvoir raised the question of gender essentialism in feminist theory, a matter hotly debated even today. The question of whether there are characteristics that essentially constitute the nature of a woman, or if we can even speak of a woman's essential nature, is not only discussed within women's studies, gender studies, and feminist theory, but it also has permeated other disciplines within the academy. Primarily led by feminist scholars influenced by postmodern theory and cultural studies, many thinkers emphasize the construction of gender identity and the sociopolitical consequences of gender essentialism.[26] Emerging from a different camp are those women who have been excluded from the operating definition of women's identity and whose critique emerges not from abstract theorizing but from their concrete daily lives.

One cannot deny that the category of women's experience is fundamental to understanding feminist theology. In its emphasis on experience as foundational for the theological task, feminist theology is not novel. As noted by Sheila Briggs, this emphasis on experience is a hallmark of modern theology: "I do not think that one can deny that feminist theology began as a modernist discourse. Although it mounted its critique of all previous, male-defined theology, it nonetheless retained one of the central assumptions of modern theology since Schleiermacher—that theology proceeds out of experience."[27] As we saw in the previous chapter, theologians such as Karl Rahner and Paul Tillich view human experience as a fundamental starting point for theology. What is novel, as stated above, is feminist theology's emphasis on *women's* experience. In a sense, as Briggs's citation implies, feminist theology does not create a new theological discourse but remains wedded to the very discourse it critiques so vehemently. Feminist theology is, for better or worse, yet another incarnation of modern theology.

The category of women's experience and the manner in which theologians define it, however, are sources of contention within feminist theology. As we saw above, with the emergence of women of color upon the theological scene, as well as the use of feminist theory that engages questions of identity, women's experience has become problematized within feminist theology. While feminist theologians want to speak of a shared women's experience, one cannot deny that such a generalization obscures the diversity and particularity of women across the globe. At the same time, one cannot deny that women have been uncritically lumped into one group throughout the history of theology, and one must respond to that essentialized, patriarchal understanding of women.

In this section I explore the debate surrounding the category of women's experience within feminist theology. Before exploring my colleagues' voices, I should confess that I find an overarching, uncritical understanding of women's experience extremely problematic, especially as a norm within feminist theology. As a Cuban American woman, a minority in the United States, and an even greater minority in theological studies, I am well aware of the dangers contained in generalizations such as women's experience. It is a category that has been used to oppress and silence women of color in feminist discourse. The "we" of women has more often than not blurred the distinctiveness of women's concrete realities, where the minority voice is often ignored or forgotten. The claims I make are not in any way novel. This is a debate that is currently ringing in the halls of academia. It is a critique recognized by both white Anglo women and women of color.

Anne E. Carr is well aware of the dangers of universalizing any form of women's experience, noting the diversity and unique individuality of women. Carr points out that while women's experience can be a source for feminist theology, it cannot be a norm: "As normative, it fails to provide for self-criticism, and thus feminist theology would be open to self-deception and a new kind of oppression."[28] Women's experience can refer to various things: bodily experience, socialized experience, feminist experience, historical experience, individual experience, or Christian experience, that is, interpreted experience of the Bible and Christian tradition. Carr sees women's experience as a vital source for theology, one that must be nuanced in light of the diversity of women. While Schüssler Fiorenza embraces women's experience as normative within her theology, she attempts to maintain the distinctiveness of women's identity within that category. As mentioned earlier, her work replaces the anthropological construction of woman with a political one. In her writing Schüssler Fiorenza uses the spelling *wo/men* "to indicate that women are not a unitary social group but rather are fragmented and fractured by structures of race, class, religion, heterosexuality, colonialism, age, and health."[29] While women's struggles for liberation, or women-church, are normative within Schüssler Fiorenza's theology, she does not collapse all women into a homogenous social group.

Elizabeth Johnson raises the question of differences among women's experiences, especially as raised by the voices of US minority and third-world women. She notes the universalizing, obscuring tendency found when white women ignore the voices of women of color. At the same time Johnson raises the need for a shared experience to mobilize women: "Commonality is essential to the fight against cruelty at the concrete level."[30] Johnson offers a paradigm in which one is aware of one's particularity and therefore open to different women's voices, simultaneously building solidarity among women. Johnson's work is characterized by her desire to link the category of women's experience to human experience in general. It is here where one finds a bit of dissonance within Johnson's theology. Her work is influenced by the theology and anthropology of Karl Rahner. In Johnson's theology one finds a description of human experience that echoes Rahner's. Johnson thus attempts to speak of human experience as a whole in an abstract manner. One finds in Johnson's theology a tension between her attention to differences among women and her statements about humanity as a whole. This is ironic for while Johnson does not want to essentialize woman, she is quick to essentialize human experience.

Carr, Schüssler Fiorenza, and Johnson are all white European American women. Their approaches to diversity within feminist theology come from a position of dominance. Too often, feminists of color point out, white women engage difference and diversity only when challenged based on the viability of such categories as women's experience. In her critical essay "On the Logic of Pluralist Feminism," Latina philosopher María Lugones challenges the articulation and treatment of "the problem of difference" in feminist theoretical discourse.[31] She points out two major pitfalls of white Anglo theoretical frameworks concerning this topic, the first being the initial lack of importance given to difference. This is a concern that women of color, as the "other," cannot avoid. "Women of color always knew that white women and women of color were different; white women all knew they were different from women of color. But white women never considered these differences important, because they did not really *notice* us."[32] In other words, women of color do not have the option of engaging the question of race, ethnic prejudice, and diversity; they live this reality in their everyday lives. The second pitfall is the formulation of this "problem" as theoretical. In other words, this concern only came to the forefront when it threatened the theoretical framework of feminist discourses, not due to the protests of women of color. Lugones proposes the need for an interactive theoretical framework inclusive of plurality in order to address this problem.

Lugones's second point is vital. A point of tension between scholars of color and white scholars is that the question of difference and diversity only became significant when feminist theologians began to engage feminist theory on this question. In other words, only when the theoretical foundations of the category of women's experience was challenged—for example, by postmodern theorists—did white feminists take notice of the women of color surrounding them, in spite of the fact that women of color had always been around them. Scholars of color are also wary of the fact that much critical theory can lead to a relativism that disempowers people of color. Because the dominant group has power, it is not challenged by the claim of relativism. The dominant group merely remains in power. Isasi-Díaz is suspicious of the political implications of postmodern discourse for people of color: "I believe that the relativism endorsed by postmodernism is an effective way of maintaining present power systems based on race, ethnicity, class, economic status, sex, sexual orientation."[33] In other words, Isasi-Díaz is concerned that a purely theoretical approach to difference and diversity allows power to remain within the status quo. In a similar vein, theorist bell hooks notes the ambiguity of appropriating postmodern theory as a black feminist. Since this theory is in large part a response to modernism, it does not take into consideration black experience, especially that of black women. "It is sadly ironic that the contemporary discourse which talks the most about heterogeneity, the decentered subject, declaring breakthroughs that allow the recognition of Otherness, still directs its critical voice primarily to a specialized audience that shares a common language rooted in the very master narratives it claims to challenge."[34] Hooks is also critical of the elitist nature of this discourse, which mirrors the very discourse it maintains that it critiques. Nonetheless, hooks argues, postmodernist thought can serve as a critical tool in deconstructing essentialized notions of black identity. In a similar vein, postmodern theory also helps unpack essentialized notions of women's identity.

In a fruitful discussion published in the *Journal of Hispanic/Latino Theology* Susan Secker and Jeanette Rodríguez wrestle with women's experience as a source for theology.[35] It is interesting to note that, resonating with Lugones's above-mentioned quotation, Secker, a white woman, deals more with her surprising discovery of the "problem of difference" in feminist theology, while this "problem" is presupposed by Latina Rodríguez. Without entering into a detailed account of the essays, I highlight two quotations that raise the essence of this issue. The first citation concerns the language of difference. Secker writes, "To say that something is different is to imply that there is a criterion of sameness from which this person deviated."[36] The difference imported by the voices of women of color, being labeled different, implies an atypical contribution. It is weighed against a norm of sameness from which they are excluded. Women of color's voices remain intrinsically "other." In labeling women of color and their experiences different, they are marginalized as abnormal and deviant from authentic women's experience.

I would add to Secker's comment a critique of the use of *problem*. It is only in cultures where hegemony is viewed as favorable that plurality is seen as problematic. If we maintain a language that essentially labels plurality as a difficulty, we will remain in a paradigm where multiplicity is seen as negative. This is a dangerous camp for feminist thought. The second quotation I cite comes from Rodríguez: "Although I think the search for a common ground is a worthy cause I am not convinced that the common ground is experience. Perhaps a more appropriate question is: What is that we can all stand behind? What is that we can work toward?"[37] Rodríguez's work, much like Schüssler Fiorenza's, is pushing for a more political notion of women's identity.

The work of Mary McClintock Fulkerson is shaped by a critical engagement with theoretical sources. She argues: "Feminist theology has failed to offer theories of language, social location, power, and gender capable of displaying difference. When it relies upon appeals to women's experience as the origin of or evidence for its claims, feminist theology cannot account for the systems of meaning and power that produce experience."[38] The goal of McClintock Fulkerson's work is not to purge the category of women of its values but instead to transform the manner in which woman as subject is constructed. She does not want to erase the subject woman; rather, she wants to create a subject that allows for multiplicity in identity. McClintock Fulkerson strives to honor the diversity of women while at the same time arguing that one must be able to say something meaningful about women as a whole.

In her analysis of the various methodologies used to examine women's experience in feminist, womanist, and *mujerista* theologies, Serene Jones comes to a similar conclusion.[39] Jones's essay maps the conception of woman in the work of various feminist theologians from different cultural and racial contexts in the United States. On one end of the spectrum are those feminist theologians who continue to employ universalizing and/or ahistorical frames of reference to structure their accounts of human experience. On the other end one finds "the work of those theologians who self-consciously avoid universalizing gestures and opt instead for descriptions of experience which are historically localized and historically specific."[40] Critiquing the essentializing of the term *experience* by some theologians versus the historicizing trend in others, Jones concludes that there is a need for a middle ground between these two, one that has yet to be articulated. The latter extreme suffers from an inability to claim any normativity, while the former suffers from abstract generalizations.

This section began by noting the use of women's experience as a tool of feminist theology used to challenge the dominant male paradigm that claims objectivity. It appears that in the course of this struggle, feminist theology has fallen victim to a similar universalizing claim. Instead of critiquing the use of experience as a norm, this challenge solely addressed its male exclusivity. The underlying theory of experientially based authority was not sufficiently challenged. In a similar vein, the manner in which this challenge is to be posed has yet, in my eyes, to be thoroughly examined. Until women begin to realize that the "problem" of difference is actually the blessing of plurality, we will continue the vicious cycle of a discourse that favors hegemonic conformity over intercultural diversity.

Nonessential Woman

Having posed the problem of women's experience within feminist theology, we conclude with those scholars who are attempting to articulate a notion of woman's identity that is informed by the debates explored above. Underlying this debate is the question of gender essentialism versus constructivism. This is a lively issue in current feminist theology, especially as theologians increasingly turn to feminist theory as a resource for theological reflection.

Serene Jones has addressed this question. As she frames it: "This debate wrestles over the origin and character of our understanding of women's nature in particular and of human nature in general. . . . Put another way, does 'womanhood' express an inborn, natural, female disposition or follow from socially learned behaviors?"[41] Jones proceeds by designating two camps in this debate, essentialism and constructivism, concluding with a middle ground that she deems a viable alternative. She traces the roots of essentialism in Greek philosophy, where things were classified based on their unchanging essences: "In contrast to accidental properties that may vary over time, essential properties were thought immune to historical forces; they inhere in an object naturally and cannot be attributed to culture or convention. Essential properties are thus *universal* in that they must be present in all instances of the object."[42] Essentialists make claims surrounding women's nature that are based on the assumption that these properties are universal and inherent in women. Often, Jones notes, classic philosophical texts that articulate an essentialist understanding of woman do so in a disorganized and ungrounded manner. Women are not even mentioned by some authors, which leads one to assume that they are included under the broad heading of man/humanity, defined with no reference to women's experiences. Feminist critiques of essentialism focus on the naturalism and determinism of this position and the reduction of women's nature to a function of male identity. Another manifestation of essentialism is the "sex-gender scheme" that identifies women in terms of biology and sociology.[43] There are feminists, however, that embrace essentialism as a manner of celebrating female distinctiveness.

The other side of the debate surrounds the question of constructivism. Tracing this notion to Greek philosophy, Jones writes, "What these theorists share is a profound appreciation for the constitutive role of nurture or socialization in the construction of 'women.'"[44] Jones makes the further distinction between weak and strong constructivists. Weak constructivists argue for the significance of culture and socialization in identity formation, yet maintain a "bottom-line given" of biological sex. Strong constructivists hold that it is impossible to ascertain any such givens based on the profound stamp of one's social context. There is a fear in some feminist circles of constructivism in any form, for it could lead to cultural determinism and hamper the political organizing of women. A third alternative proposed by Jones is what she calls strategic essentialism: "The position goes by other names as well: normative constructivism, pragmatic utopianism, and pragmatic universalism. This in-between position applauds constructivist critiques of gender but feels nervous about giving up universals (or essences) altogether."[45] A strategic essentialist is a pragmatist with regard to the role of theory. While embracing the significant insights of constructivism, strategic essentialists hold that a normative understanding of human nature is necessary. They are bridge figures between constructivism and essentialism.

Following a similar vein as strategic essentialists, Linell Elizabeth Cady argues that there is a third way to approach women's identity within feminist theology. Feminist essentialism argues that women share a common identity and a common oppression. Postmodern feminism speaks of the fragmentation of the subject. As a third alternative, Cady proposes a historicist alternative, "distinguished, in my view, by a commitment to a historical perspective that seeks to situate the individual within a particular social and historical location. The specificity of discourses and practices is, in this approach, critical to an excavation of the subject which turns out to be multiple, though not necessarily fragmented."[46] This historicist construction of identity understands subjectivity as fluid and multiple; it is not limitless. Similarly, Latin American feminist theologian Ivone Gebara understands gender as both a biological reality and a social construct. Gebara does not ignore the function of difference in gender, yet she sees it as a viable social and political analytic category. Gender is the foundation of power relationships that ground social and religious orders that subordinate some at the expense of others. Gebara does not want to universalize gender as the only manner of encompassing the experiences of women, yet she wants to maintain gender as a hermeneutic tool.[47]

Sheila Greeve Davaney argues that feminist theology must have a more pragmatic historicist perspective when it comes to the question of theological norms. First, the category of women's experience must be reconceptualized in historicist terms. Second, the plurality and complexity of historical location must be asserted. Not only must diversity within traditions be asserted but also the multiplicity of traditions. Third, female agency must not be removed from constructions of women's subjectivity. Feminists must remain aware of the historical character of their work and recognize that diverse feminist norms exist. Multiplicity becomes an expression of the historicity of theological discourse. In terms of assessing the adequacy of theological claims, Greeve Davaney argues that feminists must "assess the adequacy of our constructive proposals in terms of the pragmatic repercussions that we anticipate might result from adopting one set of values and visions rather than another."[48] This dialogical model highlights the ambiguity of human life, in which there are no clear dualisms and in which one must adopt an acritical stance.

In the feminist classic *Inessential Woman* Elizabeth Spelman reminds us of the ambiguous role of the category of woman within feminist theory; that is, it can be used to dominate and marginalize as well as negate differences among those it seeks to name. She writes: "Thus the phrase 'as a woman' is the Trojan horse of feminist ethnocentrism. Whatever else one does, or tries to do, when one is thinking of a woman 'as a woman,' one is performing a feat of abstraction as sophisticated as the one Plato asks us to perform in thinking of a person not as her body but as her soul. What is it to think of a woman 'as a woman'?"[49] In short, an essentialized understanding of women's nature and writings is reflected in the tendency to segregate women's contributions. In emphasizing women's experience as a source for feminist theology, feminists may inadvertently marginalize their own work, for their scholarship can be deemed a side project with little relevance to theology as whole.

Rebecca Chopp reminds us that while we must always exercise caution when speaking of women as a whole, feminist theologians must not abandon the category of women:

> The rich diversity of voices forces the recognition there is no "woman's" experience. The notion that all women share [in] some essence called "woman" is limiting, narrow, and even dangerous to the health of all! Yet the terms "woman" and "women" are heuristically helpful, as they remind us that women must speak and be heard, and that gender continues to influence not only our personal lives but how culture, knowledge, and politics are organized.[50]

As Chopp points out, gender continues and will continue to shape men's and women's lives. While we must be wary of essentialist claims surrounding women's identity, as a political and social category women remain a vital voice within theology and society at large. For feminist theologians, however, the discussion does not end here. Christian feminist theologians inadvertently accept an essentialist claim about humanity as created in the image of God. No theory can undermine this Christian belief. In the following chapter we explore feminist theological anthropologies informed by the issues raised by the question of gender essentialism and whether one can say something meaningful about women, and consequently humanity, as a whole.

Chapter 5

Feminist Theological Anthropology

Using their critical methodologies feminist theologians address the major themes in theology and tradition, unpacking the patriarchal impulses that have shaped Christianity and offering an alternative vision grounded in feminist hermeneutics. Their understanding of Christianity, they argue, is more authentic, for it embraces an egalitarian vision of humanity as created in the image of God. In order to overcome the marginalization of women throughout Christian history, however, feminist theologians privilege women's experiences. For many feminist theologians, women's struggle for full humanity is the normative principle, used as a corrective to overcome centuries of privileging men and naming men's experiences as normative for all of humanity.

Feminist theologians argue that through their privileging of women's experience they are in no way placing women in an honored place within the construction of humanity. The centrality of women's lives and histories is not a way of replacing male normativity with female normativity. This methodological practice is instead a manner of "curing" the Christian tradition of its one-sided understanding of humanity and ultimately producing a more authentic, egalitarian, and Christian vision. Feminist theological anthropology, in its self-critical stance, does not seek to create a (falsely) universal depiction of humanity based exclusively on women's experiences. Also, feminist theologians attempt to address more than biological sex as the sole dimension that characterizes humanity. Feminist theologians struggle to recognize and maintain diversity while not falling into complete fragmentation and losing any sense of shared humanity.

This chapter explores central themes found in contemporary feminist anthropologies. The emphasis will be on constructive moments within these theologies, namely, step three in the threefold methodology outlined in Chapter 4. I begin with an overview of various typologies presented by feminist theologians in order to enter into the field of theological anthropology. This summary examines the development and variety of feminist approaches to theological anthropology. The remainder considers gender complementarity as the theological anthropology that an overwhelming number of feminists reject. A reaction to gender complementarity is the starting point of much feminist scholarship in this area. The second half of the chapter addresses four central themes within contemporary feminist theologies: egalitarianism, relationship and community, the body, and the *imago Dei*. Given its centrality within feminist theology, comments on the *imago Dei* are not limited to this last section, for it appears in relationship to the other three areas. Through their constructive work feminists present an authentic vision of the human, one in which both male and female reflect God's image in its fullness.

Setting the Stage

Various typologies outline the manners in which feminists approach theological anthropology. Mary Aquin O'Neill highlights three models of the human found in feminist thought: polarity (men and women are essentially different), androgyny (differences between men and women are merely social), and unisex (men and women are essentially the same).[1] The first perspective argues that while men and women share a common human nature, because of their distinctive biological sex they are essentially distinctive. The second perspective emphasizes the social construction of gender identity, reminiscent of the gender constructivism explored in the previous chapter. The third perspective downplays biological sex, instead strongly emphasizing the shared human nature. Drawing from the work of Ann O'Hara Graff and Mary Ann Hinsdale, Donna Teevan offers a slightly different typology, outlining four models of theological anthropology that are predominant in feminist theology: the dual-nature, complementary model; the single-nature model; the person-centered justice-infused model of Mary Buckley; and Elizabeth Johnson's "multi-polar" model.[2] The dual-nature model presents men and women as different but complementary. The single-nature model corresponds with the unisex model above. The justice model proposes a more sociopolitical construction of the human, emphasizing the role of social structures and the need for their transformation. Johnson's model argues that there are certain elements that constitute humanity, such as relationality, embodiment, and social location. These four models, Teevan argues, share certain assumptions, for example, "that although we are to a great degree shaped by our social context, we remain relatively stable subjects. In other words, despite historical variables, subjectivity is characterized by relative coherence, unity, and stability."[3] These anthropological models attempt to address diversity at varying degrees while emphasizing a unified subject.

Mary Ann Hinsdale offers an excellent overview of the different significant impulses in Roman Catholic feminist theological anthropology in the past three decades. She cites a 1978 report by the Catholic Theological Society of America that outlines two essential models in theological anthropology:

> 1) *the dual-nature model* (a "different-but-equal" model that stressed the complementarity of the sexes, seeing sex-role duality as part of the created order, "the divine plan"; in short, a biological determinism) and 2) the androgynous

single-nature model (neither sex has any pre-ordained roles, biology is "accidental," important for reproduction but not constitutive of personhood). Henceforth these two models became the chief analytic tools used by theologians engaged in critical reflection on the underlying theological anthropology of church teaching and praxis.[4]

The dual-nature model, many feminists contend, falls into a hierarchical construction of gender complementarity where women are devalued. The single-nature model is also problematic, for it presents a narrow, assimilationist vision of the human that is constructed by those in power. In 1980 Anne Carr proposed an alternative, transformative model of theological anthropology based in the theology of Karl Rahner. Hinsdale comments: "Rahner, noted Carr, always repudiated any idea of 'nature' as static essence. She found his emphasis on freedom and decision making quite appropriate to . . . the possibility of fashioning a 'third' model that would be *critical* of the hidden social bias present in any model of being human while insisting at the same time on social *transformation*."[5] This model became in vogue among feminists in the 1980s. Elizabeth Johnson's "multi-polar" anthropology emphasizes six elements that are intrinsic to human identity: embodiment, personal relationships, structural relationships, time and spatial context, culture, and orientation toward the future. Her intention is not to limit humanity to sexuality and to view human diversity as normative. She writes: "The goal is to reorder the two-term and one-term systems into a multiple term schema, one which allows connection in difference rather than constantly guaranteeing identity through opposition or uniformity."[6] Within Hinsdale's overview one finds a shift from a static understanding of the human to a more dynamic and multifaceted depiction of humanity. This parallels the evolution of feminist theology's understanding of women's experience outlined in the previous chapter. No matter which typology one embraces, for ultimately they are all heuristic, what is clear is that there are distinctive voices within feminist theology that offer a variety of views on human nature. It is due to this diversity in the field that I have chosen a more thematic approach for the second part of this chapter.

Gender Complementarity

Perhaps no other anthropological construction of humanity is vilified more by feminists than the gender-complementarity model. This view of humanity, feminists argue, while pretending to offer an egalitarian, "distinct but equal" vision of the human is instead a patriarchal construction that devalues women. As noted by Daphne Hampson, "Feminist women are adamant in rejecting the concept of a 'complementarity' between the male and the female. . . . A good way then of marking the male concept of 'complementarity' is to note that the female is always to 'complement' the male and never *vice versa*. That is to say, he is subject, while she is 'the other.'"[7] Women are defined as complementing men, and those attributes associated with men are of central value, leaving women in the margins. Too often this model, feminists argue, reduces women's identity to motherhood. This leads to a reduction of theological anthropology to biology. Mary Catherine Hilkert argues: "While women's bodily experience and female sexuality provide appropriate images and metaphors for the divine, the way that women image God or the destiny and vocation of women cannot be extrapolated solely from biology. One can recognize and celebrate the sacredness of women's bodies without falling into the error of 'anatomy is destiny.'"[8] Women cannot be reduced to their biological roles as mothers. Just because some women can have babies does not mean that their entire identity must be reduced to that possibility. This is not an affront to motherhood, yet it is a plea not to reduce women to that one dimension of some women's identity. Men, feminists argue, are rarely reduced to their role as fathers.

Mary Aquin O'Neill provides a succinct definition of the gender complementarity that feminists contest:

This anthropology of complementarity, as it came to be known, posits a theology in which the sexes complete one another, not only on the level of reproduction, but in the full range of human existence: social, intellectual, psychological, spiritual. There is a male way of being and a female way, and these can be known from an examination of the bodies of the two and given a fair degree of specificity. Thus men are supposed to be, by nature, active, rational, willful, autonomous beings whose direction goes outward into the world; women are to be passive, intuitive, emotional, connected beings whose natural inclination is inward. This bipolar vision of the sexes leads to an equally bipolar understanding of their respective places, namely, the world and the home.[9]

As O'Neill emphasizes, this bipolar anthropology essentializes sexual identity and social roles. What is deemed feminine is the male projection of attributes that are excluded from the construction of masculine identity. Taking a slightly different path, Carr, commenting on the work of O'Neill, argues that gender complementarity is "fraught with problems, the chief of which is that defining male and female polarities (activity/passivity, reason/intuition, emotion/will, etc.), denies the wholeness of human experience and the hopes of women themselves. In this vision of humanity, the activities of each sex are rigidly limited, as is the scope of human freedom, judgment, and responsibility over nature."[10] Gender complementarity denies the fullness of the individual human and his or her nature by characterizing certain attributes based on biological sex. Too often the dualisms found within the complementarity model are grounded in an outdated, essentialist biology. This is seen, for example, in the labeling of women as passive and men as active. This incorrect

Aristotelian biology, canonized in Aquinas's theology, remains the norm of Roman Catholic anthropologies even today.

Rosemary Radford Ruether, in her now classic *Sexism and God-Talk,* outlines a feminist anthropology that undermines patriarchal understandings of humanity.[11] Ruether begins by presenting the dual structure of Christian theological anthropology, essence and existence, which represent human authentic potential and historical humanity. This framework echoes Tillich's anthropology. Central to Ruether's anthropology is the notion of humanity created in the image of God. There is tension, however, between the notions of male and female created in the image of God and the tradition that correlates female with lower human nature: "Males, as the monopolizers of theological self-definition, project onto women their own rejection of their 'lower selves.' Women, although equivalent in the image of God, nevertheless symbolize the lower self, representing this in their physical, sexual nature."[12] Citing figures such as Augustine, Aquinas, Luther, and Barth, Ruether presents the classic patriarchal paradigms of women's humanity. In a similar vein Ruether argues that romantic and liberal feminist anthropologies are unsatisfactory models of egalitarian anthropologies. In her analysis of romantic feminism Ruether emphasizes that gender complementarity is part of the feminist tradition. Romantic feminism describes male and female differences as complementary, with maleness associated with the spiritual and femaleness with the carnal. Critiquing gender complementarity Ruether argues that such models perpetuate gender stereotypes, undermining a notion of human personhood that embraces human nature as both male and female. Women, Ruether emphasizes, "need to appropriate and deepen the integration of the whole self—relational with rational modes of thought—that is already theirs."[13] Ruether concludes by offering a relational anthropology that emphasizes our interconnectedness with others.

In attempting to salvage gender complementarity, philosophical historian Prudence Allen offers her own reworking of complementarity as an anthropological category. In contrast to the "fractional sex complementarity" that dominates anthropologies, Allen proposes "integral sex complementarity" as a viable option for Christian anthropologies.[14] Fractional sex complementarity sees men as providing certain characteristics, women others; when combined they make an integrated whole. Instead, Allen offers her integral approach:

> If man and woman are considered whole already as self-defining individuals and self-giving persons, then they are more like integers than like fractions. Furthermore, the interaction of two whole beings leads to a more fertile result than simply one whole composed of two fractional beings. In fact, in integral sex complementarity, the bonding of two persons creates what can be called a *synergetic* effect, or one plus one adds up to more than two.[15]

Allen argues that men and women can have distinctive complementary roles while still reflecting humanity in its fullness. However, one sex expresses certain attributes more than the other. Therefore, when male and female come together, what they express is even greater than what they would reflect alone. While a step ahead of most complementarity anthropologies, feminists would still find issue with this model, which reduces men and women to distinctive social roles and attributes and in which men reflect certain attributes more than women and vice versa.

Lisa Sowle Cahill stands out as a feminist ethicist who embraces a positive interpretation of gender complementarity. For Cahill, the biological roles of the sexes within reproduction have implications for male and female social roles: "Sexual complementarity involves a partnership of life in the service of community—of the species and of the whole created order." Cahill does not, however, argue for gender essentialism outside of reproduction. She writes, "I do not believe it is now, or ever will be, possible for Christian ethics to enumerate fixed

normative lists of male and female characteristics and concomi-
tant social roles."[16] In other words, while Cahill maintains
gender complementarity within the realm of reproduction, this
does not translate into an essentialist list of attributes for men
and women.

Egalitarianism

The common ground for feminist theological anthropologies
is an egalitarian vision of men and women. Contained in the
work of every feminist theologian one finds a statement referring to the equality of men and women as a fundamental dimension of their corpus. This section examines this egalitarian
vision through the work of Latin American feminist theologians, bringing their particular voice to the conversation. Both
Latin American feminist movements and Latin American liberation theology inform Latin American feminist theology.
With the overwhelming poverty of Latin American peoples,
especially women, and the preferential option for the poor
embraced by Latin American liberation theologians, one finds
a heavy analysis of sexism and classism within the work of
Latin American feminist theologians. Elsa Tamez highlights
concrete daily experience as a starting point for Latin American feminist theology: "Theology is transformed by the incorporation of women's life experience, especially that of poor
women."[17]

María Pilar Aquino's ground-breaking *Our Cry for Life* is
an exploration of the historical marginalization of Latin American women from both systematic theology and the church.[18]
Building on the work of Latin American theologians, Aquino
examines the features of theology done by women in Latin
America, with special emphasis on women's experiences of
oppression and liberation. A theology emerging from such a
context, Aquino emphasizes, cannot be removed from the concrete reality of suffering, struggle, and liberation. Aquino sees
her work as "an attempt to grasp the re-creating work of the

Spirit that activates the strength, word, memory, and liberating struggles of women."[19] While building on the work of liberation theologians, Aquino is critical of the exclusion of the historical and spiritual struggles of women within that discourse. The inclusion of women's voices will reveal the androcentrism of liberation theology and involve women in the production of knowledge, calling liberation theology to expand its hermeneutics, epistemology, and social analysis.[20]

I briefly highlight here three areas in Aquino's book, for they offer significant contributions to theological anthropology. The first is her use of *lo cotidiano* (daily life). The inclusion of daily life as crucial to theology contests a dichotomous understanding of the public and private that seeks to segregate *lo cotidiano* into the irrelevant sphere of private life. "Although it is often regarded as autonomous, daily life is in fact at the center of history, invading all aspects of life."[21] Daily life is seen both as an analytic category and a point of departure for Aquino's work. A second feature is the *primacy of desire* in Aquino's work. Citing the work of María Clara Bingemer, Aquino emphasizes that the primacy of desire must be incorporated into theology, for purely rational concepts are insufficient in accounting for experience. This affects both the method and form of theology. She writes, "The language of poetry, play, and symbol becomes an appropriate way of expressing the understanding and wisdom of the faith, because it is the means of expressing the human person's deepest and most genuine aspirations and desires."[22] The primacy of desire refutes what Aquino and Bingemer name as the reductionistic primacy of rationality in systematic theology. A primacy of desire seeks to uncover the spirituality of oppressed peoples while also expanding the sources and language of theology.

The third area is the locus of theological anthropology. A foundational tenet in Aquino's work is the indebtedness of theology to anthropology. Using a feminist hermeneutic, Aquino strives to overcome the dualistic and androcentric anthropologies of Augustine and Aquinas, seeking an anthropology that does not deny the full humanity of women. Building on the work of Ivone Gebara and María Clara Bingemer, she instead offers an egalitarian anthropology that rejects a paradigm of domination and subordination. As Gebara and Bingemer state: "We believe that the human-centered perspective is actually revelatory of divine and human transcendence because it does not diminish the human by dividing it into higher and lower beings."[23] This is a human-centered and unitarian anthropology, situating both men and women at the center of history, overcoming a gendered dualistic framework. Challenging an idealist anthropology, Aquino outlines a realist position that takes history and concrete struggles seriously. This is multidimensional anthropology that accounts for the diversity of humanity.

Relationship and Community

In addition to an egalitarian vision of humanity, an emphasis on the centrality of relationships is fundamental for understanding of feminist theological anthropologies. The relational nature of humanity is grounded in God's trinitarian nature as relational and our reflection of this nature through the *imago Dei*. Catherine Mowry LaCugna grounds her theological anthropology in her trinitarian theology, emphasizing a relational God in communion with humanity. LaCugna's relational ontology "understands being as being-in-relation, not being-in-itself." "Relationship, personhood, and communion" become the heart of *theologia* and *oikonomia*. "The mysteries of human personhood and communion have their origin and destiny in God's personal existence."[24] This relational ontology understands God's nature as in relationship, and God's relationship with us reveals God's nature. LaCugna defines personhood as interpersonal, intersubjective, and unique. Personhood must balance autonomy and heteronomy, individuality and relationality. Right relationship in communion becomes LaCugna's foundation for Christian faith.[25]

Elizabeth Johnson's theological anthropology starts with the relationship between men and women, not merely their creation as male and female. Nancy Dallavalle observes, "For Johnson, patriarchy obscures the *imago Dei* because its system of dominance and subordination is an ungodly social order, not because it obscures the image of God revealed in the creation of humanity as male and female."[26] Understanding the *imago Dei* as relational, Johnson adds interpersonal relationships as a vital dimension of our humanity. Drawing from the Genesis accounts, Johnson emphasizes that humanity was not just created as individual male and female, but as male and female in relationship. We are not intended to exist in isolation but in relationship.

Basing her work on recent developments in feminist psychology, Ann O'Hara Graff offers a relational anthropology that understands humans as selves-in-relation: "The use of the term *self-in-relation* is an attempt to name identity in the fluid context of ongoing growth in and through relational development."[27] This model of the human emphasizes mutuality and empathy and strives to honor the diversity and function of power within social relationships. For Graff, this adds a dynamic dimension to creation in the image of God. Like LaCugna, she turns to the Trinity as the foundation of a relational construction of human nature: "As the Trinity is the event of the distinct persons who are God in full, continuous relation with one another—God as selves-in-relation—so we human beings are creating ourselves continually out of our ongoing relations, each of us structuring those relations uniquely to be our own dynamic self."[28] Through our relationships with others we are in a dynamic process of constant creation. This process mirrors the relational nature of God as Trinity and invites us into the *imago Dei*.

The trinitarian nature of God fuels an anthropology that envisions the human as social. These relationships must be characterized by mutuality and equality. As Mary Catherine Hilkert indicates, "If the Trinitarian model offers the ideal paradigm for social and political relations, then unity-in-diversity and radical equality become ethical and political mandates."[29] The nature of humanity is relational. The mystery of what it means to be human is grounded in the relational Mystery that is the triune God. Human beings do not image God as individuals but in their right relations. Hilkert adds the dimension of justice to her relational vision of the human: "The image of God is reflected most clearly in communities characterized by equality, respect for difference and uniqueness, and mutual love."[30] Jesus' life, ministry, and death reveal the true nature of the Trinity. This image of Christ is grounded in Jesus' teachings, where the last are first. Through baptism and embracing a Christian life we image Christ. The image of Christ reveals the image of the Trinity, which is reflected in our practical actions. In a world marked by the systematic degradation of other human beings, the image of God is found in the crucified people who image the crucified Christ. Only through our protest and action against that which violates the image of God in all of humanity is the image as "compassionate love in solidarity" revealed. The image of Christ is a vocation we are called to fulfill. Hilkert's dynamic notion of the *imago Dei* presents the image as something we embody through our ethical actions, a challenge we must meet in order to reflect our intended nature. We are called to image God through our actions and relationships with one another.

Linked to feminist theological work on relationships is the importance of community. In Ada María Isasi-Díaz's *mujerista* theology three phrases are critical to her anthropology: *la lucha* (the struggle), *permítame hablar* (allow me to speak), and *la comunidad/la familia* (the community/family).[31] These are not the only sources, nor are they necessarily exclusive to Latinas. However, "these phrases offer a valid starting point for an anthropological exploration of Latinas."[32] To speak of these three phrases is to offer an arena for Latinas' theological contributions: Latinas' daily lives *(lo cotidiano)*, their contributive voices, and their relational concept of selfhood. Family and community are fundamental dimensions of human nature. "*Familia/comunidad* for Latina/os does not subsume the person but rather emphasizes that the person is constituted by this entity and that the individual person and the community have a dialogic relationship through which the person reflects the *familia/comunidad.*"[33] In other words, the communities to which we belong, from the most personal to the broader, constitute humanity. In her emphasis on community Isasi-Díaz not only highlights the relational nature of humanity but also adds the dimension of humanity's established relationships.

Body

Through their retrieval of the body, feminist theologians transform a dimension of our humanity that was once the source of women's marginalization into a site of our *imago Dei*. In her overview of the feminist theoretical concerns that inform feminist theology, Mary Ann Zimmer notes that the body has always been a central concern for feminist theorists: "This is true partly because women have often been identified with the bodily aspects of being human while men have been assigned the project of transcending the body through culture and thought."[34] The body, feminists note, is always devalued, and reason comes to symbolize the essence of humanity. Because of women's historical and contemporary association with the body, this is of vital concern for feminist theologians. Questions that plague feminist writings on this topic are: What difference does it make that human persons are embodied? What difference does it make that bodies are gendered? Ultimately, as Lisa Cahill points out, "the issue for contemporary feminists is whether, in a nondualistic perspective, the differential embodiment of men and women must be assumed to make a difference in their way of being in the world, even if not a difference which implies hierarchy, or even very extensive or firmly demarcated role allocation."[35] Feminist theologians must wrestle with the theological value of the body and the role of distinctive embodiment as male or female within theological anthropology.

Womanist theologian Stephanie Mitchem understands the Christian theological emphasis on the separation and privileging of the soul/mind over the body as rooted in Greco-Roman philosophy. This world view, she argues, isolates the human and places one aspect of our humanity in contention with the other. "As a result of this perspective, all life can be viewed as disconnected fragments that can be hierarchically arranged, flowing from ideas of the body as 'bad' and the soul as 'good.'"[36] Such an understanding of the body fuels a devaluing of women and people of color, who are seen as more closely associated with the physical than with the spiritual or mental. This also fuels the lack of interest in and vilification of, for example, black women's religiosity, which is at best ignored and at worst disparaged and misrepresented. Womanist theology seeks to correct this absence and misrepresentation, drawing from a variety of disciplines. Black women's lives become the starting point of all womanist reflection.

African feminist theologian Mercy Amba Oduyoye sees feminist theology's appreciation of the body and its acceptance of human sexuality as a gift from God as one of its most significant contributions to contemporary theology. The body is the site through which we express our humanity. However, even with her emphasis on distinctive embodiment as male and female, Oduyoye does not present a theological anthropology of gender complementarity. "In consequence, women posit that the female and male bodies are not complementary, as each is capable of expressing the fullness of humanness."[37] Oduyoye wants to value distinctive embodiment as male and female while not conceding to a biological determinism that ultimately reduces male and female identity to their bodily functions. This is a fine line.

Ivone Gebara presents a theological anthropology whose starting point is the body. Her emphasis is moral theology. The body is the center of all human relationships, the primary reality that we know and live. To begin with the body is to acknowledge the goodness of all creation and to redeem all human bodies, male and female. Moral theology has often been used to destroy the body, marginalizing it as decadent and inventing a spiritual body in order to ignore the divine glory of material bodies. "To consider the body as the starting point of moral theology is to choose a unified anthropology that attempts to overcome dualisms and encompass the ambiguities that are inherent in human existence."[38] Gebara attempts to recover the body in order to give it value as a reflection of the image of God instead of viewing it as an impediment to authentic spirituality. Gebara argues that churches fear the body, especially women's bodies. They fear women's bodies because they demand a new organization and understanding of power and sacred space. Women's physical presence calls for a new vision of humanity and, consequently, of church.

Susan Ross argues that one can have neither an essentialist nor an engendered understanding of the body. Through their scholarship feminists challenge three interpretations of the body: the dualistic construction of the body and mind; the liberal emphasis on the universality of humanity and insignificance of the body for this position, which ignores concrete contexts and inadvertently normatizes male experience; and essentialist constructions of masculine and feminine nature. She explores the ambiguity surrounding the body within Christian theology:

> The understandings of the body that have emerged over two thousand years of Catholic tradition's history are complex. On the one hand, the Christian tradition has affirmed the goodness of creation and, in the doctrine of the incarnation, has declared that God's very being has become inevitably connected with embodiment. . . . The sacramentality of marriage and the belief in the resurrection of the body are examples of the Christian tradition's

affirmation that the body is good. But on the other hand, the tradition's ambivalence toward, and sometimes even hatred of, the body is as much a part of its history as is its reverence of it. While the Christian elevation of the celibate life over marriage has complex origins, there is no question that, far too often, bodily pleasures—usually food or sex—have been seen as evil, and that women's identification with the body has led elements in the tradition to see women as evil, or at least as potentially more evil than men.[39]

The body is both vilified and glorified within the Christian tradition. When it is vilified, however, it is most often linked to woman. The ambiguity surrounding the body mirrors, in many ways, the ambiguous views of woman throughout Christian theology, where she is both celebrated and disparaged.

Imago Dei

Creation in the image of God has been at the heart of this text. Throughout Christian history the belief that humanity reflects God in some manner has been a focal point of theological anthropology. The *imago Dei* is at the heart of Christian understandings of the human and it reveals something about humanity as created and about our Creator. As O'Neill puts it, "Implicit in this belief are the twin realities of being created and being creator. Between these poles hangs every human life, holding together on the one hand a desire for the infinite—for the totality—and on the other, the all-too-real limitations of bodily, historical, actualized human existence."[40] Humanity is limited by its created nature yet transcends its very nature through the *imago Dei*. For theologians such as Paul Tillich, this creates the existential crisis that characterizes the angst of the human condition. Karl Rahner interprets this as the infinite horizon to which we are open, creating the possibility for us to receive the gift of God's grace. Historically the image has been represented by human intellect and rationality. Early church fathers understood the image as something dynamic, something that increases as we grow closer to God. The image has been understood as the image of Christ and the image of the Trinity. Because humanity is responsible for sin and in need of redemption, Jesus Christ represents the image of redeemed humanity and consequently the *imago Dei*. Ultimately, however, our understandings and explanations of the *imago Dei* are limited by our very humanity. We will never fully understand or define it in its fullness.

Genesis 1 teaches us that humanity was not only created in the image of God but also created in that image as male and female. Throughout Christian tradition men have overwhelmingly been viewed as reflecting God's image while women have been judged to reflect the *imago Dei* deficiently. This theological anthropology views women's bodies as a particular obstacle, seeing their embodiment and women's consequent association with bodies in general as the source of their distance from the divine. This is rooted, in part, in a theological anthropology that combines the two Genesis accounts, using a misinterpretation of Genesis 2—3 to blame woman for the Fall and the corruption of the *imago Dei*. Elisabeth Gössmann accuses the Christian tradition of neglecting Genesis 1 and instead focusing on Genesis 2—3 to ground views of male and female within theological anthropology.[41] For feminist theologians, creation in the image of God is reclaimed and transformed into a rallying call for women's equality. Feminist theologians interpret Genesis 1:27 as expressing that male and female are created in the image of God equally. Feminist theologians use the *imago Dei* to reclaim the full humanity of women. Their writings also offer their own theological interpretation of the image of God, one informed by their feminist theological commitments.

Womanist theologian Delores S. Williams understands creation in the image of God as a manner of denouncing sin against the body, in particular, black women's bodies. For Williams, since we are all created in the image of God, both body and soul, abuse of the body is sin. "Black womanhood and humanity are synonymous and in the image of God; Black women's sexual being is also in the image of God; therefore to devalue the womanhood and sexuality of Black women is sin."[42] Williams rejects the notion that the body is somehow dissociated from the divine image and is something that must be overcome in order to lead a spiritual life. Linked to her emphasis on embodiment is her celebration of sexuality as a reflection of the image of God. This claim is in direct contrast to centuries of sexuality being vilified as an impediment to relationship with the divine. When these claims are made in light of the historical oppression of black women, the doctrine of the *imago Dei* becomes a justice-infused denouncement of violence against black women. Womanist theologian Cheryl A. Kirk-Duggan takes this analysis in another direction, defining slave spirituals as a "language of power and survival that celebrates African Americans as *imago Dei*."[43] Kirk-Duggan draws from traditional African American religious expression to tap into awareness of the creation in the image of God in spite of brutal oppression within slave society. Spirituals become a source of empowerment, offering a vision of a community moving from struggle to liberation.

African theologian Mercy Amba Oduyoye also offers a justice-infused interpretation of the *imago Dei*. In defining her work Oduyoye is clear that she does not wish to speak for all African women, only those whose voices and contexts she cites. Storytelling plays a key role in African women's theology, giving it a narrative quality. While not naming their theology explicitly feminist, Oduyoye describes African women theologians as participants in feminist theology. The area of theological anthropology is fundamental in the effort to create a more egalitarian understanding of human relationships. A key resource in this anthropology is African myths, which undermine the unique authority of the Genesis account. The *imago Dei* in all of humanity is foundational in Oduyoye's theology. As defined by Oduyoye, "The emphasis on justice, caring, sharing and compassion, even in a hostile world, is the expression of the divine image all human beings are expected to reflect."[44] This dynamic understanding of the divine image is something we are challenged to express in spite of the world that surrounds us. Oduyoye emphasizes the patriarchal nature of Christian anthropologies, which deny the true claims of Genesis 1:26. Her anthropology rejects dualisms, especially the separation of the spiritual and the material. Oduyoye, like other feminists, argues that patriarchal anthropologies are grounded in a misreading of the Genesis text. In Oduyoye's work we find embodiment recovered as a central dimension of the image of God, which is interpreted through the lens of justice.

Rosemary Radford Ruether defines the *imago Dei* as the authentic human united with God. She highlights, however, that there is tension between the notion of male and female created in the image of God and the tradition that correlates female with lower human nature; this ambiguity is a "case of projection"—males project their rejected lower selves onto women.[45] Her analysis is linked to the critique of gender complementarity explored earlier in the chapter. For Ruether, and for many of her feminist colleagues, one cannot have it both ways. A Christian anthropology cannot claim that male and female are equal while simultaneously associating women with those attributes of humanity that are devalued by that tradition. Feminist theologians reject this hypocrisy. Not only do they embrace male and female as fully reflecting the divine image, but they also reclaim those attributes deemed lesser by tradition—for example the body—as central features and expressions of that image.

Feminist theologians are not acritical in their acceptance of the image, which has been used to justify human (historically male) authority in hierarchical and abusive manners. They are well aware that creation in the image of God has been interpreted as giving humans free reign over the earth. This has led to abuses of the environment. One must recognize that the very passage that states that male and female are created in the image of God (Gn 1:26–29) is the same one that has been used to warrant humanity's dominion over and submission of the earth. Instead of rejecting the *imago Dei*, however, feminist theologians offer a reinterpretation of humanity's relationship with the divine and the rest of creation. Anne Clifford's eco-feminist account of the *imago Dei* emphasizes humanity's relatedness with God and all of creation. This is a model grounded in solidarity, stressing the diverse yet interdependent nature of all of creation. Humans are no longer seen as the center and goal of creation. Clifford emphasizes mutuality based on the interconnectedness of all of creation, which reflects the glory of God in all its diversity.[46]

Mary Catherine Hilkert reminds us that despite the fact that the image of God has been interpreted historically to oppress women, it is also a symbol that is used to fuel justice, human rights, and social transformation. "Official statements of all Christian churches today unconditionally affirm that women and men are created equally in the image of God and are to be accorded equal human dignity with men. This is true even of those churches who deny ordination to women or argue that women are divinely intended to be subordinate to men."[47] In spite of cultural views and church practices to the contrary, we must use the official teaching of creation in the image of God as equally shared by all humanity to empower social justice movements. Hilkert embraces an eschatological approach to the image of God, seen not as a primordial state from which humanity has fallen but as a destiny we are called to fulfill. We grow in the image throughout our lives. Similarly, the image of Christ is a vocation to which we are called to convert constantly and deeply: "In a real sense, the full meaning of what it means to 'image God' or 'image Christ' remains in the future."[48] In her retrieval of the symbol of the image of God, Hilkert disputes the body-soul division that has plagued so much of historical Christian thought on this subject. She bases her vision on an incarnational, sacramental theology that emphasizes the embodied nature of humanity (including sexuality) and the Word.

Returning to the theme of relationality as fundamental for feminist anthropologies, Mary McClintock Fulkerson reminds us that creation in the image of God is the foundation for humanity's relationship with God: "The *imago Dei* indicates the attributes of the human being that make it capable of a relationship to God. More important, it conveys the theologically appropriate affirmation of the goodness of finitude—of creatures."[49] McClintock Fulkerson does not situate the image in rationality but instead in the ability to achieve communion with God and have the divine touch our lives. McClintock Fulkerson notes that while feminist theologians see the divine image as the foundation of a feminist anthropology, ultimately we are at a loss to define it: "As a naming of subjects of God's saving care, the *imago Dei* entails no essential definition of the subject, characterized only by finitude and God-dependence."[50] We know that we are created in the image of God, but we do not know with absolute certainty what that means. As an alternative to this perspective McClintock Fulkerson proposes a narrative understanding of the *imago Dei* based on stories. Her interpretation is a bit sharper than other feminist theologians, for McClintock Fulkerson contends that we cannot merely add women to the current understanding of the *imago Dei,* which is tainted by its patriarchal nature and must be transformed. Therefore, given the discursive construction of the *imago Dei* men must be excluded from its reenvisioning. McClintock Fulkerson is not claiming that only women are created in the image of God, but that her assertion "is to make a contextual, contiguity-based judgment about the effects of the reigning hegemonic (white male) identities that control the current accompanying contrast/exclusion. If this is not recognized, then the exclusions operative in any definition of *woman* and its supporting discursive setting will continue to go unrecognized."[51] Until women are allowed a privileged status in redefining creation in the image of God, McClintock Fulkerson argues, our interpretations of this doctrine will remain tarnished by patriarchal and hierarchical misinterpretations.

Asian feminist theologian Chung Hyun Kyung notes the centrality of Genesis 1:27 for Asian women and their theological anthropologies: "'In God's Image' is an important biblical phrase Asian women have adopted to define their perspectives on humanity."[52] The foundation of Asian women's theology is anthropology, not vice versa. In other words, Asian women's experience, not Christian doctrinal claims, is the starting point for Asian feminist theology. The centrality of the *imago Dei* emerges from its values for Asian women, therefore, and not from its value within Christian doctrine. Chung's *imago Dei* is based on a vision of God as both male and female, as community, as creator, as life-giving spirit, and as mother and woman. Her sources inform a theological anthropology that sees the human reflecting the *imago Dei* in an egalitarian relationship between the sexes; in community and relationship; in our role as co-creators; in the spirit within us; and in our ability as givers of life. Chung's theological anthropology emphasizes relationship and community while reclaiming women's images and sources as fundamental for understanding creation. Asian women's suffering is the epistemological starting point of their theological anthropology. To be human, says Chung, "is to suffer and resist."[53] Here again the theme of justice emerges as a dimension of the image of God.

Elizabeth Johnson argues that Christian anthropology exists in tension with the belief in women's full participation in the *imago Dei*. Johnson highlights that historically the Christian understanding of the image has shifted. In Genesis it is linked to stewardship over the earth. Patristic authors connect it to our relationship to the divine. Medieval authors associate the divine image with the soul and human rationality. The Reformers link it to our original connection with the divine. Women, Johnson argues, are *imago Dei* in the wholeness of who they are. "Women are *imago Dei* in the exercise of stewardship over the earth and the capacity to rule as representatives of God, with ecological care; in their kinship by nature with holy mystery; in their rationality and intelligence and in their freedom capable of union with God; in their creativity, their sociality, their community with each other and with men, children, and the whole earth; in their bodiliness, their destiny."[54] Johnson's theological anthropology is an eco-feminist analysis that reenvisions humanity's relationship with creation as one of care and not dominion. Contrary to historical interpretations, she embraces women's rationality as an expression of the image in its fullness. Like many of her colleagues, she sees embodiment as connected with the divine image. Johnson argues that sexual embodiment is not a hindrance: "The fundamental capacity to be bearers of the image of God and Christ is a gift not restricted by sex."[55] The image of Christ is found in one's participation in Jesus' liberating vision in the world, empowered by the Spirit. These moves in Johnson's theology are contrasted with her efforts to embrace her "multi-polar" anthropology, which looks at the diversity and differences among humans. Johnson grounds her vision of the image of God in a relational anthropology of the Spirit-Sophia, in which the human is viewed holistically, not divided by dualisms. Suffering women, created in the image of God, point to the compassionate God who accompanies humanity in its suffering. Johnson's theology culminates with a feminine symbol of God as "she who is," the creative ground of all being. She who is "discloses women's human nature as *imago Dei*, and reveals divine nature to be the relational mystery of life who desires the liberated human existence of all women made in her image."[56] Through her incorporation of female imagery within the divine, which Johnson argues is theologically grounded in the biblical tradition, she not only includes women within the image of God fully as created but also reclaims feminine imagery of the Creator.

I have concluded with Johnson's interpretation of the *imago Dei* because it artfully weaves the various themes that have been explored throughout this chapter. In her recovery of women as reflecting God's image equally Johnson reflects the egalitarian impulse underlying all feminist scholarship. Her symbol of God as "she who is" is a relational concept of God, one that posits the relational, triune nature of God as the essence of God's nature, and consequently is reflected in humanity as creatures of God. Johnson's positive retrieval of woman's body rejects the notion that embodiment is a hindrance to reflecting the divine image. Finally, Johnson's theological anthropology is grounded in the *imago Dei*, demonstrating its centrality within feminist thought. In addition to its implications for theological anthropology, Johnson's work also demonstrates the influence the *imago Dei* has on other areas of Christian theology, namely, Christology and the concept of God. As seen in Johnson's work, as well as in the work of the other theologians explored in this chapter, the image of Christ, and therefore Jesus Christ, is envisioned as a justice-filled call to practical commitment here on earth. This has immediate implications for how we understand Jesus' message and Christian discipleship. We are challenged to reflect the image of Christ through our sociopolitical commitments. In a similar vein, emphasizing women's equal reflection of the divine image opens the door for female images and symbols of the divine. Since we cannot reduce God's nature to male or female, both male and female symbols are appropriate for expressing our limited understanding of God. The *imago Dei* is not relevant exclusively in the area of theological anthropology; it is a starting point for conversations in other areas of Christian theology as well.

Chapter 6

Our Trinitarian *Imago Dei*

An egalitarian notion of the *imago Dei* is the foundation of feminist theological anthropologies. However, in order to achieve this vision of the human, the underlying patriarchal world view that has shaped the Christian tradition must be challenged and transformed. One cannot simply "add" women as equals and produce an egalitarian anthropology. This would merely insert women into a patriarchal structure while maintaining that structure. Ultimately, true equality will occur only with the radical reconstruction of Christian theology in light of critical insights. This project entails several lifetimes of collaborative work, not merely one text. The focus of this study has been theological anthropology in light of the *imago Dei* with special attention to male and female. This is but one contribution in light of a broader feminist theological project. In this chapter I offer my own constructive contribution to the conversations elaborated throughout the text. Drawing from contemporary feminist scholarship, my reflection on the *imago Dei* is situated within the feminist theological tradition that strives to offer a critical analysis of the Christian tradition while remaining in continuity with that tradition.

Intimately linked to the manner in which we express our creation in the divine image is our notion of the divine. In other words, *imago Dei* theological anthropology has strong implications for our concept of God, Jesus Christ, and the Trinity. The way we envision our God as Creator, Savior, and Trinity deeply affects how we understand ourselves as human beings. Consequently, the misinterpretation of the Christian tradition that has led to a patriarchal anthropology also has informed patriarchal understandings of the divine. The two feed off each other, especially in the context of the *imago Dei*. To redefine the divine image as a dimension of humanity that is shared by women and men equally, therefore, we must also reexamine how we understand the divine. In fact, this chapter argues, it is the Christian vision of God, especially as revealed in Jesus Christ through the saving work of the Trinity, that is the key to an egalitarian anthropology.

This chapter begins with a return to the question of women's experience and identity within feminist theology. Due to the importance of this methodological starting point, as well as its contested nature within feminist theology, the manner in which women's identity and experience function within theological anthropology must be reexamined. Here I do not contest that experience is the starting point of theology, for as Ann O'Hara Graff states: "We have only our own lives with our experiences. This is our medium and reality. This is where theological anthropology begins. We seek understanding of ourselves in the context of our inevitable and primal relationship to God."[1] This experience of the divine is always situated within our broader relationships with other human beings. What I do wish to revisit, however, is the methodological function of experience within feminist theology. Following this more theoretical section, the rest of the chapter addresses the theology of theological anthropology. I begin by returning to the theology of gender complementarity and its viability for feminist theology in light of embodiment. I continue by examining the implications of the *imago Dei* for Christian understandings of God. I then turn to Christology and trinitarian theology as the foundations for my feminist reconstruction of the image of God.

Rethinking Women's Experience

A central question in feminist theology is the role and nature of women's identity and experience. As we explored in Chapter 4, women's experience is a fundamental starting point for feminist theologians regardless of their race or ethnicity. Within early feminist theological texts written by white, European American women, for example, the category of women's experience functions as a blanket statement for all women. US minority and third-world feminist theologians challenged this claim, arguing that the general category of women's experience ultimately translates into white or first-world women's experiences and ignores the diversity among women. Women of color offer a more complex picture of women's experience, including race, ethnicity, culture, and class. Instead of women's experience in general, women of color speak of, for example, African American women's experiences or Latinas' experiences. One could argue, however, that such a rhetorical move is just as essentializing as the broader notion of women's experience. In other words, when Stephanie Mitchem states that "womanist theology is the systematic, faith-based exploration of the many facets of African American women's religiosity. Womanist theology is based on the complex realities of black women's lives," she is proposing a definition of womanist theology that claims to represent the lives and religiosity of all black women in the United States.[2] While focusing on the African American community narrows the category of women's experience, a broad essentialized category remains.

The category of women's experience has also been challenged by feminist theoretical insights that dispute the unified subject of traditional Western philosophy and theology and instead argue for a more fragmented understanding of identity. On one extreme of this debate one finds philosophers and theologians who maintain an essentialized understanding of gender identity, arguing that biological destiny determines the nature of sexual identity. Those at the other extreme argue that gender is constructed, noting how culture and society shape male and female identity. A middle ground is proposed by those feminists who maintain a normative definition of human identity while acknowledging that gender is simultaneously a socially constructed phenomenon. Whether labeled strategic essentialism or a pragmatic historicist perspective, these feminist theorists and theologians attempt to bridge and learn from the insights of the two extremes.

My work is situated in this middle ground. I acknowledge that there is a biological human nature that we share and that biology is a factor in shaping human identity. Biology, however, is not destiny, and our social location plays an equally important role in the formation of our identity. I am especially wary of essentialist anthropologies that reduce women to the role of mother. Motherhood is not the quintessential, all-encompassing marker of women's experiences. Similarly, while I wholeheartedly embrace the constructed nature of gender identity, biological sex cannot be reduced to social conditioning. My work is informed by the philosophies of María Lugones and Iris Marion Young. The starting point for my entry into the question of subjectivity is not an abstract theoretical debate informed by academics but the everyday struggles of people of color. Here I resonate with philosopher María Lugones, who writes: "I am giving up the claim that the subject is unified. Instead I am understanding each person as many. In giving up the unified self, I am guided by the experience of bicultural people who are also victims of ethnocentric racism in a society that has one of those cultures as subordinate and the other as dominant."[3] The starting point of Lugones's fragmented yet unified self is the experience of bicultural and biracial people. As a Cuban American, I resonate with a hybrid and complex reality where one exists within two communities/realities yet never fully belongs to either one. The concrete starting point of this notion of subjectivity, in my case, is the everyday lives of Latinos/as.

Lugones fleshes out her construction of the subject with her notion of world traveling. Worlds are the different realities/contexts in which we live and which shape our identity. One can be in more than one world at the same time, belong to different worlds, travel between worlds. World traveling is our movement among the various contexts that we enter into or have imposed upon our lives. For US minorities, this notion of world traveling rings true. We spend our lives living in the world of the dominant culture, while the insiders of the mainstream culture can avoid our worlds quite easily. "I am different persons in 'different' worlds and can remember myself in both as I am in the other. I am a plurality of selves."[4] The way in which we experience ourselves within a world depends on our position of value or power within that world. This notion of world, however, is not only descriptive. World traveling is Lugones's suggestion for a way of being in the world: "The reason I think that traveling to someone's 'world' is a way of identifying with them is because by traveling to their 'world' we can understand *what it is to be them and what it is to be ourselves in their eyes.* Only when we have traveled to each other's 'worlds' are we fully subjects to each other."[5] Lugones is suggesting a relational manner of existing in community. She is also presenting a relational subject who is constituted by his or her contexts and relationships with the "other." There remains a subject who is at the core of her proposal, yet this subject is not a neatly, unified self but is "messy," complicated by the different dimensions that inform identity (race, gender, class, ethnicity, sexual identity) and the different relationships that shape individuals.

Feminist political philosopher Iris Marion Young offers another critical voice through her contention that searching for common characteristics of women's identity in order to define women's nature will only lead to essentialist constructions of women.[6] However, Young insists, there are valid political motives for conceiving of women as a group. The flaw in most feminist thinking, Young holds, is the desire to construct a systematic theory within feminist discourse. As an alternative Young offers a pragmatic view of theory: "By being 'pragmatic' I mean categorizing, explaining, developing accounts and arguments that are tied to specific practical and political problems, where the purpose of this theoretical activity is clearly related to those problems. Pragmatic theorizing is . . . driven by some problem that has ultimate practical importance and is not concerned to give an account of a whole."[7] For Young, the current practical problem is the simultaneous acknowledgment of the dangerous implications of essentialist notions of womanhood in feminist discourse and the need for a political subject for feminism.

Young contends that a reconceptualization of social collectivity, through Sartre's notion of seriality as articulated in his *Critique of Dialectical Reason*, offers us a way to view women as a collective without attributing a common or essential identity shared by all women. Young defines a series as "a collective whose members are unified passively by the relation their actions have to material objects and practico-inert histories. . . . Their membership is defined not by something they are, but rather by the fact that in their diverse existences and actions they are oriented around the same objects or practico-inert structure."[8] Series differ from groups, which are "a collection of persons that recognize themselves and one another as in a unified relation with one another."[9] The series *women* is not based on attributes shared by all women. Instead, womanhood is situated in the social realities that are exterior to one's personal identity and that condition women's lives. In one's relationship to these social realities, gender is constructed. A key dimension in Young's understanding of identity is choice. One can decide which aspects of one's serial memberships are central to one's identity: "No individual woman's identity, then, will escape the markings of gender, but how gender marks her life is her own."[10] This statement removes the paradox of identity as choice and as imposed.

I would add to Lugones and Young's work the historical dimension of women's shared identity. Resonating with Sheila

Greeve Davaney and Linell Elizabeth Cady, a more historicist perspective must inform the category of women's experience. Within Christianity, women share a tradition of marginalization that constructs their identity in a limited and essentialist manner. They have this shared history of marginalization. However, one cannot essentialize women's responses to and experiences of this marginalization, for to do so would grossly limit and silence the diversity of women's experiences. I am wary of speaking, in a sociological manner, of a contemporary collective of women, whether it is women in general, Latinas, Asian American women, or others. Such categorizations must be clearly defined so that their scope does not claim to speak for all women who are placed under these labels. Young's contribution is helpful on this point, for it highlights the political function of the category of women. Nonetheless, while I agree with Young that often when feminists refer to women they are speaking of women as a political serial, as a theologian I cannot reduce women solely to a socially constructed collective. To use Young's language, I see women as a serial and as a group. To use more theological terminology, as created in the image of God as female, all women share a God-given nature. This nature, however, is always expressed through the particularities of their social location. Therefore, it is impossible to arrive at the core of women's identity stripped of its social location, for our relationships and contexts, as Lugones points out, constitute our identity. Within feminist theology the category of women functions on these two levels, as a serial and a group. Feminist theologians, however, must be clear when they are speaking of women as a socially constructed collective versus a group that shares an essential nature.

Linked to defining women's experiences is its function as a methodological starting point for feminist theology. I find an essentialized notion of women's experience, even when it is qualified by race or ethnicity, to be problematic. I am not contesting the need to be intentional in our critical inclusion of women's experiences both in historical and contemporary

Christian studies. I am flagging the manner in which we introduce women's lives and writings into the discourse of theology. Humanity's experience or response to the divine will always be the starting point of theology. I do not want to erase that which unites humanity as created in the image of God and the manner in which that shared creation marks our relationship with the divine. However, our expression of God's revelation is always shaped by our context and culture; human particularity will always color the experience of God's grace. Therefore, theology must walk a fine line between naming both the universality and the particularity of its subject matter. One method of approaching this is to enter into the particularity of a community in order to address these broader questions. This entails more critical studies that do not generalize women as a sociological whole but rather examine the distinctiveness of different communities and the function of gender within them.

The claim that human beings are created equally in the image of God as male and female is a theological statement. It must be examined as a theological claim and not merely analyzed on a political or social level. Therefore, while the philosophers explored above aid in my formulation of women's identity, ultimately I must turn to theology as the primary source for my theological anthropology. In other words, it is my contention that there is a difference between a sociological or political construction of gender identity and a theological one. The theological construction of gender acknowledges that men and women are created in the image of God, sharing a common humanity yet distinctive in their sexuality. This is of particular concern in light of feminist theology's value of embodiment. If we are going to take human embodiment seriously as a reflection of our *imago Dei*, and we are going to acknowledge that men and women are embodied in different and significant manners, then we must explore the theology of the body and the meaning of the embodied differences between the sexes. A theological understanding of gender acknowledges that biological sex cannot be reduced to social location; however, it recognizes that our creation as male and female is only expressed through the contextuality that marks our humanity.

Gender Complementarity and Embodiment

As explored in Chapter 5, a theological anthropology of gender complementarity is practically anathema among feminist theologians. Their reasons are varied. Rosemary Radford Ruether argues that gender complementarity "draws on sophiological and mariological traditions of the 'good feminine.' Women are called to exemplify this good femininity associated with altruistic love and service to 'others,' that is, men and children, in a way that re-enforces women's passive, auxiliary relation to male agency."[11] A complementary vision of the sexes, Ruether contends, is based on a limited, idealized, patriarchal notion of women's identity, one that serves only men. Susan Ross dismisses gender complementarity for its "highly questionable understandings of human biology and sociology; they also perpetuate a psychology of women as 'receptive' and men as 'active' that has tremendously destructive consequences for relationships between the sexes."[12] The foundation of gender complementarity is an outdated and false biology that labels women as essentially receptive. Margaret Farley points out that the vision of mutual love within gender complementarity is not one of full complementarity and equality. Instead, it is constructed based on hierarchical relationships such as parent and child, ruler and servant. Farley is not arguing that differences between men and women do not exist: "The question, of course, for a right love of women as human persons is, whether or not the differences between men and women are relevant in a way that justifies differentiating gender roles and consequent inequality of opportunity for women to participate in the public sphere or to determine the mode of their participation in the private sphere."[13] Acknowledging that men and women are different, Farley contends, does not ultimately lead to such drastic differentiation between men's and women's social roles.

Perhaps one of the most classic contemporary examples of a theology of gender complementarity is the position of the Vatican, outlined in John Paul II's 1988 apostolic letter *Mulieris Dignitatem (On the Dignity and Vocation of Women)*. The document argues that *"both man and woman are human beings to an equal degree*, both are created *in God's image"* (no. 6). This egalitarian anthropology is quickly amended with a gender complementarity that defines the ethical vocation of women as one in which she *"can only find herself by giving love to others"* (no. 30). Woman is characterized as giving by her nature, almost to the point that she appears naturally self-effacing. Women have a special capacity to care and love based on a Marian anthropology of motherhood. John Paul II grounds his anthropology in the inner-trinitarian life. The male God reveals God's love for humanity through Jesus Christ, and humanity is receptive of this love as female. The foundation of this anthropology is, of course, Aristotelian biology. Within this model Jesus' embodiment as a male confirms the Vatican's association of masculinity with divinity, while femininity is associated with humanity. This position echoes that of Hans Urs von Balthasar explored in Chapter 3.

Mirroring my position on the essentialist-constructivist debate regarding women's identity, my work is informed by the insights of advocates of gender complementarity and its critics. Two feminist theologians help shape my views: Nancy Dallavalle and Lisa Cahill. In an attempt to bridge the insights of essentialist understandings of the human and what she labels agnostic, constructivist notions of selfhood, Dallavalle argues for critical essentialism as a response to the either/or paradigms of current discussions between feminist theory and theology.[14] Rejecting essentialist claims surrounding human relationships, Dallavalle notes, "Male and female are to be understood as essential differences, but this difference need not imply an anthropology of complementarity in which male and female only find their meaning in the other."[15] Dallavalle acknowledges that gender dualisms saturate theological anthropologies, especially models where women are deemed subordinate to men. Dalla-valle critiques feminist theology's "agnostic" position on bio-logical sexuality. "Since biological sexuality is never available to human knowing without the cultural construction of gender, no claims at all shall be made about 'maleness' and female-ness.'"[16] Dallavalle begins a critical conversation between gen-der theory and the understanding of biological sexuality in the Catholic theological tradition. Her critical essentialism at-tempts to create a theological understanding of biological sexu-ality. Dallavalle writes:

> By the word "essentialism" I mean to indicate that the creation of humanity as "male" and "female" should continue to stand as a fixed point of reference for theo-logical reflection. By the word "critical" I mean to indi-cate that we have no unconstructed access to this fixed point, and that therefore all theological interpretation of humanity as "male" and "female" is provisional—no fi-nal, positive theological interpretation of biological sexu-ality can be asserted.[17]

In other words, to assert that distinctive biological sexuality is a given is not to impose any meaning on that given.

Dallavalle does not want to separate the insight that we are created as male and female from its reception in the life of the church. She also holds that this biological distinction need not lead to a theology of gender complementarity. Dallavalle argues that while humanity as male and female is revelatory, male and female together are not somehow more revelatory. In a similar vein, relationality does not automatically lead to complemen-tarity: "the (never accessed) starting points for theological re-flection are males and females—both are made in the image of God, each bears whatever fullness of that image is given to any concrete particular, and each bears whatever limitation being male or female might necessarily entail."[18] Dallavalle contends that while an emphasis on embodiment in all its dimensions is important, embodiment as male or female is the sole site for profound theological reflection.

Cahill attempts to balance an awareness of the socially constructed nature of gender roles while not erasing what makes the sexes distinctive: "This does not necessarily mean that the sexes have no innate differences; it does mean such differences—whatever they may be—will not be accepted as warrants for social systems which grant men in general authority and power over women in general."[19] To embrace the distinctiveness and importance of motherhood, for example, is not to reduce women to mothers. Cahill notes that the recent interest in the body found in philosophical and theological writings follows two directions: "affirmation of the body as constitutive of personhood or deconstruction of the body as produced by social discourse."[20] Cahill assumes the distinction between bodies as male and female sexes. "[But] what must be taken for granted at the same time is that sexual dimorphism need not provide the basic category for organizing human persons into social relations, and especially not for establishing social hierarchies."[21] The differences between males and females does not have to lead to a hierarchy. While one cannot reduce women to their sexual and reproductive experiences, one also cannot deny that these experiences are a significant aspect of women's sense of self: "Women's sexual and, more so, reproductive experiences have not only set them apart from men, but have bound women together historically. Why are we so willing to deconstruct them now?"[22] Cahill highlights that more is at stake here than merely a patriarchal, essentialist construction of women. If one strips women of all shared sense of self, one removes a very significant tie that has linked women throughout history.

Building on Farley's, Dallavalle's, and Cahill's contributions, a theological understanding of gender, informed by biological sex, views humanity as created equally yet distinctively male and female in the image of God. Male and female are different, yet these embodied differences do not lead to a limitation of either men or women in their reflection of the divine or in their concrete everyday lives. Women and men share the image of God equally and fully. One sex does not have a monopoly on certain attributes. While women's sexual and reproductive roles play a central part in women's lives and shared experiences, women cannot be reduced to reproduction. In addition, the relationship between women and men and how this relationship expresses the divine image cannot be reduced to the sexual act. Echoing Dallavalle's critical essentialism, while creation as male and female is a theological certainty, the possibility of arriving at that created nature despite one's social location is impossible. Therefore, we can only offer provisional statements about male and female created in the image of God. My contribution to *imago Dei* anthropology is grounded in feminist theological reflection regarding the nature of God and how this informs our understanding of the human. I do not specifically address how male or female reflects that image in his or her particularity, but instead focus on the relational nature of God, whose image all humanity reflects.

Image of God

Any study that addresses the *imago Dei* within feminist theology would be remiss if it did not critically engage the God that is behind this image. There is a clear relationship between Christian understandings of the divine and the degree to which men and women reflect God. A patriarchal concept of God clearly informs a patriarchal anthropology. As Eleazar S. Fernandez points out:

> The notion of the image of God is still considered by feminist theologians as very important to the anthropological reconstruction of the devalued and denigrated woman's image. But this is not and cannot be a simple "me too" theological claim, for the notion of the image of God in a patriarchal and sexist society is itself problematic. Yes,

women must reclaim their being created in the image of God, but there are questions that cannot be bypassed: What images of God do we embrace in the context of a patriarchal and sexist society? Whose image is God's image in a patriarchal society? These questions must be asked first, if women are not to be continually colonized by male images of God.[23]

In order for women to claim God's image fully, they must undermine the male as paradigmatic of the *imago Dei*. Patriarchal constructions of the image of God are based on a hierarchy that values men at the expense of women. The value system underlying this theological notion must be completely deconstructed and reconstructed using a critical feminist hermeneutic. Margaret Farley highlights this deeper concern when she writes, "If we are to pursue the question of whether women as women can be understood to be in the image of God, we must ask whether God can be imaged in feminine as well as masculine terms."[24] To embrace men and women fully as equal bearers of the image of God, Christians must become comfortable with male and female symbols and language about God sharing equal value. This is an extremely difficult task for Christians, for male images of God are overwhelmingly the norm. To understand the Christian God as "she" is a radical notion for the majority of Christians. For Catholics, this is compounded by the exclusive ordination of men, which reinforces male similarity to the divine. The expansion of our images of the divine is a pressing concern, however, for "to take one image drawn from one gender and in one sociological context as normative for God," Rosemary Radford Ruether argues, "is to legitimate this gender and social group as the normative possessors of the image of God and representatives of God on earth. This is idolatry."[25] In addition, to draw exclusively from male imagery, feminists contend, limits the very nature of God. While none of our language, symbols, and names for God can be taken literally, exclusively imaging God as male leads to the conclusion that God is literally a man.

In addition to idolizing the male, exclusive male God language contributes to women's own alienation from the sacred. It is more difficult to see oneself as created in God's image if that God is limited to men. "When women imagine God to be a male deity, they tend to relate to God as 'the other' but 'not like me.'"[26] One could also add to this analysis that if God is imaged exclusively representing one racial or ethnic group, this is also idolatry. Black theologians in the United States created a wave of confusion and outrage when they claimed that both God and Jesus were black. James H. Cone, for example, offers a trinitarian image of God as black in solidarity with marginalized peoples. To know God is to be in solidarity with the oppressed in their struggles for liberation. One must become black like God and participate in liberation struggles.[27] In my eyes, the most revolutionary implication of these claims is not that the divine is somehow racially black, but instead that, in the minds of many, God and Jesus are white. Many who retorted that God has no race were quite comfortable with the blond, blue-eyed Jesus and the white, male images of God on their church walls. Imaging the divine as one social group or gender distances those outside those groups from their creation in the *imago Dei*. It is a lot easier to say and believe that women do not share the divine image equally when only male images of the divine are normative. Incorporation of female images, however, should not be construed as an essentialized feminine that complements the already established masculine. Instead, both male and female images of God, with all the limitations they contain based on their human origin, must equally express the fullness of God's nature.

Patriarchal images of God have implications for how we understand not only humanity but also the rest of creation. Eco-feminist theologians link the exploitation of women to the exploitation of the rest of creation. Since women have been symbolically linked with the body and materiality, the same world views that degrade women fuel the disregard and abuse of the environment. "Ecofeminism by definition refers to a connection between patriarchy's domination of women and of nonhuman nature. Ecofeminists argue that in the drive to dominate, patriarchy forgets that humans, including those in power positions, have a natural biological connectedness with all of Earth's life forms."[28] Within eco-feminist theology the *imago Dei* is critiqued as a doctrine that has misinterpreted humanity's relationship with the rest of creation and fueled the abuse of nonhuman creation. Eco-feminist theologian Sallie McFague critiques traditional theological anthropologies for divorcing the human from the cosmos in its focus on our divine image. Today, humanity must resituate itself and accept its appropriate role in creation: "This proper place has decentered and recentered us: we are no longer the point of the whole show, as Kant and the Christian tradition both thought, but have emerged as bearing heavy responsibilities for the well-being of the whole, responsibilities that will be difficult and painful to carry out, such as limiting both our population and its insatiable appetite for material goods."[29] McFague criticizes feminist and liberation theologies for being anthropocentric. Her evolutionary, ecological perspective highlights our interrelationship with the cosmos as a prerequisite for theology. Humanity, McFague argues, must come to terms with its interrelationship with and dependency on the rest of creation:

> What is significant, however, for a theological anthropology is not only a continuity from the simplest events in the universe to the most complex, but also their inverse dependency, which undercuts any sense of absolute superiority. That is, the so-called higher levels depend on the lower ones rather than vice-versa. . . . *The higher and more complex the level, the more vulnerable it is and dependent on the levels that support it.*[30]

Humans are not autonomous rulers of creation. On the contrary, they are heavily dependent on the created world.

Rosemary Radford Ruether argues that while traditional interpretations of the divine image have fueled abuse of the rest of the creation, this is a misreading of the original intent of the Genesis account.[31] Human beings, created in the image of God, are representatives of God on earth. We are stewards of the earth. As Anne Clifford points out, while the word *steward* appears nowhere in the Genesis passage, many biblical scholars link the *imago Dei* with royalty practices: "These scholars believe that the words 'image' and 'likeness' echo language used of ancient Middle Eastern kings, the sovereigns who represented their gods as rulers in theocratic societies. The representatives of rulers were known as 'stewards.' The king represented God as God's steward."[32] An interpretation of the divine image within this stewardship models implies that both male and female, as created in the image of God, are God's representatives here on earth.

As women reclaim the divine image they share equally with men, the very nature of our symbols and language of the divine is transformed. Elizabeth Johnson writes, "Simultaneously, it becomes obvious that the *imago* is flexible and returns to its giver, so that women who are genuinely in God's image in turn become suitable metaphors for the divine."[33] There is a mutual transformation of the manner in which human beings understand themselves and how we name and describe the God who is our Creator. As eco-feminists teach us, this also has deep implications for our relationship with the rest of creation. It is clear that to transform the *imago Dei* into an egalitarian vision for all humans, we must do away with patriarchal constructions of God. The image of God must be grounded in our understanding of God as God has been revealed to us within human history. Therefore, Christology is central to the *imago Dei*. Jesus Christ's ministry and message become the basis of our reworking of theological anthropology in order to offer an inclusive, egalitarian vision.

Image of Christ

Christian understandings of the image of God are intimately linked to Jesus Christ. As God's concrete revelation within human history, as the center of Christian belief, Jesus' ministry, suffering, death, and resurrection are normative for Christian theology. Too often, however, it is Jesus' maleness that becomes normative within patriarchal theological claims, limiting women's ability to reflect God and implying that men reflect God's image more appropriately. Feminists deny these claims, arguing that "the image of Christ does not lie in sexual similarity to the human man Jesus, but in coherence with the narrative shape of his compassionate, liberating life in the world, through the power of the Spirit."[34] Feminist theologians situate the *imago Christi* in Jesus' liberating message and in his concrete outreach to and inclusion of the marginalized. Grounded in this liberating Christology is an image of Christ that we are challenged to reflect in our spirituality and actions.

Christology is an ambiguous area for feminist theologians, given the adamant use of Jesus' masculinity as a weapon to oppress women. As Ruether asked in *Sexism and God-Talk*, "Can a male savior save women?"[35] Feminist theologians answer yes, arguing that Jesus' maleness is insignificant. As womanist theologian Jacquelyn Grant states: "If Jesus Christ were a Savior of men then it is true the maleness of Christ would be paramount. But if Christ is a Savior of all, then it is the humanity—the wholeness—of Christ which is significant."[36] For Roman Catholic feminists, Christology has been a particularly problematic area because it serves as a fundamental justification against the ordination of women. The exclusive presence of the twelve male apostles at the institutionalization of the Eucharist, in the Vatican's eyes, supports this claim. As *Mulieris Dignitatem* argues, "Since Christ, in instituting the Eucharist, linked it in such an explicit way to the priestly service of the Apostles, it is legitimate to conclude that he thereby wished to express the relationship between man and woman, between what is 'feminine' and what is 'masculine'" (no. 26). This perspective ignores the importance of women in Jesus' ministry and in the early church. Ruether argues that a concept of God as exclusively male, a Logos Christology that emphasizes reason (which is historically associated with men) and the belief that women reflect the divine image deficiently "threaten to undermine the basic Christian belief that women are included in the redemption of 'man' won by Christ."[37] To render Jesus' masculinity an idol undermines Jesus' universal salvation of all humans, regardless of biological sex. Patriarchal Christologies that divinize Christ's maleness marginalize woman. Presenting the ways in which Christology contributes to the marginalization of women, Johnson pinpoints two effects: "First, it comes to be taken for granted that the maleness of Jesus reveals the maleness of God, or that the only proper way to present God is in male images." And second, "The gender of Jesus has been taken to be the mode or paradigm of what it means to be human."[38] The divinizing of Jesus' maleness has implications for our concept of God, anthropology, and soteriology that negate authentic Christian claims.

Feminist theologians offer alternative christological visions that emphasize Jesus' ministry and message versus his masculinity. African theologian Thérèse Souga emphasizes Jesus' liberationist vision to the oppressed, especially suffering women. Two biblical accounts fuel her Christology: Jesus' healing of the woman with a hemorrhage (Mt 9:18–22) and his curing of the Canaanite woman's daughter (Mk 7:24–30; Mt 15:21–28). In both cases Jesus reaches out to marginalized women, one for her medical condition, another for her ethnicity. He does this in spite of society's norms. Through his incarnation and crucifixion Jesus assumes the condition of weakness. In his weakness, Souga argues, he takes on the condition of suffering African women: "Christ is in solidarity with women, for they incarnate the suffering of the African people. It is within this situation that he liberates them and entrusts them with his message of life for both men and women today."[39] The suffering Christ accompanies suffering Africans in their struggles against oppressive social structures. This vision of the suffering Christ empowers African women and contrasts with a model of Christ's suffering that glorifies women's suffering.

A Christology that emphasizes Christ's suffering and humility runs the danger of appearing to endorse the unjust suffering of peoples throughout history. Womanist theologian Delores S. Williams asks, "Can there be salvific power for black women in Christian images of oppression (for example, Jesus on the cross) meant to teach something about redemption?"[40] After examining and critiquing atonement theories, Williams comes to the conclusion that it is Jesus' *ministerial vision* that is redemptive: "The cross thus becomes an image of defilement, a gross manifestation of collective human sin."[41] The resurrection is God's triumph over this manifestation of human sin.

While noting the dangers of an uncritical acceptance of vulnerability in Christian thought, Sarah Coakley holds that there is an equal danger in Christian feminist thought's rejection of vulnerability as victimology: "The failure to embrace a feminist reconceptualizing of the power of the cross and resurrection. . . . What I have elsewhere called the 'paradox of power and vulnerability' is I believe uniquely focused in this act of silent waiting on the divine in prayer. This is because we can only be properly 'empowered' here if we cease to set the agenda, if we 'make space' for God to be God."[42] Coakley's understanding of vulnerability does not concern suffering or self-abnegation. She writes, "On the contrary, this special 'self-emptying' is not a negation of self, but the place of the self's transformation and expansion into God."[43] Kenosis is understood by Coakley as humans' openness to God, the ability for us to make room for God in our lives. Instead of understanding vulnerability as opposed to power and thus leading to victimhood, Coakley defines vulnerability in terms of transformation and openness to receive and give. Humanity's relationship with God is kenotic—an openness and vulnerability to God's love. This is a relational anthropology that does not glorify suffering but grounds it christologically as empowering for marginalized communities.

As an alternative to patriarchal Christologies, Ruether highlights the praxis and message of the historical Jesus, whom she portrays as "an iconoclastic prophet of God who stands in judgment on social and religion systems that exclude subordinated and marginalized people from divine favor. Jesus' mission is seen as one of bringing 'good news to the poor,' hope to despised people whom the priestly and clerical classes regarded as unworthy of redemption."[44] Among the despised embraced in Jesus' ministry were, of course, women. Building on this foundation Ruether offers a Christology grounded in an egalitarian anthropology, one in which women and men are equally theomorphic. In this Christology, Jesus' maleness has nothing to do with his divine nature. In other words, it is Jesus' message and action and not his biological sex that is important. In her overview of feminist Christologies, Elizabeth Johnson offers nine elements as foundational: (1) Jesus' inclusive message of justice; (2) Jesus naming God Abba contrary to patriarchal models of authority; (3) Jesus' inclusivity of the oppressed, including women; (4) Jesus' inclusion of women as disciples; (5) women's accompaniment of Jesus to Jerusalem; (6) the ministry of women in the early church; (7) the persecution of Jesus and his message and its critique of patriarchal power; (8) the outpouring of the Holy Spirit to both men and women; and (9) early images of Jesus as Sophia (Wisdom), a female symbol of God.[45] These elements inform an authentic Christology, one that is grounded in the fullness of Jesus' message and ministry and not in an unfounded overemphasis on his biological sex. "The guiding model for this *imago Christi* is not replication of sexual features but participation in the life of Christ, which is founded on communion in the Spirit: those who live the life of Christ are icons of Christ."[46] For Johnson, the image of Christ does not lie in biological sex but is instead found in one's coherence with Christ's liberating message.

Ada María Isasi-Díaz's Christology is inextricably linked to social justice. She places an emphasis on a praxiological and ethical understanding of *Jesucristo*, where discipleship requires active participation in the kingdom of God as it is realized here and now: "All who commit themselves to proclaim with their lives and deeds the kingdom of God are mediators of the kingdom."[47] This mediation is grounded in humanity's *imago Dei* and calls followers of *Jesucristo* to realize God's kingdom concretely here on earth, though never in its fullness. The commitment is informed by the concrete struggles of the poor and oppressed. Underlying Isasi-Díaz's Christology is the sense that we grow in the image of Christ as we engage in these concrete struggles. It is through one's active participation in Jesus' liberating message that we come to reflect the image of Christ.

In highlighting the image of Christ within us, Sallie McFague goes to what some would call an extreme in arguing that Jesus is not unique among humanity: "Jesus is not ontologically different from other paradigmatic figures either in our tradition or in other religious traditions who manifest in word or deed the love of God for the world. He is special to us as our foundational figure: he is our historical choice as the premier paradigm of God's love."[48] Jesus, McFague argues, is only special in his paradigmatic status within Christianity. While some may feel uncomfortable with this view, ultimately McFague shares with her feminist sisters a call to follow Jesus' model as Christians.

Contrary to patriarchal theologies that wield Christology as a weapon to deny the full humanity of women, feminist theologians argue that the life and ministry of Jesus Christ are the foundation of an egalitarian anthropology. As Catherine Mowry LaCugna emphasizes, "The life of Jesus Christ is at odds with the sexist theology of complementarity, the racist theology of white superiority, the clerical theology of cultic privilege, the political theology of exploitation and economic injustice, and the patriarchal theology of male dominance and control."[49] Jesus' ministry, his message, his suffering, and his accompaniment of the marginalized denounce theologies that attempt to justify any hierarchical subordination of one human group to another. Christologies that render Jesus' masculinity an idol are not only wrong, they are also in direct conflict with Jesus' liberating message of inclusive love. The image of Christ teaches us that we grow in God's image as we model our lives and behavior on Jesus. This notion is grounded in patristic theology. Underlying this christological anthropology is a vision of the human where relationship is central. Perhaps no other area of theology highlights the relational nature of being, and consequently of humanity, than the doctrine of the Trinity.

Image of the Trinity

A strong component of trinitarian theology's historical legacy has been an overemphasis on rationality as a fundamental dimension of the image of the Trinity within humanity. This undue prominence of the rational is not surprising, given that masculinity is most often associated with rationality within traditional anthropologies. Feminist theologians, however, contest this claim, arguing that relationality is the foundation of the Trinity. A feminist trinitarian understanding of the *imago Dei* places relationships and not rationality front and center: "Relationship is constitutive of who we are and what we can become. Relationality, not rationality, is decisive for our humanity."[50] Relationality replaces rationality as that which reflects the image of God within us. It is through our relationships that we most concretely reflect God's image. This trinitarian notion of the image of God also gives us a theological grounding for relational anthropology. This prevents relationality from being viewed as a "tacked on" feminist contribution grounded in women's experience. I often worry that when feminist theologians ground the importance of relationship within their theologies in sociological terms, the association of women with feeling and emotion unwittingly accompanies this claim. Grounding a relational theological anthropology in the

Trinity, however, avoids this confusion and strengthens the theological claims of feminists. Relationality becomes the essence of God's image and our human nature.

The doctrine of the Trinity, however, has also been seen as problematic for feminists. As LaCugna points out, historically the relationship among the divine Persons has been interpreted as hierarchical, reinforcing an anthropology of gender complementarity. Second, the male images used to refer to the divine Persons (Father and Son) contribute to imaging God exclusively as male.[51] Often feminist theologians attempt to resolve the second concern by offering feminine images of the divine. Latin American feminist theologian María Clara Bingemer argues that traditional interpretations of the Trinity are grounded in a theomorphous vision of man that comes to represent the form and image of God, and consequently an andromorphous concept of God.[52] Feminine images of God, she argues, seek to correct this vision. Bingemer turns to feminine biblical images as her sources for her reworking of the Trinity. While it is important to broaden our symbols, images, and language referring to the divine, she falls into very essentialist language regarding the feminine as compassionate and emotional. Nonetheless, Bingemer's overall presentation of the implications of trinitarian theology for theological anthropology and vice versa is significant. To include women fully in the *imago Dei* forces us to reconceive God in terms of the feminine and masculine. Building on the work of Kari Elisabeth Børreson, Bingemer argues for an anthropomorphous notion of God that reflects the fullness of humanity as created in God's image. This trinitarian theology also serves as a foundation for relationships as central to the *imago Dei:* "Basically, the Trinitarian mystery of God is a mystery of the community; it has social implications. For this reason, a lone individual cannot be the image of this God except insofar as he or she is open to relationship and communitarian being."[53] Foundational to feminist retrievals of the Trinity, therefore, is this emphasis on nonhierarchical relationship. An emphasis on relationality, however, must clarify what sorts of relationship reflect God's image. In other words, while relationality constitutes the image of God, not all relationships reflect that image. It is here where the area of Christology and the *imago Christi* are most helpful. Our definitions of right relationships must claim the ministry, life, death, and resurrection of Jesus Christ as normative.

A trinitarian understanding of the divine image is grounded in historical Christian theology. Beginning with Augustine, the *imago Dei* bears a trinitarian stamp. LaCugna writes:

> Augustine's premise is that the soul is created in the image and after the likeness of God (Gen. 1:26). The journey of the soul is cyclic: The soul loves God and seeks to return to God. Moreover, in drawing the soul back to Godself, God bestows on the soul the true knowledge of itself. Thus if God is a Trinity, then the soul must resemble that which it images and that to which it seeks to return.[54]

Augustine's trinitarian *imago Dei*, however, is one where relationship is self-contained. In other words, as LaCugna points out, "God and the soul are alike in that they are both self-enclosed, self-related." The soul's imaging of God is a result of inward, self-reflection. In this inner process the soul mirrors the inner life of the Trinity. However, LaCugna argues, Augustine's theology ignores the fact that the life of the Trinity is not self-contained but instead flows into the economy of creation and salvation. Augustine's anthropology, where "the soul knows itself apart from social relations, and the soul knows God apart from God's economy of redemption," ignores the interrelational nature of both God and humanity.[55] This individualistic anthropology is also found in the theology of Karl Rahner. With their emphasis on the interrelationship between humanity's relationship with God and our relationships with one another, as well as their emphasis on community, feminist theologians safeguard against this self-contained vision of the human.

In her monumental study of the Trinity, LaCugna reminds us that "Trinitarian theology is par excellence a theology of relationship: God to us, we to God, we to each other. The doctrine of the Trinity affirms that the 'essence' of God is relational, other-ward, that God exists as diverse persons united in communion of freedom, love, and knowledge."[56] Trinitarian theology is the foundation for a relational ontology where being is defined as "being-in-relation." The economy of salvation shows us that this relational being is not "by-itself" but "with-us." "God's To-Be is To-Be-in-relationship, and God's being-in-relationship-to-us *is* what God is."[57] LaCugna affirms that this relational understanding of the Trinity is a firm foundation for a relational theological anthropology, yet one that must be grounded in the Trinity as revealed in the economy of salvation through the concrete revelation of Christ and the Spirit. To ground this theological claim in the intra-trinitarian life is to tread on fragile ground, for one could be accused of perpetuating an ideology similar to patriarchy. We only have a window into the Trinity as it is revealed to us in our concrete human condition.

The doctrine of the Trinity also becomes the foundation for Christian understandings of community and consequently of church. Within Susan Ross's sacramental theology the feminist principle of mutuality becomes the foundation of community:

> Feminist conceptions of self and community challenge the hierarchical model of relationships that tend to characterize the magisterial Catholic understanding of church as community. In contrast, the feminist principle of *mutuality* suggests an egalitarian model for community. This principle also demands that human beings not see themselves in isolation from each other, but rather in positions of mutual responsibility.[58]

However, Ross warns, feminists cannot maintain a romanticized notion of community and relationships and must always be guided by feminist theology's struggle against any form of domination. As Leonardo Boff writes, "Communion, which is the nature of the Trinity, means a critique of all kinds of exclusion and nonparticipation that exist and remain in society and also in the churches."[59] The mutual relational love of the Trinity as expressed through the Christ becomes the foundation for an egalitarian understanding of our relationships and their formalizations within community.

Through their critical work feminist theologians also remind us of the importance of respecting difference within community, where difference is not reduced to biological sex:

> As they look at women's communities, women in community, and the play of gender constructs throughout community, feminists also recognize the significant roles of race, class, sexuality, geography, and ethnicity play in forming and maintaining communal practices and identities. . . . Feminists also recognize that as factors such as race, gender, and geography intermingle in community, the definition of community shifts as contexts change.[60]

Communities must remain open to changes and growth within them and always respectful of differences among us. In the spirit of a trinitarian anthropology, such a vision of the human strives to image who we are in all of our distinctiveness and unity.

My contribution to *imago Dei* anthropology is grounded in the trinitarian life as relational, which constitutes the inner nature of the Trinity as revealed in its relationship with humanity within salvation history. Our *imago Dei* is our ability to be relational. Through our relationship with God, our fellow human beings, and the rest of creation we reflect the image of God within us. The human being is not self-contained but rather is constituted by relationships. This is not an uncritical and romanticized understanding of relationships. Not all relations reflect the image of God. Instead, relationships are judged against the norm of Jesus' concrete life, ministry, death, and resurrection. Through our mirroring of Jesus' justice-infused ministry we grow in the image of Christ and, consequently, in the image of God. Hierarchical relationships that privilege certain sectors of humanity are deemed unrevelatory, for they contradict Jesus' inclusive vision of community. The relationship between men and women must use the criteria of Jesus, embracing an egalitarian vision of the human who is embodied distinctively as male and female. While we must take our biological sex seriously, we cannot reduce humanity to biology and assume that biological distinction equals a hierarchical and complementary model of gender relations. Instead, male and female reflect the image of God equally and express this image through their own historical, social, and cultural particularity. The image of God calls us to be in relationship and community with one another as we mirror the relational life of the trinitarian God.

Conclusion

The focus of this study is the manner in which gender functions within Christian understandings of creation in the image of God. The category of gender is not a new arrival within Christian theology; it has always marked Christianity. Genesis 1:27, which is the biblical foundation of the *imago Dei*, includes "male and female" within the *imago*. Christian theologians have struggled with the meaning behind the link between gender and the image of God, often basing their insights on philosophies that predate the Christian tradition. Too often, this study demonstrates the Christian theological tradition has defined the *imago Dei* in a manner that degrades women. Men, it is too often argued, reflect the image fully. Women, on the other hand, reflect the image in a deficient or secondary manner. This is most often due to women's bodies, which are constructed in opposition to rationality and spirituality. This denigration of women's bodies has led to women's association with bodies in general. Women as symbolic of embodiment is constructed in contrast to the rational, spiritual male, who is seen as closer to and consequently more reflective of the divine.

Contemporary feminist theologians respond to this unjust, patriarchal construction of women by revealing the biased and flawed manner in which women's nature is depicted within Christian theology. This understanding of humanity, feminists argue, not only denies both male and female their full humanity, but also is contrary to the authentic Christian message. Privileging the male at the expense of the female leads to valuing men theologically as closer to the divine. The consequences

161

of this abound, including the exclusive and idolatrous use of male imagery for the divine. As Eleazar S. Fernandez states, "Sexism, like other forms of oppression, is a form of idolatry. . . . Sexism is the worship of male genitalia as an idol."[1] Using biblical studies, historical theology, and contemporary constructive theology, feminist theologians reconstruct Christian theological understandings of the human revealing, they stress, the authentic Christian vision of the human. The Christian tradition has, in their eyes, been tainted by patriarchy, but not to the extent that it is not unsalvageable. My contribution to this area of study falls in line with mainstream feminist theology, embracing this spirit of uncovering a more just vision of the human informed by Christian theological insights.

My work is fueled by the scholarship of feminist theologians, in particular those who have a strong commitment to the Christian tradition. Because our understanding of the image of God is intimately tied to our understanding of God, Jesus Christ, and the Trinity, my proposal constructs the image of God through those theological loci. Beginning with the concept of God, I argue that authentic transformation of the *imago Dei* into an egalitarian model will never occur unless Christians radically transform their imaging of God. As long as God is imaged exclusively as male, men will be viewed as closer to the divine. Exclusively male God-language divinizes masculinity. As Catherine LaCugna points out, "Theological feminism is in part a critique of the propensity to literalize metaphors for God and forget the dissimilarity in every analogy."[2] I argue for a more inclusive imaging of God, one in which masculine and feminine metaphors reveal the fullness of God, always acknowledging the limitations of human God-talk. My christological section emphasized the image of Christ in humanity, grounded in Jesus' radical message of inclusive love. Jesus Christ becomes normative for understanding how we must embody the image within us. "Each and every one of us is an image of God, an *imago Dei*," Ada María Isasi-Díaz emphasizes. "Each and every one of us carries seeds of divinity that make who we are capable of being and what we are capable of doing essential to the unfolding of the kingdom of God."[3] The final section proposes a trinitarian vision of the divine image grounded in the relational nature of God and consequently human nature. This anthropology highlights the intra-relationship between Creator and creature and the external relationships within the human community as the sites of our divine image. Humanity shares this image equally, yet our expression of the image is always conditioned by our social location.

Christian theology has perpetuated an understanding of the divine image that grants men normative status as human beings. As María Clara Bingemer points out: "There is a gap between humanity and femininity. As long as she is female, a woman is not the image of God; thus, in order to be saved (that is, in order to become one with God) she must find another form."[4] Women reflect the image of God in spite of their femaleness. Their nature becomes an obstacle to overcome in order to be fully human. Too often, the culprit is women's bodies. As a result of the vilification of women's bodies, women come to be associated with all bodies, while men become equated with higher reason and spirituality. Elizabeth Johnson writes: "In the battle between the spirit and the flesh, waged by men who aspired to God, women were placed on the side of the flesh owing to their role as marriage partners as well as their messy connection with pregnancy and childbirth. You can watch it develop in the literature of early Christian centuries: an increasingly strong torrent of misogyny against women and their bodies."[5] Women's bodies become the battlefield for their full humanity. In response to this disparagement, feminist theologians emphasize embodiment as a fundamental site of the divine image. Human beings reflect the image of God within their bodies, not in spite of them. This positive retrieval of embodiment is one of feminist theology's greatest contributions to the Christian tradition. In this concluding section I emphasize five other areas within feminist theological anthropologies that also offer substantial contributions to Christian theology.

These are areas that I hope my colleagues will continue to explore in their own work, for they are of utmost concern.

The first of these issues that merit further attention is the role of anthropology to the doctrine of creation. Here the eco-feminist insight into the interrelationship between the hierarchical ordering of humanity over the natural world and the male over the female is essential. Susan Ross states: "One of feminist theology's most important contributions to the discipline has been its disclosure of ways in which women, the human body, and the natural world have been, at best, relegated to a lower position in relation to men and the spiritual, and at worst, seen to be inherently evil."[6] Linked to this, Ross points out, is the feminist retrieval of the body. However, the feminist concern for creation cannot merely come out of their shared marginalization within the dominant patriarchal world view. Instead, it must emerge from an appreciation of the interrelationship among all of creation. The same relational anthropology that envisions humanity's *imago Dei* must extend its partners to include all of God's creation. The current ecological crisis is but one grave example of the effects of the hierarchical ordering of humanity over the rest of the natural world. If we are to take the claims and concerns of eco-feminist theologians seriously, then we must begin to speak of a theology of creation or cosmology versus a theological anthropology. As Anne Clifford observes: "Contemporary theology with its strong focus on history could benefit greatly from a parallel focus on the cosmos. Creation theology needs to attend to nature and to the cosmos not as a replacement for the concerns for human emancipation and liberation, but as a complement to them."[7] The justice element, Clifford emphasizes, is fundamental, for the mistreatment of the earth affects not only women but also the poor and dispossessed. Creation theology need not do away with the doctrine of the *imago Dei*, but it must reenvision the relationship between humanity and nonhuman creation as one of stewardship and not dominion.

The question of redemptive suffering is a second area that warrants more extensive study. As Chapter 6 highlights, redemptive suffering is a point of debate for many feminist theologians. Those scholars that reject redemptive suffering claim that any theology that glorifies suffering requires people to suffer. This leads to an unhealthy emphasis on self-denial and sacrifice, which historically have been used as weapons of sexism to subordinate women. "And while Christian love in all persons has indeed always included the notion of self-sacrifice," Margaret Farley remarks, "there have been ways of attributing that element of love especially to women—reinforcing, on the one hand, a sense of subservience in women, and leading, on the other hand, to such strange conclusions as that the woman is the 'heart' of the family and the man is the 'mind.'"[8] On the other side of the debate is the recognition that a theology of redemptive suffering can be empowering for marginalized communities that see Jesus' suffering as the way in which he accompanies them in their suffering. M. Shawn Copeland proposes a womanist theology of suffering in which suffering is redemptive and resistant: "And, by their very suffering and privation Black women under chattel slavery freed the cross of Christ. Their steadfast commitment honored that cross and the One who died for all and redeemed it from Christianity's vulgar misuse. . . . With sass, Black women survived, even triumphed over physical and emotional assault."[9] The crucified Jesus accompanies suffering peoples both in their suffering and in their struggles to transform their suffering. A healthy discussion (even debate) over the question of redemptive suffering would be a fruitful collaboration for feminist theologians, demonstrating the influence of culture and social location and the manner in which it fuels diversity within feminist theologies.

This book repeatedly has emphasized the critical and liberationist impulses behind feminist theologies, a third area of interest. Most often, feminist theology is situated as a liberationist discourse among other liberation theologies. Nancy Dallavalle, however, challenges this privileging of justice concerns and calls for the expansion of feminist theology's agenda. Dallavalle argues that while the theme of justice is central within the New Testament, this liberationist agenda does not exhaust the possibilities for feminist theologians: "Indeed, reducing either the insights of feminism or the complexities of Catholic theology to justice concerns ignores the fact that some feminist theories reflect exclusively on being female *and* the fact that the object of Christian theology, and the ground of the Catholic tradition's catholicity, is God, not human concerns for justice."[10] Feminist theologians describe their work as liberationist through their ethical critique of patriarchy and theological because of their emphasis on the patriarchal nature of Christian theology. However, Dallavalle contends, this is only one portion of the fullness of the Christian message. "The New Testament has many messages—about repentance, about plentitude, about piety, and, most clearly, about the person of Jesus Christ—that cry out for feminist analysis without in the first place being messages about justice."[11] Dallavalle is not critical of the justice emphasis, just of its exclusive use.

While not wanting to undermine the primacy of justice, I echo Dallavalle's concerns. Given feminist theologians' intended goal of offering a more authentic vision of the Christian message in its entirety, the self-imposed limitation to justice concerns hampers their broader objectives. Indeed, I would argue that an emphasis on piety and repentance need not be in contrast to justice concerns. This narrow liberationist concern contributes to the overall marginalization of feminist theology as a women's "side project" to authentic Christian theology. Marcella María Althaus-Reid argues that liberation theologies have been coopted and rendered powerless in the face of dominant Western discourse. Liberation theologies become "theme parks" that Western theologians can visit while not having to alter the nature and structure of their theology. As theme-park theologies, Althaus-Reid contends, liberation theologies become a commodity for Western capitalism: "The centerpiece of theological thinking is constituted by systematic Western theology, and it is done even in opposition. The theme parks, in the case of Liberation Theology, are divided into subthemes, such as 'Marxist Theology,' 'Evangelical Theology,' 'Indigenous Theology,' 'Feminist Theology'—and all of them with a central unifying theme ending with 'and the poor.'"[12] As theme parks, they can be visited at one's leisure; one is never forced to take them seriously. Broadening the language and agenda of feminist theologies, while never losing the liberationist impulse, would not only assist the progress of feminist theology's objectives, but also, I suspect, broaden its audience.

A fourth area for further study is the apparent tension within feminist theologies between the recognition of the situated nature of all knowledge and the normative critique of patriarchy. As defined by Elizabeth Johnson, "Christian feminism labors to bring the community, its symbols and practices, into a closer coherence with the reign of God's justice."[13] This statement maintains that there is an authentic Christian message that feminists can uncover. Yet such assertions regarding the possible retrieval of a more accurate version of Christianity free of patriarchal elements are contrasted to feminists' repeated emphasis on the contextual nature of all knowledge. Therefore, even if feminists were able to retrieve a more authentic Christianity, this retrieval would always be mediated and limited by a particular theologian's social location. This ambiguity fuels the debates surrounding the nature of women's experience, which often functions as an antidote to patriarchy. "It is certainly true that Catholic feminist theologians invoke 'women's experience' often with great nuance," Dallavalle observes, "but the tendency thus far is to invoke it medicinally, as a corrective to androcentric perspectives."[14] I am not suggesting that feminist theologians continue this debate within the realm of identity politics. However, there needs to be clear definition of feminist theology's norms. Women's experience, as I argued in Chapter 6, is not a sound norm for feminist theological projects.

Related to the question of normativity is the construction of gender as a theological category, the fifth area I am highlighting for further study. Feminist theologians must continue to ground their constructive work soundly within the discipline of theology. While theology is an interdisciplinary task, ultimately theologians must remain grounded in their particular field as an entry point to other areas of study. Here European American feminist theologians have made excellent contributions. The work of US minority and third-world women, in contrast, is often characterized by their emphasis on identity politics and expressing the particular sources of their racial or ethnic group. While this work is vital, it must be complemented by more constructive work. While offering a more critical presentation of women's experiences and the sources for Christian theology, these theologies lack the weight of the substantive constructive claims offered by the European American sisters. It is my hope that feminists of color will begin to tackle more explicitly constructive theological work.

Feminist theology proposes a vision of God as relational, mutual love, whose image we are called to embody. As Catherine LaCugna poetically writes, "Humanity is created in the image of God, and God exists as the communion of love, as a reciprocal exchange of love and persons in which humanity has been graciously included as a partner."[15] Humanity is challenged to respond to this gracious invitation and reflect the image through our actions and relationships. While we will never fully image the fullness of the trinitarian God, we can grow in the divine image through our relationships with the divine, our fellow human beings, and nonhuman creation, modeling our behavior on the liberating and prophetic message and life of Jesus Christ. For centuries the doctrine of the *imago Dei* has been misinterpreted to benefit male authority and render women subservient in their "defective" humanity. A critical feminist reconstruction counters centuries of misreading the Christian tradition, arguing that both men and women reflect the divine image fully. This theological anthropology presents an egalitarian vision of humanity that reflects the relational, trinitarian God in whose image we are created.

Notes

Introduction

The first epigraph to this chapter is drawn from Kristen E. Kvam, Linda S. Schearing, and Valerie H. Ziegler, *Eve and Adam: Jewish, Christian, and Muslim Readings on Genesis and Gender* (Bloomington: Indiana University Press, 1999), 15; the second from Adrien Janis Bledstein, "The Genesis of Humans: The Garden of Eden Revisited," *Judaism* 26 (1977): 187.

1. Gustavo Gutiérrez, *A Theology of Liberation*, 15th anniv. ed. (Maryknoll, NY: Orbis Books, 1988), 11.

2. Francis Schüssler Fiorenza, "Systematic Theology: Task and Methods," in *Systematic Theology: Roman Catholic Perspectives*, vol. 1, ed. Francis Schüssler Fiorenza and John P. Galvin (Minneapolis, MN: Fortress Press, 1991), 6–7.

3. Anne E. Carr, "The New Vision of Feminist Theology: Method," in *Freeing Theology: The Essentials of Theology in Feminist Perspective*, ed. Catherine Mowry LaCugna (San Francisco: HarperSanFrancisco, 1993), 7.

4. Ibid.

5. Orlando O. Espín, for example, expands the sources of theology to include the *sensus fidelium* of Christians, what he defines as "'faith-full' intuition." For Espín, this *sensus fidelium* is infallible, for its origin is the Holy Spirit and the Spirit working in the Christian community throughout history. Also, this *sensus fidelium* is always expressed in a contextual manner, building on the symbols and language of a particular community. However, Espín does not propose an acritical acceptance of the Spirit working within Christians. Instead, he offers three criteria to judge whether an expression of the *sensus fidelium* is just: scripture, the written texts of tradition, and the historical and sociological contexts from which it manifests itself. See Orlando O. Espín, "Tradition and Popular Religion: An Understanding of the *Sensus Fidelium*," in *The Faith of the People: Theological*

Reflections on Popular Catholicism (Maryknoll, NY: Orbis Books, 1997), 63–90.

6. Serene Jones, *Feminist Theory and Christian Theology: Cartographies of Grace* (Minneapolis: Fortress Press, 2000), 11.

7. Kristen E. Kvam, "Anthropology, Theological," in *Dictionary of Feminist Theologies*, ed. Letty M. Russell and J. Shannon Clarkson (Louisville, KY: Westminster John Knox Press, 1996), 10.

8. M. Shawn Copeland et al., "Human Being," in *Constructive Theology: A Contemporary Approach to Classical Themes*, ed. Serene Jones and Paul Lakeland (Minneapolis, MN: Fortress Press, 2005), 79.

9. Ibid.

10. Ibid., 84.

11. For an excellent introduction to the Christian notion of original sin, see Tatha Wiley, *Original Sin: Origins, Developments, and Contemporary Meanings* (Mahwah, NJ: Paulist Press, 2002).

12. Prudence Allen, *The Concept of Woman*, vol. 1, *The Aristotelian Revolution, 750 B.C.—A.D. 1250* (Montreal: Eden, 1985; Grand Rapids, MI: Eerdmans, 1997), 1.

13. Elisabeth Schüssler Fiorenza, "Breaking the Silence—Becoming Visible," in *The Power of Naming: A* Concilium *Reader in Feminist Liberation Theology*, ed. Elisabeth Schüssler Fiorenza (Maryknoll, NY: Orbis Books, 1996), 161–62.

14. Some would argue that Valerie Saiving's essay "The Human Situation: A Feminine View" (*The Journal of Religion* [April 1960]) is the first feminist theological text. While not disputing this fact, I find the impact of Mary Daly's book to be the fundamental public moment for feminist theologians.

15. In her excellent introduction to feminist theologies, Anne M. Clifford offers a helpful typology of what she categorizes as the three types of feminist theologies: revolutionary feminist theology, reformist Christian feminist theology, and reconstructionist Christian feminist theology. Revolutionary feminist theologians are post-Christian. "Many of these women originally participated in Christian churches, but their own feminist consciousness led them to conclude that Christianity is irredeemably patriarchal, even anti-woman." Reformist Christian theologians "are looking for far more modest changes within existing church structures" and share a common "commitment to the Christian tradition." "Reconstructionist feminist theologians

seek a liberating theological core for women within the Christian tradition, while also envisioning a deeper transformation, a true reconstruction, not only of their church structures but also of civil society." Anne M. Clifford, *Introducing Feminist Theology* (Maryknoll, NY: Orbis Books, 2001), 32–33. The majority of feminist theologians examined herein would fall under the reconstructionist heading.

16. Donna Teevan, "Challenges to the Role of Theological Anthropology in Feminist Theologies," *Theological Studies* 64 (2003): 583.

17. Robin May Schott, "Introduction," in *Feminist Interpretations of Immanuel Kant*, ed. Robin May Schott (University Park: The Pennsylvania State University Press, 1997), 4.

1. Foundations: Scripture and Philosophy

1. Phyllis Trible, *God and the Rhetoric of Sexuality* (Minneapolis, MN: Fortress Press, 1978), 1.

2. Sandra M. Schneiders, "The Bible and Feminism: Biblical Theology," in *Freeing Theology: The Essentials of Theology in Feminist Perspective*, ed. Catherine Mowry LaCugna (San Francisco: HarperSanFrancisco, 1993), 47.

3. Pauline A. Viviano, "Genesis," in *The Collegeville Bible Commentary*, ed. Dianne Bergant and Robert J. Karris (Collegeville, MN: The Liturgical Press, 1988), 39–40.

4. Claus Westermann, *Genesis 1:11: A Commentary*, trans. John J. Scullion, SJ (Minneapolis, MN: Augsburg Publishing House, 1984), 148–55, cited in Kristen E. Kvam, Linda S. Schearing, and Valerie H. Ziegler, *Eve and Adam: Jewish, Christian, and Muslim Readings on Genesis and Gender* (Bloomington: Indiana University Press, 1999), 24.

5. Westermann, *Genesis 1:11*, 155.

6. Trible, *God and the Rhetoric of Sexuality*, 16–18.

7. Ibid., 21.

8. Anne M. Clifford, "When Being Human Becomes Truly Earthly: An Ecofeminist Proposal for Solidarity," in *In the Embrace of God: Feminist Approaches to Theological Anthropology*, ed. Ann O'Hara Graff (Maryknoll, NY: Orbis Books, 1995), 183.

9. Phyllis A. Bird, "Sexual Differentiation and Divine Image in the Genesis Creation Texts," in *The Image of God: Gender Models in*

Judaeo-Christian Tradition, ed. Kari Elisabeth Børreson (Minneapolis, MN: Fortress Press, 1991), 11.

10. Kvam, Schearing, and Ziegler, *Eve and Adam*, 24–25.

11. Trible, *God and the Rhetoric of Sexuality*, 80.

12. Ibid., 98.

13. Kvam, Schearing, and Ziegler, *Eve and Adam*, 29.

14. Trible, *God and the Rhetoric of Sexuality*, 110.

15. Bird, "Sexual Differentiation and Divine Image," 15–16.

16. Lone Fatum, "Image of God and Glory of Man: Women in the Pauline Congregations," in Børreson, *The Image of God*, 62.

17. Ibid., 71.

18. Ibid., 76.

19. Ibid., 78–79.

20. Francis Schüssler Fiorenza, "Systematic Theology: Task and Methods," in *Systematic Theology: Roman Catholic Perspectives*, vol. 1, ed. Francis Schüssler Fiorenza and John P. Galvin (Minneapolis, MN: Fortress Press, 1991), 7–8.

21. Schneiders, "The Bible and Feminism," 36.

22. As Rosemary Radford Ruether writes, "Feminist readings of the Bible can discern a norm within Biblical faith by which the Biblical texts themselves can be criticized. To the extent to which Biblical texts reflect this normative principle, they are regarded as authoritative. On this basis many aspects of the Bible are to be frankly set aside and rejected" (*Sexism and God-Talk: Toward a Feminist Theology* [Boston: Beacon Press, 1993], 23).

23. Schneiders, "The Bible and Feminism,"49.

24. Nicholas D. Smith, "Plato and Aristotle on the Nature of Women," *Journal of the History of Philosophy* 21, no. 1 (October 1983): 467–68.

25. Prudence Allen, *The Concept of Woman*, vol. 1, *The Aristotelian Revolution, 750 B.C.—A.D. 1250* (Montreal: Eden, 1985; Grand Rapids, MI: Eerdmans, 1997), 63. My analyses of Plato and Aristotle are heavily indebted to Allen's excellent scholarship.

26. Ibid., 68.

27. Plato, *Republic*, in *The Collected Dialogues of Plato, including His Letters*, ed. Edith Hamilton and Huntington Cairns (New York: Pantheon Books, 1961), 455c-e.

28. Ibid., 455e-56a.

29. Beverly Clack, ed., *Misogyny in the Western Philosophical Tradition: A Reader* (New York: Routledge, 1999), 13.

30. L. D. Derksen, *Dialogues on Women: Images of Women in the History of Philosophy* (Amsterdam: VU University Press, 1996), 24.

31. Smith, "Plato and Aristotle on the Nature of Women," 469–470.

32. Allen, *The Concept of Woman*, 83.

33. Aristotle, *On the Generation of Animals*, trans. and ed. A. L. Peck (Cambridge, MA: Harvard University Press, 1943), 729b 15–20.

34. Ibid., 737a 26–30.

35. Aristotle, *Politics*, in *The Complete Works of Aristotle in English: The Revised Oxford Translation*, ed. Jonathan Barnes (Princeton, NJ: Princeton University Press, 1984), 1254b 13–15.

36. Ibid., 1260b.

37. Allen, *The Concept of Woman*, 103–4.

2. Historical Theology

1. P. Th. Camelot, OP, "La Théologie de L'Image de Dieu," *Revue des Sciences Philosophiques et Théologiques* 40 (1956): 471.

2. Rosemary Radford Ruether, "Misogynism and Virginal Feminism in the Fathers of the Church," in *Religion and Sexism: Images of Woman in the Jewish and Christian Traditions*, ed. Rosemary Radford Ruether (New York: Simon and Schuster, 1974), 153.

3. Kari Elisabeth Børreson, "God's Image, Man's Image? Patristic Interpretation of Gen. 1,27 and 1Cor. 11,7," in *The Image of God: Gender Models in Judaeo-Christian Tradition*, ed. Kari Elisabeth Børreson (Minneapolis, MN: Fortress Press, 1991), 187.

4. Mary Ann Donovan, *One Right Reading? A Guide to Irenaeus* (Collegeville, MN: The Liturgical Press, 1997), 3. Much of the insights in this section are gleaned from Donovan's impressive work on Irenaeus.

5. George A. Maloney, SJ, *Man, the Divine Icon* (New Mexico: Dove Publications, 1973), 34.

6. Jacques Fantino, *L'homme Image de Dieu chez Saint Irénée de Lyon* (Paris: Éditions du Cerf, 1986), 113.

7. Ibid., 121.

8. All citations from this section are taken from Irenaeus of Lyons, *Against Heresies,* trans. Dominic J. Unger (New York: Paulist Press, 1992).

9. Donovan, *One Right Reading?*, 88.

10. Maloney, *Man, the Divine Icon*, 37.

11. Mary Ann Donovan, "Alive to the Glory of the Lord: A Key Insight in St. Irenaeus," *Theological Studies* 49, no. 2 (1988): 294.

12. Donovan, *One Right Reading?* 81.

13. "Jesus Christ, the Son, Word and image of God, is the visible image who makes visible the invisible God. Since humans are the image of the Son, the appearance of the Son in flesh made visible the one in whose image they are, and established the likeness to the Father." Donovan, *One Right Reading?*, 155, commenting on Irenaeus, "When the Word of God was made flesh, it confirmed two things: it showed the image true, he himself being that which was his image, and it established the likeness, making humanity like to the invisible Father through the Visible Word" (V,16,2).

14. Maloney, *Man, the Divine Icon*, 138.

15. Ibid., 144.

16. All citations from Gregory of Nyssa are taken from *On the Making of Man,* in *A Select Library of Nicene and Post-Nicene Fathers of the Christian Church*, second series, ed. Philip Schaff and Henry Wace, vol. 5, *Gregory of Nyssa: Dogmatic Treatises, Etc.* (New York: The Christian Literature Company, 1893).

17. All citations from chapter 12 of Gregory of Nyssa, *On Virginity* are taken from Schaff and Wace, *Gregory of Nyssa.*

18. Børreson, "God's Image, Man's Image?" 197.

19. John Edward Sullivan, OP, *The Image of God: The Doctrine of St. Augustine and Its Influence* (Dubuque, IA: The Priory Press, 1963), ix.

20. See Augustine, *The Trinity*, in *Augustine: Later Works*, ed. John Burnaby (Philadelphia: Westminster Press, 1955).

21. Book 3, chap. 19. All citations in the text are taken from Augustine, *The Literal Meaning of Genesis*, vol. 1, *Books 1–6*, trans. John Hammond Taylor, SJ (New York: Paulist Press, 1982).

22. Tatha Wiley, *Original Sin: Origins, Developments, and Contemporary Meanings* (Mahwah, NJ: Paulist Press, 2002), 65.

23. John Burnaby, "Introduction," in Augustine, *The Trinity*, 30–31.

24. Augustine, *The Trinity*, book 12, chap. 7.

25. Augustine, *The Literal Meaning of Genesis*, vol. 2, *Books 7–12*, trans. John Hammond Taylor, SJ (New York: Paulist Press, 1982), book 9, chap. 5, 9.

26. Prudence Allen, *The Concept of Woman*, vol. 1, *The Aristotelian Revolution, 750 B.C.—A.D. 1250* (Montreal: Eden, 1985; Grand Rapids, MI: Eerdmans, 1997), 229.

27. Kari Elisabeth Børreson, *Subordination and Equivalence: The Nature and Role of Woman in Augustine and Thomas Aquinas* (Oslo: Universitetsforlaget, 1968; Kampen: Kok Pharos Publishing House, 1995), 26.

28. Børreson, "God's Image, Man's Image?" 200.

29. All citations in the text are taken from Aquinas, *The Disputed Questions on Truth*, in *Truth*, vol. 2, *Questions X-XX*, trans. James V. McGlynn, SJ (Chicago: Henry Regnery Company, 1953).

30. D. Juvenal Merriell, *The Image of the Trinity: A Study in the Development of Aquinas' Teaching* (Toronto: Pontifical Institute of Mediaeval Studies, 1990), 245.

31. All citations in the text are taken from Aquinas, *Summa Theologiae*, in *Basic Writings of Saint Thomas Aquinas*, ed. Anton C. Pegis (New York: Random House, 1945).

32. Børreson, *Subordination and Equivalence*, 171.

33. L. D. Derksen, *Dialogues on Women: Images of Women in the History of Philosophy* (Amsterdam: VU University Press, 1996), 38.

34. Allen, *The Concept of Woman*, 385.

35. Margaret R. Miles attributes Hildegard's lack of influence to her isolation in a monastery and the egalitarian vision of her theology, which did little to support reigning social institutions. Margaret R. Miles, *Carnal Knowing: Female Nakedness and Religious Meaning in the Christian West* (Boston: Beacon Press, 1989), 105.

36. Caroline Walker Bynum, *Jesus as Mother: Studies in the Spirituality of the High Middle Ages* (Berkeley and Los Angeles: University of California Press, 1982), 210.

37. Caroline Walker Bynum, *Holy Feast and Holy Fast: The Religious Significance of Food for Medieval Women* (Berkeley and Los Angeles: University of California Press, 1987), 263.

38. Catherine of Siena, *The Dialogue*, cited in ibid., 377 n. 139.

39. Walker Bynum, *Holy Feast and Holy Fast*, 296.

40. Allen, *The Concept of Woman*, 295.

41. Walker Bynum, *Holy Feast and Holy Fast*, 264.

42. Ibid., 265.

43. Allen, *The Concept of Woman*, 292.

44. Kristen E. Kvam, Linda S. Schearing, and Valerie H. Ziegler, *Eve and Adam: Jewish, Christian, and Muslim Readings on Genesis and Gender* (Bloomington: Indiana University Press, 1999), 171.

45. Anthony O. Erhueh, *Vatican II: Image of God in Man* (Rome: Pontificia Universitas Urbania, 1987), 54.

46. Martin Luther, "Lectures on Genesis," in *Luther's Works*, ed. Jaroslav Pelikan (Saint Louis: Concordia Publishing House, 1958), 1:61–62.

47. Ibid., 1:68–69.

48. Jane Dempsey Douglass, "The Image of God in Woman as Seen by Luther and Calvin," in Børreson, *The Image of God*, 251.

49. Ibid.

50. Luther, "The Disputation Concerning Justification," in *Luther's Works*, vol. 34, *Career of the Reformer IV*, ed. Lewis W. Spitz (Philadelphia: Muhlenberg Press, 1955), Argument XV.

51. Beverly Clack, ed., *Misogyny in the Western Philosophical Tradition: A Reader* (New York: Routledge, 1999), 95.

52. Genevieve Lloyd, *The Man of Reason: 'Male' and 'Female' in Western Philosophy*, 2nd ed. (Minneapolis: University of Minnesota Press, 1993), 45.

53. Ibid., 50.

54. Louis Dupré, *Passage to Modernity: An Essay in the Hermeneutics of Nature and Culture* (New Haven, CT: Yale University Press, 1993), 3.

55. Clack, *Misogyny in the Western Philosophical Tradition*, 145.

56. Immanuel Kant, *Observations on the Feeling of the Beautiful and Sublime,* trans. J. T. Goldthwait (Berkeley and Los Angeles: University of California Press, 1960), section 3.

57. Robin May Schott, "The Gender of Enlightenment," in *Feminist Interpretations of Immanuel Kant*, ed. Robin May Schott (University Park: The Pennsylvania State University Press, 1997), 323.

3. Twentieth-Century Theology

1. Clifford Green, "Introduction: Karl Barth's Life and Theology," in *Karl Barth: Theologian of Freedom*, ed. Clifford Green (Minneapolis, MN: Fortress Press, 1991), 17–18.

2. Barth's theology is also referred to as Word-of-God theology. The Word is expressed in three ways in Barth's theology: (1) Jesus Christ; (2) the Bible (where the Bible is not static but rather an event through which God speaks); and (3) the church's proclamation of the gospel.

3. Green, "Introduction," 33.

4. Karl Barth, *Church Dogmatics: A Selection*, trans. Helmut Gollwitzer (Louisville, KY: Westminster John Knox Press, 1994), 194–221.

5. Ibid., 195.

6. Ibid., 202.

7. Ibid., 205.

8. Ibid., 219.

9. Ibid., 221.

10. Karl Barth, *Church Dogmatics*, III/1, *The Doctrine of Creation* (Edinburgh: T & T Clark, 1956), 191–92.

11. Rosemary R. Ruether, *Sexism and God-Talk: Toward a Feminist Theology* (Boston: Beacon Press, 1993), 98–99.

12. Geffrey B. Kelly, "Introduction," in *Karl Rahner: Theologian of the Graced Search for Meaning*, ed. Geffrey B. Kelly (Minneapolis, MN: Fortress Press, 1992), 1.

13. J. A Di Noia, OP, "Karl Rahner," in *The Modern Theologians*, ed. David F. Ford (New York: Blackwell, 1997), 120.

14. Kelly, "Introduction," 1.

15. Karl Rahner, *Foundations of Christian Faith: An Introduction to the Idea of Christianity*, trans. William V. Dych (New York: Crossroad, 1997), 172.

16. Ibid., 21.

17. Kelly, "Introduction," 42.

18. William V. Dych, *Karl Rahner* (Collegeville, MN: The Liturgical Press, 1992), 36.

19. Rahner, *Foundations of Christian Faith*, 128.

20. Ibid., 53.

21. Miguel H. Díaz, *On Being Human: U.S. Hispanic and Rahnerian Perspectives* (Maryknoll, NY: Orbis Books, 2001), chap. 4.

22. David H. Kelsey, "Paul Tillich," in Ford, *The Modern Theologians*, 87.

23. James C. Livingston and Francis Schüssler Fiorenza, *Modern Christian Thought*, vol. 2, *The Twentieth Century* (Upper Saddle River, NJ: Prentice-Hall, 2000), 141.

24. Paul Tillich, *Systematic Theology*, vol. 2, *Existence and the Christ* (Chicago: University of Chicago Press, 1975), 3.

25. Ibid., 13.

26. Ibid., 7.

27. Kelsey, "Paul Tillich," 93.

28. Tillich, *Systematic Theology*, 2:22.

29. Ibid., 32–33.

30. Ibid., 35.

31. Ibid., 57.

32. Alexander J. McKelway, *The Systematic Theology of Paul Tillich: A Review and Analysis* (Richmond, VA: John Knox Press, 1964), 21.

33. Judith Plaskow, *Sex, Sin, and Grace: Women's Experience and the Theologies of Reinhold Niebuhr and Paul Tillich* (Lanham, MD: University Press of America, 1980).

34. See, e.g., Louis Dupré, "The Glory of the Lord: Hans Urs von Balthasar's Theological Aesthetic," in *Hans Urs von Balthasar: His Life and Work*, ed. David L. Schindler (San Francisco: Ignatius Press, 1991), 183.

35. Hans Urs von Balthasar, *My Work: In Retrospect* (San Francisco: Ignatius Press, 1993).

36. Lucy Gardner and David Moss, "Something Like Time; Something Like the Sexes—An Essay in Reception," in *Balthasar at the End of Modernity*, ed. Lucy Gardner et al. (Edinburgh: T & T Clark, 1999), 78.

37. I agree with John O'Donnell, who writes, "Moreover, the reader comes to see that Balthasar's understanding of sexuality is central to his vision and sheds light on every facet of his theology" (John O'Donnell, SJ, "Man and Woman as *Imago Dei* in the Theology of Hans Urs von Balthasar," *Clergy Review* 68, no. 4 [1983]: 117).

38. Angelo Scola, *Hans Urs von Balthasar: A Theological Style* (Grand Rapids, MI: Eerdmans, 1995), 85–86.

39. "He exists as a limited being in a limited world, but his reason is open to the unlimited, to all of being. The proof exists in the recognition of his finitude, of his contingence: I am, but I could not-be" (Balthasar, "A Résumé of My Thought," in Schindler, *Hans Urs von Balthasar*, 1).

40. Gerard Loughlin, "Erotics: God's Sex," in *Radical Orthodoxy: A New Theology*, ed. John Milbank, Catherine Pickstock, and Graham Ward (New York: Routledge, 1999), 150.

41. Hans Urs von Balthasar, *Theo-Drama: Theological Dramatic Theory*, vol. 2, *Dramatis Personae: Man in God*, trans. Graham Harrison (San Francisco: Ignatius Press, 1990), 411.

42. Hans Urs von Balthasar, *Theo-Drama: Theological Dramatic Theory*, vol. 3, *Dramatis Personae: The Person in Christ, Christus*, trans. Graham Harrison (San Francisco: Ignatius Press, 1992), 285.

43. Loughlin, "Erotics," 153.

44. Balthasar, *The Christian State of Life* (San Francisco: Ignatius Press, 1983), 227.

45. Balthasar, *Dramatis Personae: The Person in Christ*, 286.

46. David Moss and Lucy Gardner, "Difference—The Immaculate Concept? The Laws of Sexual Difference in the Theology of Hans Urs von Balthasar," *Modern Theology* 14, no. 3 (July 1998): 385.

47. Balthasar, *Dramatis Personae: The Person in Christ*, 287.

48. In Balthasar's theology, Gardner and Moss hold, woman is "chronologically, temporally, historically, accidentally second" (Gardner and Moss, "Something Like Time," 86).

49. For an excellent introduction to the influence of Henri de Lubac on the prominence of *ressourcement* in Balthasar's theology, see Kevin Mongrain, *The Systematic Thought of Hans Urs von Balthasar: An Irenaean Retrieval* (New York: Crossroad, 2002).

4. Feminist Theology

1. Daphne Hampson, *After Christianity* (Valley Forge, PA: Trinity Press International, 1996), 116.

2. Rosemary Radford Ruether, *Sexism and God-Talk: Toward a Feminist Theology* (Boston: Beacon Press, 1993), 13.

3. Mary Ann Hinsdale, "Heeding the Voices: A Historical Overview," in *In the Embrace of God: Feminist Approaches to Theological Anthropology*, ed. Ann O'Hara Graff (Maryknoll, NY: Orbis Books, 1995), 23.

4. Valerie Saiving, "The Human Situation: A Feminine View," in *The Journal of Religion* (April 1960).

5. Elizabeth A. Johnson, *She Who Is: The Mystery of God in Feminist Theological Discourse* (New York: Crossroad, 1997), 29. In another work Johnson uses a fourfold method of ideological suspicion; historical reconstruction; ethical assessment of texts; and hermeneutics of suspicion, of remembrance, of proclamation, and of

celebration. See Elizabeth A. Johnson, *Friends of God and Prophets: A Feminist Theological Reading of the Communion of Saints* (New York: Continuum, 1998), 160–61.

6. Elisabeth Schüssler Fiorenza, "Breaking the Silence—Becoming Visible," in *The Power of Naming: A* Concilium *Reader in Feminist Liberation Theology,* ed. Elisabeth Schüsser Fiorenza (Maryknoll, NY: Orbis Books, 1996), 168.

7. Ibid., 171.

8. Elisabeth Schüssler Fiorenza, *Bread Not Stone: The Challenge of Feminist Biblical Interpretation* (Boston: Beacon press, 1995), x.

9. Ibid., xiv.

10. Ruether, *Sexism and God-Talk,* 18.

11. Johnson, *She Who Is,* 30.

12. Anne M. Clifford, *Introducing Feminist Theology* (Maryknoll, NY: Orbis Books, 2001), 25.

13. Stephanie Y. Mitchem, *Introducing Womanist Theology* (Maryknoll, NY: Orbis Books, 2002), 4.

14. Jacquelyn Grant, "Womanist Theology: Black Women's Experience as a Source for Doing Theology, with Special Reference to Christology," in *Black Theology: A Documentary History*, vol. 2, *1980–1992,* ed. James H. Cone and Gayraud S. Wilmore (Maryknoll, NY: Orbis Books, 1993), 278. As echoed by Mitchem "Simply put, womanist theology is the systematic, faith-based exploration of the many facets of African American women's religiosity. Womanist theology is based on the complex realities of black women's lives. Womanist scholars recognize and name the imagination and initiative that African American women have utilized in developing sophisticated religious responses to their lives." Mitchem, *Introducing Womanist Theology,* ix.

15. Ada María Isasi-Díaz, "Introduction," in *Mujerista Theology: A Theology for the Twenty-First Century* (Maryknoll, NY: Orbis Books, 1996), 1.

16. Ada María Isasi-Díaz, *En la Lucha/In the Struggle: Elaborating a Mujerista Theology* (Minneapolis, MN: Fortress Press, 1993), 4.

17. Ada María Isasi-Díaz, "*Mujeristas*: A Name of Our Own," in *The Future of Liberation Theology: Essays in Honor of Gustavo Gutiérrez,* ed. Marc H. Ellis and Otto Maduro (Maryknoll, NY: Orbis Books, 1989), 410.

18. Aquino argues that feminism is indigenous to Latin Americans. Ignoring this reality erases the struggles of women against

sexism and patriarchy. To those who call themselves *mujeristas*, Aquino writes, "With these views, not only do they show their ignorance regarding the feminist tradition within Latin American communities, but they also attempt to remove from us our authority to name ourselves according to our own historical roots" (María Pilar Aquino, "Latin American Feminist Theology," *Journal of Feminist Studies in Religion* 14 [Spring 1998]: 94).

19. Kwok Pui-lan, *Introducing Asian Feminist Theology* (Cleveland, OH: The Pilgrim Press, 2000), 9.

20. Serene Jones, *Feminist Theory and Christian Theology: Cartographies of Grace* (Minneapolis, MN: Fortress Press, 2000), 3.

21. See Seyla Benhabib, *Situating the Self: Gender, Community, and Postmodernism in Contemporary Ethics* (New York: Routledge, 1992); Judith Butler, *Gender Trouble: Feminism and the Subversion of Identity* (New York: Routledge, 1990); Lorraine Code, *What Can She Know? Feminist Theory and the Construction of Knowledge* (Ithaca, NY: Cornell University Press, 1991); Linda Nicholson, ed., *Feminism and Postmodernism* (New York: Routledge, 1990); Elizabeth V. Spelman, *Inessential Woman: Problems of Exclusion in Feminist Thought* (Boston: Beacon Press, 1988).

22. Rebecca S. Chopp, "Feminist Queries and Metaphysical Musings," *Modern Theology* 11, no. 1 (January 1995): 47.

23. Ibid., 53.

24. Ibid., 56.

25. Simone de Beauvoir, *The Second Sex* (New York: Vintage Books, 1989), 267.

26. Gender essentialism is the belief that there are certain qualities that are essentially or a priori natural to men and women.

27. Sheila Briggs, "A History of Our Own; What Would a Feminist History of Theology Look Like?" in *Horizons in Feminist Theology: Identity, Tradition, and Norms*, ed. Rebecca Chopp and Sheila Greeve Davaney (Minneapolis, MN: Fortress Press, 1997), 167.

28. Anne E. Carr, "A New Vision of Feminist Theology," in *Freeing Theology: The Essentials of Theology in Feminist Perspective*, ed. Catherine Mowry LaCugna (San Francisco: HarperSanFrancisco, 1993), 21.

29. Elisabeth Schüssler Fiorenza, *Jesus: Miriam's Child, Sophia's Prophet: Critical Issues in Feminist Christology* (New York: Continuum, 1995), 24.

30. Johnson, *Friends of God and Prophets*, 39.

31. María C. Lugones, "On the Logic of Pluralist Feminism," in *Feminist Ethics*, ed. Claudia Card (Lawrence: University Press of Kansas, 1991), 35–44.

32. Ibid., 40.

33. Ada María Isasi-Díaz, "Doing Theology as Mission," *Apuntes* 18, no. 4 (Winter 1998): 105.

34. bell hooks, "Postmodern Blackness," in *Yearning: Race, Gender, and Cultural Products* (Boston: South End Press, 1990), 25.

35. Susan Secker, "Women's Experience in Feminist Theology: The 'Problem' or the 'Truth' of Difference," *Journal of Hispanic/Latino Theology* 1, no. 1 (1993): 56–67, and Jeanette Rodríguez, "Experience as a Resource for Feminist Thought," *Journal of Hispanic/Latino Theology* 1, no. 1 (1993): 68–76.

36. Secker, "Women's Experience in Feminist Theology," 65.

37. Rodríguez, "Experience as a Resource for Feminist Thought," 75.

38. Mary McClintock Fulkerson, *Changing the Subject: Women's Discourses and Feminist Theology* (Minneapolis, MN: Fortress Press, 1994), vii.

39. Serene Jones, "Feminist Theology between a Rock and a Hard Place: Feminist, Womanist, and *Mujerista* Theologies in North America," in Chopp and Greeve Davaney, *Horizons in Feminist Theology*, 33–53.

40. Ibid., 34.

41. Jones, *Feminist Theory and Christian Theology*, 23.

42. Ibid., 25.

43. Ibid., 27.

44. Ibid., 32.

45. Ibid., 44.

46. Linell Elizabeth Cady, "Identity, Feminist Theory, and Theology," in Chopp and Greeve Davaney, *Horizons in Feminist Theology*, 24.

47. Ivone Gebara, *Out of the Depths: Women's Experience of Evil and Salvation* (Minneapolis, MN: Fortress Press, 2002), 62–66.

48. Sheila Greeve Davaney, "Continuing the Story, but Departing the Text: A Historicist Interpretation of Feminist Norms in Theology," in Chopp and Greeve Davaney, *Horizons in Feminist Theology*, 212.

49. Spelman, *Inessential Woman*, 13.

50. Rebecca S. Chopp, "Feminist and Womanist Theologies," in *The Modern Theologians*, ed. David F. Ford (New York: Blackwell, 1997), 392.

5. Feminist Theological Anthropology

1. Mary Aquin O'Neill, "Toward a Renewed Anthropology," *Theological Studies* 36 (1975): 725–36.

2. Donna Teevan, "Challenges in the Role of Theological Anthropology in Feminist Theologies," *Theological Studies* 64 (2003): 584.

3. Ibid., 585.

4. Mary Ann Hinsdale, "Heeding the Voices: A Historical Overview," in *In the Embrace of God: Feminist Approaches to Theological Anthropology*, ed. Ann O'Hara Graff (Maryknoll, NY: Orbis Books, 1995), 27.

5. Ibid., 28.

6. Elizabeth A. Johnson, "The Maleness of Christ," in *The Special Nature of Women? Concilium* (1991/6), ed. Anne E. Carr and Elisabeth Schüssler Fiorenza, 111, cited in ibid., 29.

7. Daphne Hampson, *After Christianity* (Valley Forge, PA: Trinity Press International, 1996), 192.

8. Mary Catherine Hilkert, "Cry Beloved Image: Rethinking the Image of God," in O'Hara Graff, *In the Embrace of God*, 199.

9. Mary Aquin O'Neill, "The Mystery of Being Human Together," in *Freeing Theology: The Essentials of Theology in Feminist Perspective*, ed. Catherine Mowry LaCugna (San Francisco: HarperSanFrancisco, 1993), 149.

10. Anne E. Carr, *Transforming Grace: Christian Tradition and Women's Experience* (New York: Continuum, 1996), 123; see O'Neill, "Toward a Renewed Anthropology," 725–36.

11. Rosemary R. Ruether, *Sexism and God-Talk: Toward a Feminist Theology* (Boston: Beacon Press, 1993), 93–115.

12. Ibid., 94.

13. Ibid., 112.

14. Prudence Allen, "Integral Sex Complementarity and the Theology of Communion," *Communio* 17 (Winter 1990): 523–44.

15. Ibid., 540.

16. Lisa Sowle Cahill, *Between the Sexes: Foundations for a Christian Ethics of Sexuality* (Philadelphia: Fortress Press, 1985), 99–100.

17. Elsa Tamez, "Introduction: The Power of the Naked," in *Through Her Eyes: Women's Theology from Latin America*, ed. Elsa Tamez (Maryknoll, NY: Orbis Books, 1989), 4.

18. María Pilar Aquino, *Our Cry for Life: Feminist Theology from Latin America* (Maryknoll, NY: Orbis Books, 1993).

19. Ibid., 3.

20. "This is not just a change of language, but also a change in liberation theology's *epistemological horizon*" (ibid., 109).

21. Ibid., 39.

22. Ibid., 111.

23. Ivone Gebara and María Clara Bingemer, *Mary, Mother of God, Mother of the Poor* (Maryknoll, NY: Orbis Books, 1989), 5. A multidimensional vision of the human is also fundamental for Ivone Gebara and María Clara Bingemer's anthropology, one that is human-centered, unifying, realist, and multidimensional. A human-centered anthropology does not privilege male over female. A unifying anthropology dismantles the dualism between material and spiritual, affirming the unity of the human. Concrete history is the starting point of an idealist anthropology. An understanding of the human in all of his or her dimensions is the foundation of a multidimensional anthropology.

24. Catherine Mowry LaCugna, *God for Us: The Trinity and Christian Life* (San Francisco: HarperSanFrancisco, 1993), 246.

25. Ibid., 288–92.

26. Nancy Dallavalle, "Neither Idolatry nor Iconoclasm: A Critical Essentialism for Catholic Feminist Theology," *Horizons* 25, no. 1 (1998): 27.

27. Ann O'Hara Graff, "Strategies for Life: Learning from Feminist Psychology," in *In the Embrace of God*, 123.

28. Ibid., 131–32.

29. Hilkert, "Cry Beloved Image," 199.

30. Ibid., 200.

31. Ada María Isasi-Díaz, "Elements of a *Mujerista* Anthropology," in *Mujerista Theology: A Theology for the Twenty-First Century* (Maryknoll, NY: Orbis Books, 1996), 129.

32. Ibid.

33. Ibid., 143.

34. Mary Ann Zimmer, "Stepping Stones in Feminist Theory," in O'Hara Graff, *In the Embrace of God*, 17. For an excellent study of

the relationship between embodiment and holiness within historical Christianity, see Peter Brown, *The Body and Society: Men, Women, and Sexual Renunciation in Early Christianity* (New York: Columbia University Press, 1988).

35. Lisa Sowle Cahill, *Sex, Gender, and Christian Ethics* (Cambridge: Cambridge University Press, 1996), 84.

36. Stephanie Y. Mitchem, *Introducing Womanist Theology* (Maryknoll, NY: Orbis Books, 2002), 35.

37. Mercy Amba Oduyoye, *Introducing African Women's Theology* (Cleveland, OH: The Pilgrim Press, 2001), 70.

38. Ivone Gebara, *Teología a ritmo de mujer* (Mexico City: Ediciones Dabar, 1995), 106.

39. Susan A. Ross, *Extravagant Affections: A Feminist Sacramental Theology* (New York: Continuum, 1998), 102–3.

40. O'Neill, "The Mystery of Being Human Together," 140.

41. Elisabeth Gössmann, "The Construction of Women's Difference," in *The Power of Naming: A* Concilium *Reader in Feminist Liberation Theology*, ed. Elisabeth Schüssler Fiorenza (Maryknoll, NY: Orbis Books, 1996), 199.

42. Delores S. Williams, "A Womanist Perspective on Sin," in *A Troubling in My Soul: Womanist Perspectives on Evil and Suffering*, ed. Emilie M. Townes (Maryknoll, NY: Orbis Books, 1993), 146.

43. Cheryl A. Kirk-Duggan, "African-American Spirituals: Confronting and Exorcising Evil through Song," in *A Troubling in My Soul*, 164.

44. Oduyoye, *Introducing African Women's Theology*, 76.

45. Ruether, *Sexism and God-Talk*.

46. Anne M. Clifford, "When Being Human Becomes Truly Earthly: An Ecofeminist Proposal for Solidarity," in O'Hara Graff, *In the Embrace of God*, 173–89.

47. Hilkert, "Cry Beloved Image," 194.

48. Ibid., 196.

49. Mary McClintock Fulkerson, "Contesting the Gendered Subject: A Feminist Account of the *Imago Dei*," in *Horizons in Feminist Theology: Identity, Tradition, and Norms*, ed. Rebecca Chopp and Sheila Greeve Davaney (Minneapolis, MN: Fortress Press, 1997), 107.

50. Ibid., 108.

51. Ibid., 114.

52. Chung Hyun Kyung, "To Be Human Is to Be Created in God's Image," in *Feminist Theology from the Third World: A Reader*, ed. Ursula King (Maryknoll, NY: Orbis Books, 1996), 252.

53. Chung, *Struggle to Be the Sun Again: Introducing Asian Women's Theology* (Maryknoll, NY: Orbis Books, 1990), 39.

54. Elizabeth A. Johnson, *She Who Is: The Mystery of God in Feminist Theological Discourse* (New York: Crossroad, 1997), 71.

55. Ibid., 75.

56. Ibid., 243.

6. Our Trinitarian *Imago Dei*

1. Ann O'Hara Graff, "Introduction," in *In the Embrace of God: Feminist Approaches to Theological Anthropology*, ed. Ann O'Hara Graff (Maryknoll, NY: Orbis Books, 1995), 1.

2. Stephanie Y. Mitchem, *Introducing Womanist Theology* (Maryknoll, NY: Orbis Books, 2002), ix.

3. María Lugones, "Structure/Antistructure and Agency under Oppression," *Journal of Philosophy* 81 (1990): 503.

4. María Lugones, "Playfulness, 'World'-Traveling, and Loving Perception," in *Making Face, Making Soul—Haciendo Caras*, ed. Gloria Anzaldúa (San Francisco: An Aunt Lutte Foundation Book, 1990), 399.

5. Ibid., 401.

6. Iris Marion Young, "Gender as Seriality: Thinking about Women as a Social Collective," in *Intersecting Voices: Dilemmas of Gender, Political Philosophy, and Policy*, ed. Iris Marion Young (Princeton, NJ: Princeton University Press, 1997), 12.

7. Ibid., 17.

8. Ibid., 27. "*Woman* is a serial collective defined neither by any common identity nor by a common set of attributes that all the individuals in the series have, but rather names a set of structural constraints and relations to practical inert objects that condition action and its meaning" (36).

9. Ibid., 23.

10. Ibid., 33.

11. Rosemary Radford Ruether, *Introducing Redemption in Christian Feminism* (Sheffield, England: Sheffield Academic Press, 1998), 65.

12. Susan A. Ross, *Extravagant Affections: A Feminist Sacramental Theology* (New York: Continuum, 1998), 59.

13. Margaret Farley, "New Patterns of Relationship," *Theological Studies* 36 (1975): 633.

14. Nancy Dallavalle, "Neither Idolatry nor Iconoclasm: A Critical Essentialism for Catholic Feminist Theology," *Horizons* 25, no. 1 (1998): 23–42.

15. Ibid., 37.

16. Ibid., 23.

17. Ibid., 30.

18. Ibid., 37.

19. Lisa Sowle Cahill, *Sex, Gender, and Christian Ethics* (Cambridge: Cambridge University Press, 1996), 1–2.

20. Ibid., 73.

21. Ibid., 82.

22. Ibid., 87.

23. Eleazar S. Fernandez, *Reimagining the Human: Theological Anthropology in Response to Systematic Evil* (St. Louis: Chalice Press, 2004), 123.

24. Farley, "New Patterns of Relationship," 640.

25. Rosemary Radford Ruether, "Feminist Theology and Spirituality," in *Christian Feminism: Visions of a New Humanity*, ed. Judith L. Weidman (San Francisco: Harper and Row, 1984), 16.

26. Anne M. Clifford, *Introducing Feminist Theology* (Maryknoll, NY: Orbis Books, 2001), 95.

27. See James H. Cone, *A Black Theology of Liberation*, 20th anniv. ed. (Maryknoll, NY: Orbis Books, 1994), chap. 4.

28. Clifford, *Introducing Feminist Theology*, 223.

29. Sallie McFague, "Cosmology and Christianity: Implications of the Common Creation Story for Theology," in *Theology at the End of Modernity: Essays in Honor of Gordon D. Kaufman*, ed. Sheila Greeve Davaney (Philadelphia: Trinity Press International, 1991), 37.

30. Sallie McFague, *The Body of God: An Ecological Theology* (Minneapolis, MN: Fortress Press, 1993), 106.

31. Rosemary Radford Ruether, *Gaia and God: An Ecofeminist Theology of Earth Healing* (San Francisco: HarperCollins, 1992), 19–22.

32. Clifford, *Introducing Feminist Theology*, 241. While Clifford interprets Ruether's model as a step in the right direction, she still

finds its anthropomorphic emphasis to be contrary to eco-feminism's core claims.

33. Elizabeth A. Johnson, *She Who Is: The Mystery of God in Feminist Theological Discourse* (New York: Crossroad, 1997), 75.

34. Ibid., 73.

35. Rosemary Radford Ruether, *Sexism and God-Talk: Toward a Feminist Theology* (Boston: Beacon Press, 1993), chap. 6.

36. Jacquelyn Grant, "Womanist Theology: Black Women's Experience as a Source for Doing Theology, with Special Reference to Christology," in *Black Theology: A Documentary History*, vol. 2, *1980–1992*, ed. James H. Cone and Gayraud S. Wilmore (Maryknoll, NY: Orbis Books, 1993), 286.

37. Ruether, *Introducing Redemption in Christian Feminism*, 85.

38. Elizabeth A. Johnson, *Consider Jesus: Waves of Renewal in Christology* (New York: Crossroad, 1997), 104–7.

39. Thérèse Souga, "The Christ-Event from the Viewpoint of African Women: A Catholic Perspective," in *With Passion and Compassion: Third World Women Doing Theology*, ed. Virginia Fabella and Mercy Amba Oduyoye (Maryknoll, NY: Orbis Books, 1994), 29.

40. Delores S. Williams, *Sisters in the Wilderness: The Challenge of Womanist God-Talk* (Maryknoll, NY: Orbis Books, 1993), 162.

41. Ibid., 166.

42. Sarah Coakley, "Kenosis and Subversion: On the Repression of 'Vulnerability' in Christian Feminist Thinking," in *Swallowing the Fishbone: Feminist Theologies Debate Christianity*, ed. Daphne Hampson (London: SPCK, 1996), 107.

43. Ibid., 108.

44. Ruether, *Introducing Redemption in Christian Feminism*, 87.

45. Johnson, *Consider Jesus*, 108–11.

46. Johnson, *She Who Is*, 72.

47. Ada María Isasi-Díaz, "Christ in *Mujerista* Theology," in *Thinking of Christ: Proclamation, Explanation, Meaning*, ed. Tatha Wiley (New York: Continuum, 2003), 162.

48. Sallie McFague, *Models of God: Theology for an Ecological, Nuclear Age* (Philadelphia: Fortress Press, 1987), 136.

49. Catherine Mowry LaCugna, "God in Communion with Us: The Trinity," in *Freeing Theology: The Essentials of Theology in Feminist Perspective*, ed. Catherine Mowry LaCugna (San Francisco: HarperSanFrancisco, 1993), 99.

50. Fernandez, *Reimagining the Human*, 187.

51. LaCugna, "God in Communion with Us," 84–85.

52. María Clara Bingemer, "Reflection on the Trinity," in *Through Her Eyes; Women's Theology from Latin America*, ed. Elsa Tamez (Maryknoll, NY: Orbis Books, 1989), 58.

53. Ibid., 79.

54. Catherine Mowry LaCugna, *God for Us: The Trinity and Christian Life* (San Francisco: HarperSanFrancisco, 1993), 93.

55. Ibid., 103.

56. Ibid., 243.

57. Ibid., 250.

58. Ross, *Extravagant Affections*, 49–50.

59. Leonardo Boff, *Holy Trinity, Perfect Community* (Maryknoll, NY: Orbis Books, 2000), 118.

60. Serene Jones, *Feminist Theory and Christian Theology: Cartographies of Grace* (Minneapolis, MN: Fortress Press, 2000), 129.

Conclusion

1. Eleazar S. Fernandez, *Reimagining the Human: Theological Anthropology in Response to Systematic Evil* (St. Louis: Chalice Press, 2004), 114.

2. Catherine Mowry LaCugna, "The Trinitarian Mystery of God," in *Systematic Theology: Roman Catholic Perspectives*, vol. 1, ed. Francis Schüssler Fiorenza and John P. Galvin (Minneapolis, MN: Fortress Press, 1991), 181.

3. Ada María Isasi-Díaz, "*Identifícate con Nosotras*: A *Mujerista* Christological Understanding," in *La Lucha Continues: Mujerista Theology*, ed. Ada María Isasi-Díaz (Maryknoll, NY: Orbis Books, 2004), 247.

4. María Clara Bingemer, "Reflection on the Trinity," in *Through Her Eyes; Women's Theology from Latin America*, ed. Elsa Tamez (Maryknoll, NY: Orbis Books, 1989), 58.

5. Elizabeth A. Johnson, *Truly Our Sister: A Theology of Mary in the Communion of Saints* (New York: Continuum, 2003), 28.

6. Susan A. Ross, *Extravagant Affections: A Feminist Sacramental Theology* (New York: Continuum, 1998), 46.

7. Anne M. Clifford, "Creation," in Schüssler Fiorenza and Galvin, *Systematic Theology*, 1:195.

8. Margaret Farley, "New Patterns of Relationship," *Theological Studies* 36 (1975): 632.

9. M. Shawn Copeland, "Wading through Many Sorrows: Toward a Theology of Suffering in Womanist Perspective," in *A Troubling in My Soul: Womanist Perspectives on Evil and Suffering*, ed. Emilie M. Townes (Maryknoll, NY: Orbis Books, 1993), 124.

10. Nancy Dallavalle, "Toward a Theology That Is Catholic and Feminist: Some Basic Issues," *Modern Theology* 14, no. 4 (October 1998): 535–36.

11. Ibid., 537.

12. Marcella María Althaus-Reid, "Gustavo Gutiérrez Goes to Disneyland: Theme Park Theologies and the Diaspora of the Discourse of the Popular Theologian in Liberation Theology," in *Interpreting beyond Borders*, ed. Fernando F. Segovia (England: Sheffield Academic Press, 2000), 42.

13. Elizabeth A. Johnson, *Friends of God and Prophets: A Feminist Theological Reading of the Communion of Saints* (New York: Continuum, 1998), 35.

14. Dallavalle, "Toward a Theology That Is Catholic and Feminist," 542.

15. LaCugna, "The Trinitarian Mystery of God," 188.

Bibliography

Allen, Prudence, RSM. *The Concept of Woman*. Vol. 1, *The Aristotelian Revolution, 750 B.C.–A.D. 1250*. Montreal: Eden, 1985; Grand Rapids, MI: Eerdmans, 1997.

———. *The Concept of Woman*. Vol. 2, *The Early Humanist Reformation, 1250–1500*. Grand Rapids, MI: Eerdmans, 2002.

———. "Integral Sex Complementarity and the Theology of Communion." *Communio* 17 (Winter 1990): 523–44.

Althaus-Reid, Marcella María. "Gustavo Gutiérrez Goes to Disneyland: Theme Park Theologies and the Diaspora of the Discourse of the Popular Theologian in Liberation Theology." In *Interpreting beyond Borders*, ed. Fernando F. Segovia, 36–58. England: Sheffield Academic Press, 2000.

Aquinas, Thomas. *The Disputed Questions on Truth*. In *Truth,* vol. 2, *Questions X–XX*. Translated by James V. McGlynn, SJ. Chicago: Henry Regnery Company, 1953.

———. *Summa Theologiae*. In *Basic Writings of Saint Thomas Aquinas*, ed. Anton C. Pegis. New York: Random House, 1945.

———. "Toward a Renewed Anthropology." *Theological Studies* 36 (1975): 725–36.

Aquino, María Pilar. "Latin American Feminist Theology." *Journal of Feminist Studies in Religion* 14 (Spring 1998): 89–107.

———. *Our Cry for Life: Feminist Theology from Latin America*. Maryknoll, NY: Orbis Books, 1993.

Aristotle. *On the Generation of Animals*, trans. and ed. A. L. Peck. Cambridge, MA: Harvard University Press, 1943.

Augustine, *The Literal Meaning of Genesis*. Vol. 1, *Books 1–6*. Translated by John Hammond Taylor, SJ. New York: Paulist Press, 1982.

———. *The Literal Meaning of Genesis*. Vol. 2, *Books 7–12*. Translated by John Hammond Taylor, SJ. New York: Paulist Press, 1982.

———. *On the Literal Interpretation of Genesis: An Unfinished Book.* Translated by Roland J. Teske, SJ. Washington, DC: The Catholic University of America Press, 1991.

———. *The Trinity.* In *Augustine: Later Works*, ed. John Burnaby. Philadelphia: Westminster Press, 1955.

Balthasar, Hans Urs von. *The Christian State of Life.* San Francisco: Ignatius Press, 1983.

———. *My Work: In Retrospect.* San Francisco: Ignatius Press, 1993.

———. *Theo-Drama: Theological Dramatic Theory.* Vol. 2, *Dramatis Personae: Man in God.* Translated by Graham Harrison. San Francisco: Ignatius Press, 1990.

———. *Theo-Drama: Theological Dramatic Theory.* Vol. 3, *Dramatis Personae: The Person in Chris.* Translated by Graham Harrison. San Francisco: Ignatius Press, 1992.

Barth, Karl. *Church Dogmatics.* Vol. III/1–4, *The Doctrine of Creation.* Edinburgh: T & T Clark, 1956.

———. *Church Dogmatics: A Selection.* Translated by Helmut Gollwitzer. Louisville, KY: Westminster John Knox Press, 1994.

———. *Karl Barth: Theologian of Freedom.* Edited by Clifford Green. Minneapolis, MN: Fortress Press, 1991.

Battersby, Christine. *The Phenomenal Woman: Feminist Metaphysics and the Patterns of Identity.* New York: Routledge, 1998.

Beauvoir, Simone de. *The Second Sex.* New York: Vintage Books, 1989.

Benhabib, Seyla. *Situating the Self: Gender, Community, and Postmodernism in Contemporary Ethics.* New York: Routledge, 1992.

Bingemer, María Clara. "Reflection on the Trinity." In *Through Her Eyes; Women's Theology from Latin America*, ed. Elsa Tamez, 56–80. Maryknoll, NY: Orbis Books, 1989.

Bird, Phyllis A. "Sexual Differentiation and Divine Image in the Genesis Creation Texts." In *The Image of God: Gender Models in Judaeo-Christian Tradition*, ed. Kari Elisabeth Børreson, 6–28. Minneapolis, MN: Fortress Press, 1991.

Bledstein, Adrien Janis. "The Genesis of Humans: The Garden of Eden Revisited." *Judaism* 26 (1977).

Boff, Leonardo. *Holy Trinity, Perfect Community.* Maryknoll, NY: Orbis Books, 2000.

Børreson, Kari Elisabeth. "God's Image, Man's Image? Patristic Inter-pretation of Gen. 1,27 and 1Cor. 11,7." In *The Image of God: Gender Models in Judaeo-Christian Tradition*, ed. Kari Elisabeth Børreson, 187–209. Minneapolis, MN: Fortress Press, 1991.

———. *Subordination and Equivalence: The Nature and Role of Woman in Augustine and Thomas Aquinas*. Oslo: Univer-sitetsforlaget, 1968; Kampen: Kok Pharos Publishing House, 1995.

Briggs, Sheila. "A History of Our Own; What Would a Feminist His-tory of Theology Look Like?" In *Horizons in Feminist The-ology: Identity, Tradition, and Norms*, ed. Rebecca Chopp and Sheila Greeve Davaney, 165–78. Minneapolis, MN: Fortress Press, 1997.

Brown, Peter. *The Body and Society: Men, Women, and Sexual Renun-ciation in Early Christianity*. New York: Columbia University Press, 1988.

Butler, Judith. *Gender Trouble: Feminism and the Subversion of Iden-tity*. New York: Routledge, 1990.

Cady, Linell Elizabeth. "Identity, Feminist Theory, and Theology." In *Horizons in Feminist Theology: Identity, Tradition, and Norms*, ed. Rebecca Chopp and Sheila Greeve Davaney, 17–32. Minneapolis, MN: Fortress Press, 1997.

Cahill, Lisa Sowle. *Between the Sexes: Foundations for a Christian Ethics of Sexuality*. Philadelphia: Fortress Press, 1985.

———. *Sex, Gender, and Christian Ethics*. Cambridge: Cambridge University Press, 1996.

Camelot, P. Th. "La Théologie de L'Image de Dieu." *Revue des Sci-ences Philosophiques et Théologiques* 40 (1956): 443–71.

Cannon, Katie Geneva. *Katie's Cannon: Womanism and the Soul of the Black Community*. New York: Continuum, 1996.

Carr, Anne E. "The New Vision of Feminist Theology: Method." In *Freeing Theology: The Essentials of Theology in Feminist Perspective*, ed. Catherine Mowry LaCugna, 1–29. San Fran-cisco: HarperSanFrancisco, 1993.

———. *Transforming Grace: Christian Tradition and Women's Expe-rience*. New York: Continuum, 1996.

Catholic Theological Society of America. *Research Report: Women in Church and Society*, ed. Sara Butler. Mahwah, NJ: Darlington Seminary, 1978.

Chopp, Rebecca S. "Feminist and Womanist Theologies." In *The Modern Theologians*, ed. David F. Ford, 389–404. New York: Blackwell, 1997.

———. "Feminist Queries and Metaphysical Musings." *Modern Theology* 11, no. 1 (January 1995): 47–63.

Chung Hyun Kyung. *Struggle to Be the Sun Again: Introducing Asian Women's Theology*. Maryknoll, NY: Orbis Books, 1990.

———. "To Be Human Is to Be Created in God's Image." In *Feminist Theology from the Third World: A Reader*, ed. Ursula King, 251–58. Maryknoll, NY: Orbis Books, 1996.

Clack, Beverly, ed. *Misogyny in the Western Philosophical Tradition: A Reader*. New York: Routledge, 1999.

Clifford, Anne M. "Creation." In *Systematic Theology: Roman Catholic Perspectives*, vol. 1, ed. Francis Schüssler Fiorenza and John P. Galvin, 192–248. Minneapolis, MN: Fortress Press, 1991.

———. *Introducing Feminist Theology*. Maryknoll, NY: Orbis Books, 2001.

———. "When Being Human Becomes Truly Earthly: An Ecofeminist Proposal for Solidarity." In *In the Embrace of God: Feminist Approaches to Theological Anthropology*, ed. Ann O'Hara Graff, 173–89. Maryknoll, NY: Orbis Books, 1995.

Coakley, Sarah. "Kenosis and Subversion: On the Repression of 'Vulnerability' in Christian Feminist Thinking." In *Swallowing the Fishbone: Feminist Theologies Debate Christianity*, ed. Daphne Hampson. London: SPCK, 1996.

Code, Lorraine. *What Can She Know? Feminist Theory and the Construction of Knowledge*. Ithaca, NY: Cornell University Press, 1991.

Cone, James H. *A Black Theology of Liberation*. 20th anniv. ed. Maryknoll, NY: Orbis Books, 1994.

Copeland, M. Shawn. "Wading through Many Sorrows: Toward a Theology of Suffering in Womanist Perspective," In *A Troubling in My Soul: Womanist Perspectives on Evil and Suffering*, ed. Emilie M. Townes, 109–29. Maryknoll, NY: Orbis Books, 1993.

Dallavalle, Nancy. "Neither Idolatry nor Iconoclasm: A Critical Essentialism for Catholic Feminist Theology." *Horizons* 25, no. 1 (1998): 23–42.

————. "Toward a Theology That Is Catholic and Feminist: Some Basic Issues." *Modern Theology* 14, no. 4 (October 1998): 535–53.

Dempsey Douglass, Jane. "The Image of God in Woman as Seen by Luther and Calvin." In *The Image of God: Gender Models in Judaeo-Christian Tradition*, ed. Kari Elisabeth Børreson, 236–66. Minneapolis, MN: Fortress Press, 1991.

Derksen, L. D. *Dialogues on Women: Images of Women in the History of Philosophy*. Amsterdam: VU University Press, 1996.

Díaz, Miguel H. *On Being Human: U.S. Hispanic and Rahnerian Perspectives*. Maryknoll, NY: Orbis Books, 2001.

Di Noia, J. A. "Karl Rahner." In *The Modern Theologians*, ed. David F. Ford, 118–33. New York: Blackwell, 1997.

Donovan, Mary Ann. "Alive to the Glory of the Lord: A Key Insight in St. Irenaeus." *Theological Studies* 49:2 (1988): 283–97.

————. *One Right Reading? A Guide to Irenaeus*. Collegeville, MN: The Liturgical Press, 1997.

Dupré, Louis. *Passage to Modernity: An Essay in the Hermeneutics of Nature and Culture*. New Haven, CT: Yale University Press, 1993.

Dych, William V. *Karl Rahner*. Collegeville, MN: The Liturgical Press, 1992.

Erhueh, Anthony O. *Vatican II: Image of God in Man*. Rome: Pontificia Universitas Urbania, 1987.

Espín, Orlando O. "Tradition and Popular Religion: An Understanding of the *Sensus Fidelium*." In *The Faith of the People: Theological Reflections on Popular Catholicism*, 63–90. Maryknoll, NY: Orbis Books, 1997.

Fantino, Jacques. *L'homme Image de Dieu chez Saint Irénée de Lyon*. Paris: Éditions du Cerf, 1986.

Farley, Margaret. "New Patterns of Relationship." *Theological Studies* 36 (1975): 627–46.

Fatum, Lone. "Image of God and the Glory of Man: Women in the Pauline Congregations." In *The Image of God: Gender Models in Judaeo-Christian Tradition*, ed. Kari Elisabeth Børreson, 50–133. Minneapolis, MN: Fortress Press, 1991.

Fernandez, Eleazar S. *Reimagining the Human: Theological Anthropology in Response to Systematic Evil*. St. Louis: Chalice Press, 2004.

Fiorenza, Francis Schüssler. "Systematic Theology: Task and Methods." In *Systematic Theology: Roman Catholic Perspectives*, vol. 1, ed. Francis Schüssler Fiorenza and John P. Galvin, 3–87. Minneapolis, MN: Fortress Press, 1991.

Gardner, Lucy, and David Moss. "Something Like Time; Something Like the Sexes—An Essay in Reception." In *Balthasar at the End of Modernity*, ed. Lucy Gardner, David Moss, Ben Quash, and Graham Ward. Edinburgh: T & T Clark, 1999.

Gardner, Lucy, David Moss, Ben Quash, Graham Ward, eds. *Balthasar at the End of Modernity*. Edinburgh: T & T Clark, 1999.

Gebara, Ivone. *Longing for Running Water: Ecofeminism and Liberation*. Minneapolis, MN: Fortress Press, 1999.

———. *Out of the Depths: Women's Experience of Evil and Salvation*. Minneapolis, MN: Fortress Press, 2002.

———. *Teología a ritmo de mujer*. Mexico City: Ediciones Dabar, 1995.

Gebara, Ivone, and María Clara Bingemer. *Mary, Mother of God, Mother of the Poor*. Maryknoll, NY: Orbis Books, 1989.

Gonzalez, Michelle A. "*Nuestra Humanidad*: Toward a Latina Theological Anthropology." *Journal of Hispanic/Latino Theology* 8:3 (February 2001): 49–72.

Gössmann, Elisabeth. "The Construction of Women's Difference." In *The Power of Naming: A* Concilium *Reader in Feminist Liberation Theology*, ed. Elisabeth Schüssler Fiorenza, 198–207. Maryknoll, NY: Orbis Books, 1996.

Grant, Jacquelyn. "Womanist Theology: Black Women's Experience as a Source for Doing Theology, with Special Reference to Christology." In *Black Theology: A Documentary History*. Vol. 2, *1980–1992*, ed. James H. Cone and Gayraud S. Wilmore, 273–89. Maryknoll, NY: Orbis Books, 1993.

Green, Clifford. "Introduction: Karl Barth's Life and Theology." In *Karl Barth: Theologian of Freedom*, ed. Clifford Green. Minneapolis, MN: Fortress Press, 1991.

Gregory of Nyssa. *On the Making of Man* and *On Virginity*. In *A Select Library of Nicene and Post-Nicene Fathers of the Christian Church*, second series, ed. Philip Schaff and Henry Wace. Vol. 5, *Gregory of Nyssa: Dogmatic Treatises, Etc.* New York: The Christian Literature Company, 1893.

Greeve Davaney, Sheila. "Continuing the Story, but Departing the Text: A Historicist Interpretation of Feminist Norms in Theology." In *Horizons in Feminist Theology: Identity, Tradition, and Norms*, ed. Rebecca Chopp and Sheila Greeve Davaney, 198–214. Minneapolis, MN: Fortress Press, 1997.

Gutiérrez, Gustavo. *A Theology of Liberation*. 15th anniv. ed. Maryknoll, NY: Orbis Books, 1988.

Hampson, Daphne. *After Christianity*. Valley Forge, PA: Trinity Press International, 1996.

Hilkert, Mary Catherine. "Cry Beloved Image: Rethinking the Image of God." In *In the Embrace of God: Feminist Approaches to Theological Anthropology*, ed. Ann O'Hara Graff, 190–205. Maryknoll, NY: Orbis Books, 1995.

Hinsdale, Mary Ann. "Heeding the Voices: A Historical Overview." In *In the Embrace of God: Feminist Approaches to Theological Anthropology*, ed. Ann O'Hara Graff, 22–48. Maryknoll, NY: Orbis Books, 1995.

hooks, bell. "Postmodern Blackness." In *Yearning: Race, Gender, and Cultural Products*, 23–31. Boston: South End Press, 1990.

Irenaeus of Lyons. *Against Heresies*. Translated by Dominic J. Unger. New York: Paulist Press, 1992.

Isasi-Díaz, Ada María. "Christ in *Mujerista* Theology." In *Thinking of Christ: Proclamation, Explanation, Meaning*, ed. Tatha Wiley. New York: Continuum, 2003.

———. "Doing Theology as Mission." *Apuntes* 18, no. 4 (Winter 1998).

———. "Elements of a *Mujerista* Anthropology." In *Mujerista Theology: A Theology for the Twenty-First Century*, 128–47. Maryknoll, NY: Orbis Books, 1996.

———. "*Identifícate con Nosotras*: A *Mujerista* Christological Understanding." In *La Lucha Continues: Mujerista Theology*, ed. Ada María Isasi-Díaz, 240–66. Maryknoll, NY: Orbis Books, 2004.

———. *En la Lucha/In the Struggle: Elaborating a Mujerista Theology*. Minneapolis, MN: Fortress Press, 1993.

———. *Mujerista Theology: A Theology for the Twenty-First Century*. Maryknoll, NY: Orbis Books, 1996.

———. "*Mujeristas*: A Name of Our Own." In *The Future of Liberation Theology: Essays in Honor of Gustavo Gutiérrez*, ed.

Marc H. Ellis and Otto Maduro, 410–19. Maryknoll, NY: Orbis Books, 1989.

Johnson, Elizabeth A. *Consider Jesus: Waves of Renewal in Christology*. New York: Crossroad, 1997.

———. *Friends of God and Prophets: A Feminist Theological Reading of the Communion of Saints*. New York: Continuum, 1998.

———. "The Maleness of Christ." In *The Special Nature of Women? Concilium* (1991/6), ed. Anne E. Carr and Elisabeth Schüssler Fiorenza, 108–16.

———. *She Who Is: The Mystery of God in Feminist Theological Discourse*. New York: Crossroad, 1997.

———. *Truly Our Sister: A Theology of Mary in the Communion of Saints*. New York: Continuum, 2003.

Jones, Serene. *Feminist Theory and Christian Theology: Cartographies of Grace*. Minneapolis, MN: Fortress Press, 2000.

———. "Women's Experience between a Rock and a Hard Place: Feminist, Womanist, and *Mujerista* Theologies in North America." In *Horizons in Feminist Theology: Identity, Tradition, and Norms*, ed. Rebecca Chopp and Sheila Greeve Davaney, 33–53. Minneapolis, MN: Fortress Press, 1997.

Jones, Serene, and Paul Lakeland, eds. *Constructive Theology: A Contemporary Approach to Classical Themes*. Minneapolis, MN: Fortress Press, 2005.

Kant, Immanuel, *Observations on the Feeling of the Beautiful and Sublime*, trans. J. T. Goldthwait. Berkeley and Los Angeles: University of California Press, 1960.

Kelly, Geffrey B., ed. "Introduction." In *Karl Rahner: Theologian of the Graced Search for Meaning*, ed. Geffrey B. Kelly. Minneapolis, MN: Fortress Press, 1992.

Kelsey, David H. "Paul Tillich." In *The Modern Theologians*, ed. David F. Ford, 87–102. New York: Blackwell, 1997.

Kirk-Duggan, Cheryl A. "African-American Spirituals: Confronting and Exorcising Evil through Song." In *A Troubling in My Soul: Womanist Perspectives on Evil and Suffering*, ed. Emilie M. Townes, 150–71. Maryknoll, NY: Orbis Books, 1993.

Kvam, Kristen E., Linda S. Schearing, and Valerie H. Ziegler. *Eve and Adam: Jewish, Christian, and Muslim Readings on Genesis and Gender*. Bloomington: Indiana University Press, 1999.

Kwok Pui-lan. *Introducing Asian Feminist Theology*. Cleveland, OH: The Pilgrim Press, 2000.

LaCugna, Catherine Mowry. *God for Us: The Trinity and Christian Life*. San Francisco: HarperSanFrancisco, 1993.

———. "God in Communion with Us: The Trinity." In *Freeing Theology: The Essentials of Theology in Feminist Perspective*, ed. Catherine Mowry LaCugna, 83–114. San Francisco: HarperSanFrancisco, 1993.

———. "The Trinitarian Mystery of God." In *Systematic Theology: Roman Catholic Perspectives*. Vol. 1, ed. Francis Schüssler Fiorenza and John P. Galvin, 151–92. Minneapolis, MN: Fortress Press, 1991.

Livingston, James C., and Francis Schüssler Fiorenza. *Modern Christian Thought*. Vol. 2, *The Twentieth Century*. Upper Saddle River, NJ: Prentice-Hall, 2000.

Lloyd, Genevieve. *The Man of Reason: 'Male' and 'Female' in Western Philosophy*, 2nd ed. Minneapolis: University of Minnesota Press, 1993.

Loughlin, Gerard. "Erotics: God's Sex." In *Radical Orthodoxy: A New Theology*, ed. John Milbank, Catherine Pickstock, and Graham Ward. New York: Routledge, 1999.

Lugones, María C. "On the Logic of Pluralist Feminism." In *Feminist Ethics*, ed. Claudia Card, 35–44. Lawrence: University of Kansas Press, 1991.

———. "Playfulness, 'World'-Traveling, and Loving Perception." In *Making Face, Making Soul—Haciendo Caras*, ed. Gloria Anzaldúa, 390–402. San Francisco: An Aunt Lutte Foundation Book, 1990.

———. "Structure/Antistructure and Agency under Oppression." *Journal of Philosophy* 81 (1990).

Luther, Martin. "The Disputation concerning Justification." In *Luther's Works*. Vol. 34, *Career of the Reformer IV*, ed. Lewis W. Spitz. Philadelphia: Muhlenberg Press, 1955.

———. "Lectures on Genesis." In *Luther's Works*, ed. Jaroslav Pelikan. Vol. 1. Saint Louis, MO: Concordia Publishing House, 1958.

Maloney, George A., SJ. *Man, the Divine Icon*. New Mexico: Dove Publications, 1973.

McClintock Fulkerson, Mary. *Changing the Subject: Women's Discourses and Feminist Theology*. Minneapolis, MN: Fortress Press, 1994.

————. "Contesting the Gendered Subject: A Feminist Account of the *Imago Dei.*" In *Horizons in Feminist Theology: Identity, Tradition, and Norms*, ed. Rebecca Chopp and Sheila Greeve Davaney, 99–115. Minneapolis, MN: Fortress Press, 1997.

McFague, Sallie. *The Body of God: An Ecological Theology.* Minneapolis, MN: Fortress Press, 1993.

————. "Cosmology and Christianity: Implications of the Common Creation Story for Theology." In *Theology at the End of Modernity: Essays in Honor of Gordon D. Kaufman*, ed. Sheila Greeve Davaney. Philadelphia: Trinity Press International, 1991.

————. *Models of God: Theology for an Ecological, Nuclear Age.* Philadelphia: Fortress Press, 1987.

McKelway, Alexander J. *The Systematic Theology of Paul Tillich: A Review and Analysis.* Richmond, VA: John Knox Press, 1964.

Merriell, D. Juvenal. *The Image of the Trinity: A Study in the Development of Aquinas' Teaching.* Toronto: Pontifical Institute of Mediaeval Studies, 1990.

Miles, Margaret R. *Carnal Knowing: Female Nakedness and Religious Meaning in the Christian West.* Boston: Beacon Press, 1989.

Mitchem, Stephanie Y. *Introducing Womanist Theology.* Maryknoll, NY: Orbis Books, 2002.

Moss, David, and Lucy Gardner. "Difference—The Immaculate Concept? The Laws of Sexual Difference in the Theology of Hans Urs von Balthasar." *Modern Theology* 14, no. 3 (July 1998): 377–401.

Nicholson, Linda, ed. *Feminism and Postmodernism.* New York: Routledge, 1990.

O'Donnell, John, SJ. "Man and Woman as *Imago Dei* in the Theology of Hans Urs von Balthasar." *Clergy Review* 68, no. 4 (1983): 117–27.

Oduyoye, Mercy Amba. *Introducing African Women's Theology.* Cleveland, OH: The Pilgrim Press, 2001.

O'Hara Graff, Ann, ed. *In the Embrace of God: Feminist Approaches to Theological Anthropology.* Maryknoll, NY: Orbis Books, 1995.

————. "Strategies for Life: Learning from Feminist Psychology." In *In the Embrace of God: Feminist Approaches to Theological*

Anthropology, ed. Ann O'Hara Graff, 122–37. Maryknoll, NY: Orbis Books, 1995.

O'Neill, Mary Aquin. "The Mystery of Being Human Together." In *Freeing Theology: The Essentials of Theology in Feminist Perspective*, ed. Catherine Mowry LaCugna, 139–60. San Francisco: HarperSanFrancisco, 1993.

———. "Toward a Renewed Anthropology." *Theological Studies* 36 (1975): 725–36.

Plaskow, Judith. *Sex, Sin, and Grace: Women's Experience and the Theologies of Reinhold Niebuhr and Paul Tillich*. Lanham, MD: University Press of America, 1980.

Plato. *Republic*. In *The Collected Dialogues of Plato, including His Letters*, ed. Edith Hamilton and Huntington Cairns. New York: Pantheon Books, 1961.

Rahner, Karl. *Foundations of Christian Faith: An Introduction to the Idea of Christianity*. Translated by William V. Dych. New York: Crossroad, 1997.

———. *Karl Rahner: Theologian of the Graced Search for Meaning*, ed. Geffrey B. Kelly. Minneapolis, MN: Fortress Press, 1992.

Rodríguez, Jeanette. "Experience as a Resource for Feminist Thought." *Journal of Hispanic/Latino Theology* 1, no. 1 (1993): 68–76.

Ross, Susan A. *Extravagant Affections: A Feminist Sacramental Theology*. New York: Continuum, 1998.

Ruether, Rosemary Radford. "Feminist Theology and Spirituality." In *Christian Feminism: Visions of a New Humanity*, ed. Judith L. Weidman. San Francisco: Harper and Row, 1984.

———. *Gaia and God: An Ecofeminist Theology of Earth Healing*. San Francisco: HarperCollins, 1992.

———. *Introducing Redemption in Christian Feminism*. Sheffield, England: Sheffield Academic Press, 1998.

———. "Misogyny and Virginal Feminism in the Fathers of the Church." In *Religion and Sexism: Images of Woman in the Jewish and Christian Traditions*, ed. Rosemary Radford Ruether, 150–83. New York: Simon and Schuster, 1974.

———. *Sexism and God-Talk: Toward a Feminist Theology*. Boston: Beacon Press, 1993.

Russell, Letty M., and J. Shannon Clarkson, eds. *Dictionary of Feminist Theologies*. Louisville, KY: Westminster John Knox Press, 1996.

Saiving, Valerie. "The Human Situation: A Feminine View." *The Journal of Religion* (April 1960).

Schindler, David L., ed. *Hans Urs von Balthasar: His Life and Work.* San Francisco: Ignatius Press, 1991.

Schneiders, Sandra M. "The Bible and Feminism: Biblical Theology." In *Freeing Theology: The Essentials of Theology in Feminist Perspective*, ed. Catherine Mowry LaCugna, 31–57. San Francisco: HarperSanFrancisco, 1993.

Schott, Robin May, ed. *Feminist Interpretations of Immanuel Kant.* University Park: The Pennsylvania State University Press, 1997.

Schüssler Fiorenza, Elisabeth. *Bread Not Stone: The Challenge of Feminist Biblical Interpretation.* Boston: Beacon Press, 1995.

———. "Breaking the Silence—Becoming Visible." In *The Power of Naming: A Concilium Reader in Feminist Liberation Theology*, ed. Elisabeth Schüssler Fiorenza, 161–74. Maryknoll, NY: Orbis Books, 1996.

———. *Jesus: Miriam's Child, Sophia's Prophet: Critical Issues in Feminist Christology.* New York: Continuum, 1995.

Scola, Angelo. *Hans Urs von Balthasar: A Theological Style.* Grand Rapids, MI: Eerdmans, 1995.

Secker, Susan L. "Women's Experience in Feminist Theology: The 'Problem' or the 'Truth' of Difference." *Journal of Hispanic/Latino Theology* 1, no. 1 (1993): 56–67.

Smith, Nicholas D. "Plato and Aristotle on the Nature of Women." *Journal of the History of Philosophy* 21, no. 1 (October 1983): 467–78.

Souga, Thérèse. "The Christ-Event from the Viewpoint of African Women: A Catholic Perspective." In *With Passion and Compassion: Third World Women Doing Theology*, ed. Virginia Fabella and Mercy Amba Oduyoye, 22–29. Maryknoll, NY: Orbis Books, 1994.

Spelman, Elizabeth V. *Inessential Woman: Problems of Exclusion in Feminist Thought.* Boston: Beacon Press, 1988.

Sullivan, John Edward, OP. *The Image of God: The Doctrine of St. Augustine and Its Influence.* Dubuque, IA: The Priory Press, 1963.

Tamez, Elsa, ed. *Through Her Eyes; Women's Theology from Latin America.* Maryknoll, NY: Orbis Books, 1989.

Tanner, Kathryn. *Jesus, Humanity, and the Trinity: A Brief Systematic Theology*. Minneapolis, MN: Fortress Press, 2001.

Teevan, Donna. "Challenges to the Role of Theological Anthropology in Feminist Theologies." *Theological Studies* 64 (2003): 582–97.

Thielicke, Helmut. *Being Human—Becoming Human: An Essay in Christian Anthropology*. New York: Doubleday, 1983.

Tillich, Paul. *Systematic Theology*. Vol. 2, *Existence and the Christ*. Chicago: University of Chicago Press, 1975.

Trible, Phyllis. *God and the Rhetoric of Sexuality*. Minneapolis, MN: Fortress Press, 1978.

Viviano, Pauline A. "Genesis." In *The Collegeville Bible Commentary*, ed. Dianne Bergant and Robert J. Karris, 35–78. Collegeville, MN: The Liturgical Press, 1988.

Walker Bynum, Caroline. *Holy Feast and Holy Fast: The Religious Significance of Food for Medieval Women*. Berkeley and Los Angeles: University of California Press, 1987.

———. *Jesus as Mother: Studies in the Spirituality of the High Middle Ages*. Berkeley and Los Angeles: University of California Press, 1982.

Westermann, Claus. *Genesis 1:11: A Commentary*, Translated by John J. Scullion, SJ. Minneapolis, MN: Augsburg Publishing House, 1984.

Wiley, Tatha. *Original Sin: Origins, Developments, and Contemporary Meanings*. Mahwah, NJ: Paulist Press, 2002.

Williams, Delores S. *Sisters in the Wilderness: The Challenge of Womanist God-Talk*. Maryknoll, NY: Orbis Books, 1993.

———. "A Womanist Perspective on Sin." In *A Troubling in My Soul: Womanist Perspectives on Evil and Suffering*, ed. Emilie M. Townes, 130–49. Maryknoll, NY: Orbis Books, 1993.

Young, Iris Marion. "Gender as Seriality: Thinking about Women as a Social Collective." In *Intersecting Voices: Dilemmas of Gender, Political Philosophy, and Policy*, ed. Iris Marion Young, 12–37. Princeton, NJ: Princeton University Press, 1997.

Zimmer, Mary Ann. "Stepping Stones in Feminist Theory." In *In the Embrace of God: Feminist Approaches to Theological Anthropology*, ed. Ann O'Hara Graff, 7–21. Maryknoll, NY: Orbis Books, 1995.

Index